BOOSTING COMPETITIVENESS THROUGH DECENTRALIZATION

Cities and Society Series

Series Editor:
Chris Pickvance, Professor of Urban Studies, University of Kent, UK

Cities and Society is a series disseminating high quality new research and scholarship which contribute to a sociological understanding of the city. The series promotes scholarly engagement with contemporary issues such as urban access to public and private services; urban governance; urban conflict and protest; residential segregation and its effects; urban infrastructure; privacy, sociability and lifestyles; the city and space; and the sustainable city.

Other titles in the series

Residential Segregation in Comparative Perspective:
Making Sense of Contextual Diversity
Edited by Thomas Maloutas and Kuniko Fujita

Opportunities and Deprivation in the Urban South:
Poverty, Segregation and Social Networks in São Paulo
Eduardo Cesar Leão Marques

Beyond the Resources of Poverty:
Gecekondu Living in the Turkish Capital
Şebnem Eroğlu

Boosting Competitiveness Through Decentralization

Subnational Comparison of Local Development in Mexico

AYLIN TOPAL
Middle East Technical University, Turkey

LONDON AND NEW YORK

First published 2012 by Ashgate Publishing

2 Park Square, Milton Park, Abingdon, Oxon OX14 4RN
711 Third Avenue, New York, NY 10017, USA

Routledge is an imprint of the Taylor & Francis Group, an informa business

British Library Cataloguing in Publication Data
Topal, Aylin.
Boosting competitiveness through decentralization :
subnational comparison of local development in Mexico. --
(Cities and society)
  1. Decentralization in government--Economic aspects--
Mexico. 2. Mexico--Economic conditions--Regional
disparities. 3. Mexico--Economic policy.
  I. Title II. Series
  338.9'72-dc23

Library of Congress Cataloging-in-Publication Data
Topal, Aylin.
Boosting competitiveness through decentralization : subnational comparison
of local development in Mexico / by Aylin Topal.
    p. cm. -- (Cities and society)
  Includes bibliographical references and index.
  ISBN 978-1-4094-2572-4 (hardback) 1. Mexico--Economic
policy--21st century. 2. Public-private
sector cooperation--Mexico. 3. Central-local government relations--Mexico.
  4. Mexico--Politics and government--21st century. I. Title.
  HC135.T66 2012
338.972--dc23

ISBN 978-1-4094-2572-4 (hbk)   2012006243
ISBN 978-1-138-26862-3 (pbk)

Contents

Abbreviations and Acronyms

AMEAC	*Asociación de Maquiladoras y Exportadoras de Chihuahua, A.C.* / Association of Maquiladoras and Exporting Companies in Chihuahua
CANACINTRA	*Cámara Nacional de la Industria de Transformación* / National Chamber of Manufacturers
CANACO	*Cámara Nacional de Comercio, Servicios y Turismo* / National Chamber of Commerce, Service and Tourism
CANACOMIN	*Cámara Nacional de Comercio y Industria* / National Chamber of Commerce and Industry
CANAGRAF	*Camara Nacional de la Industria de Artes Grafica* / National Chamber of Graphic Arts Industry
CCE	*Consejo Coordinador Empresarial* / Private Sector Coordinating Council
CDS	*Convenio de Desarrollo Social* / Social Development Agreement
CEPAC	*Comité Estatal de Participación Cuidadana* / State Committee of Citizen Participation
CEPE	*Centro Estatal de Promoción Empresarial* / State Center for Entrepreneurial Promotion
CG500ARI	*Consejo Guerrerense 500 Anos de Resistencia Indígena* / Guerrero Council of 500 Years of Indigenous Resistance
CIMADES	*Comisión Interinstitucional para el Medio Ambiente y el Desarrollo Social* / Inter-institutional Commission for Environment and Social Development
CMC	*Consejo Mesoamerica de Competitividad* / Central American Council of Competitiveness
CNC	*Confederación Nacional Campesinos* / National Peasants' Confederation
CNDH	*Comisión Nacional de los Derechos Humanos* / National Human Rights Commission
CNOP	*Confederación Nacional de Organizaciones Populares* / National Confederation of Popular Organizations

COCENTRO   *Centro de Liderazgo y Desarrollo Humano /*
            Center of Leadership and Human Development
COCOVE   *Coalición de Comités de Vecinos /*
            Committees of Neighborhood Coalition
CODECH   *Consejo Para el Desarrollo Económico del*
            Estado de Chihuahua / Council for Economic
            Development of the State of Chihuahua
CODEZPET   *Comisión para el Desarrollo de las*
            Zonas Petroléras del Estado de Tabasco /
            Commission for Development of the
            Petroleum Zones of the State of Tabasco
COLUDE   *Coordinadora de Lucha por la Democracia /*
            Fight for Democracy Coordination
CONAGO   *Conferencia Nacional de Gobernadores /*
            National Governors' Conference
CONAII   *Colegio Nacional de Ingenieros Industriales /*
            National College of Industrial Engineers
CONAMM   *Conferencia Nacional de Municipios de*
            México / National Conference of Mexican Municipalities
CONCAMIN   *Confederación Nacional de Cámaras*
            Industriales / National Confederation of Chambers of Industry
CONCANACO   *Confederación de Cámaras Nacionales de*
            Comercio / Confederation of National Chambers of Commerce
COPARMEX   *Confederación Patronal de la República*
            Mexicana / Mexican Employers Confederation
COPLADE   *Comité de Planeación para el Desarrollo del*
            Estado / State Development Planning Committee
COPLADEG   *Comité de Planeación para el Desarrollo del*
            Estado de Guerrero / Development Planning
            Committee of Guerrero
COPLADEM   *Comité de Planeación para el Desarrollo*
            Municipal / Municipal Development Planning Committee
COPLADET   *Comité de Planeación para el Desarrollo del*
            Estado de Tabasco / Development Planning
            Committee of Tabasco
COPRODET   *Comité Promotor de Desarrollo*
            Socioeconómico de Tabasco /Promoter
            Committee of Socioeconomic Development of Tabasco
CPNAB   *Consejo de Pueblos de Nahua en Alto Balsas*
            / Council of Nahua Peoples in Alto Balsas
CRECE   *Centro Regional para la Competitividad*
            Empresarial / Regional Center for Business Competitiveness.
CTM   *Confederación de Trabajadores de México /*
            Conferation of Mexican Workers

| CUD | *Convenio Único de Desarrollo* / Development Agreement |
| CUDE | *Comerciantes Unidos y Democracia* / United Traders and Democracy |

| DECJ | *Desarrollo Económico de Ciudad Juárez* / Economic Development of Ciudad Juárez |
| DESEC | *Desarrollo Económico del Estado de Chihuahua, A.C.* / Economic Development of Chihuahua |

ECG	Economic Competitiveness Group
EOI	Export-Oriented Industrialization
EPR	*Ejército Popular Revolucionario* / *Popular Revolutionary Army*
ETG	Economic Transformation Group
EXATAC	*Asociación de Exalumnos del ITESM* / Association of ITESM Alumni
EZLN	*Ejército Zapatista de Liberación Nacional* / *Zapatista Army of National Liberation*

FAT	*Frente Auténtico de Trabajo* / Autentic Labor Front
FDC	*Frente Democrático Campesino* / Peasants' Democratic Front
FDN	*Frente Democrático Nacional* / National Democratic Front
FECHAC	*Fundación del Empresariado Chihuahua, A.C.* / Chihuahua Business Foundation
FIDETAB	*Fideicomiso para el Apoyo Empresarial de Tabasco* / Trust for Business of Tabasco
FIDESUR	*Fideicomiso para el Desarrollo Sur-Sureste* / Trust for Regional Development of South-Southeast
FOGATUR	*Fondo de Garantía y Fomento del Turismo* / Tourism Guarantee and Promotion Fund
FONATUR	*Fondo de Nacional Turística* / National Tourism Fund
FSI	*Frente Sindical Independiente* / Independent Front of Trade Unions
FTAA	Free Trade Area of the Americas

| GATT | General Agreement of Tariffs and Trade |
| GERRSE | *Grupo Económico de la Región Sur-Sureste de México* / Economic Group of South-Southeast Region of Mexico |

IFI	*International Financial Institution*
ILO	*International Labor Organization*
IMCP	*Instituto y Colegio de Contadores Públicos* / Institute and College of Public Accountance
IMF	International Monetary Fund

IMPULSA	*Desarrollo Empresarial Mexicana* / Mexican Business Development
INFRATUR	*Fondo de Promoción de Infraestructura Turística* / Tourism Infrastructure Trust
IS	Import Substitution
IWG	International Women's Group
MFS	*Movimiento Sindical Ferrocarrilero* / Trade Union Movement of Railroad Workers
NAFINSA	*Nacional Financiera* / National Finance Bank
NAFTA	North American Free Trade Agreement
OCSS	*Organización de Campesinos en Sierra Sureño* / Farmers' Organization of the Southern Sierra
PAN	*Partido Acción Nacional* / National Action Party
PCM	*Partido Comunista Mexicana* / Mexican Communist Party
PDLP	*Partido de los Pobres* / Party of the Poor
PEMEX	*Petroleos Mexicanos* / Mexican Petroleum
PMS	*Partido Mexicano Socialista* / Mexican Socialist Party
PNR	*Partido Nacional Revolucionario* / Revolutionary National Party
POA	*Partido Obrero de Acapulco* / Worker Party of Acapulco
PRD	*Partido de la Revolución Democrática* / Party of the Democratic Revolution
PRI	*Partido Revolucionario Institucional* / Institutional Revolutionary Party
PRODECOT	*Programa de Desarrollo de Costa de Tabasco* / Development Program of the Coast of Tabasco
PRONASOL	*Program Nacional de Solidaridad* / National Solidarity Program
PRST	*Partido Socialista Radical Tabasqueño* / Radical Socialist Party of Tabasco
PRT	*Partido Revolucionario de los Trabajadores* / Revolutionary Workers Party
PSD	*Partido Social Demócrata* / Social Democratic Party
PSG	*Partido Socialista de Guerrero* / Socialist Party of Guerrero
PST	*Partido Socialista de los Trabajadores* / Socialist Workers' Party
PSUM	*Partido Socialista Unificado de México* / Mexican Unified Socialist Party
SECTUR	*Secretaria de Turismo* / Ministry of Tourism

SIESPLADE	*Sistema Estatal de Planeación Democrática /* State System of Democratic Planning
SNPD	*Sistema Nacional de Planeación Democrática /* National System of Democratic Planning
SNTE	*Sindicato Nacional de Trabajadores de la Educación /* National Education Workers' Union
SPP	*Secretaría de Programación y Presupuesto /* Ministry of Programming and Budget
SSRC	Social Science Research Council
STERM	*Sindicato de Trabajadores Electricistas de la República Mexicana /* Union of Electricity Workers of Mexico
STPRM	*Sindicato de Trabajadores Petroleros de la República Mexicana /* Mexican Petroleum Workers' Union
UAG	*Universidad Autónoma de Guerrero /* Autonomous University of Guerrero
USEM	*Union Social de Empresarios Mexicanos /* Social Union of Mexican Businessmen

Acknowledgements

This book draws on my PhD dissertation prepared at the New School for Social Research. It is a pleasure to express my gratitude to this institution and many of its members. The research for the dissertation would not be possible without the generous support funded by the New School Eberstadt Dissertation Fellowship, Janey Program for Latin American Studies Summer Research Grant and New School Research and Conference Travel Grant. The ideas that inspired this book developed in collaboration with numerous people. Special thanks must be given to Aristede Zolberg for his warm support and encouragement all through my PhD studies. My interest in Mexico was developed in our long conversations with him. He has been and always will be an inspring intellectual character for me. I would like to acknowledge my special thanks to my supervisor Courtney Jung for her valuable advice and criticism in shaping the arguments and for her support and help in turning the dissertation into a book manuscript. Encouragement and unconditional support of David Plotke motivated me from the very early stages of my PhD studies. I am indebted to him.

I have benefited from discussions with scholars in New York in developing the arguments. Maria Victoria Murillo and Neil Brenner gave me a lot of valuable comments in the early stages of my research. I would like to record my gratitude to Vivek Chibber for his interest, support and guidance over the PhD years.

The field research of this dissertation turned into a very fruitful and enjoyable experience. The institutional affiliation with the Centro de Investigación y Docencia Económicas as a visiting researcher allowed me to reach to key informants. I would like to thank Enrique Cabrero and everybody there for their warm welcome as well as for their interest in my research. Special thanks to Roberto Trad for his constant support in Mexico City. Beto gave me a home away from home. Doña Albina kindly shared her home with me in Tabasco. I would like to thank Nicolas Marín Martínez for his research assistantship in Tabasco. I have spent many hours at the Hemeroteca Nacional at UNAM in Mexico City. I am grateful to the staff there for helping me and other researchers in any ways they could. I am especially indebted to many people in Mexico whom I interviewed who gave their time and insight. I would like to particularly thank Manuel Camacho Solís for sharing his insights on the decentralization policies and implementation of these policies in different states of Mexico. His overview guided me through the labyrinth of the case selection process.

As I was writing the chapters I received useful comments from a number of people. Adam Morton, Alejandro Alvarez, Alfredo Saad-Filho, Cem Somel, David Plotke, Erik Olin Wright read some chapters and gave me important feedback.

Thanks to my friends and colleagues Attila Aytekin, Ebru Deniz Ozan, Daniel Kato, Jennifer Terrell, Jorge Romero Leon, Mustafa Bayırbağ, Sarah Taylor, Tom Marois, who read (some of) the chapters and provided me with insightful comments. I cannot express my gratitude enough for Galip Yalman for giving me valuable feedback for strengthening my arguments. The book carries the mark of his lectures, our illuminating conversations and exchanges.

I would especially like to thank the series editor Chris Pickvance for giving me the opportunity to publish my manuscript as part of the Cities and Society Series. I am very pleased to be part of this series. Without his encouragement and support my dissertation would not reincarnate as a book. Thanks to the editorial team at Ashgate for their quick and precise editing.

Most of all, I cannot thank my family and friends enough for their love and care. Without the warm companionship of my friends, especially Asuman Göksel, Bahar Tabakoğlu, Ebru Deniz Ozan, Laura Balbuena and Nida Alahmad, writing this book would not be as joyful. I would like to express a special thanks to my dear friend and roommate, Claudia Heiss for her constant help and support when it was most needed even if it was late at night. I owe my parents Şerife and Hasan more than can be expressed. Their support and encouragement means a lot to me. My deepest gratitude is to my partner Özgür Yılmaz, whose constant support and love has given me an inner strength when my courage faltered.

Chapter 1

Introduction

In the midst of the severe economic crisis of the 1970s in the advanced industrialized countries of the West as well as the developing world, free-market ideology of the classical economic liberalism found itself a receptive audience. Incarnation of century-old ideas as 'neoliberalism' constrained the policy priorities first in the UK and the US then spread, through different mechanism and agencies, to other advanced and developing countries. Although it is impossible to clearly define the neoliberal policy framework, neoliberalization share a common logic of process: further integration of the national economies into the world economy for enhanced capitalist competition, capital accumulation and profit maximization.

Meanwhile, decentralization policies have been an important aspect of the transformations of the territorial structure and functioning of the state. Various studies show that central governments around the world have transferred a broad array of resources, responsibilities and authorities to subnational governments.[1] These transfers have rendered the subnational level an important part of the policy-making process, especially of funding, delivery and management of various public services including education, health, transportation and poverty alleviation.

Observing this policy shift, decentralization has become a subject of widespread academic interest. Students of state theories, democratization and development studies have begun to pay scholarly attention to these policies. These scholars agree that decentralization has been an important aspect of the transformations of the territorial structure and functioning of the state with important implications for development. While state theorists problematize the transformation of statehood in the process of decentralization, students of democratization and development studies focus on the impact of decentralization on local participation patterns, political party systems and development policies.[2] The current research agenda

---

1 For studies on decentralization in various countries, see Bardhan and Mookherjee (eds) (2006), Bosch and Duran (eds) (2008), Cheema and Rondinelli (eds) (1983), Crook and Manor (1998), Falletti (2010), Montero and Samuels (eds) (2004), Oxhorn,Tulchin and Selee (eds) (2004), Pickvance and Pretecielle (eds) (1991), Ribot (2004), Tulchin and Selee (eds) (2004).

2 For state theories, see Brenner (2004), Jessop (2002: 172–216), Peck (2001), Smith (1993), Taylor (1996), and Treisman (2007); for development studies and democratization, see Adib et al. (eds) (2008), Canel (2010), Chávez and Goldfrank (eds) (2004), Connerly, Eaton and Smoke (eds) (2010), Fung and Wright (eds) (2003), Goldfrank (2011), Grindle (2009), McNulty (2011), Mullen (2011), Sellers (2002), Selee (2011), Smith (1984), Stohr et al. (eds) (2001).

of these scholars is primarily concerned with uncovering the dynamics that help explain the impact of decentralization policies on local, national and global political economic relations and on social regulation.

Two theoretical approaches dominate the debate regarding the sources and impact of decentralization policies: liberal-individualist and statist approaches. The liberal-individualist approach, especially advocated by the World Bank, promotes decentralization policies on the premises of efficiency, equity and responsiveness to local demands. Advocates of this approach claim that decentralization is the key to implementing the deregulation mechanisms of the state and democratization; decentralization policies open new channels for ethnic minorities and social groups to participate in the policy-making process.[3]

The second theoretical approach to decentralization became eminent especially in the early 1990s. The experiences of the Asian Tigers such as Taiwan and South Korea attracted attention on state institutions, suggesting that particular state institutions could have significant impact on socioeconomic development. The official launch and public manifesto of this approach can be traced back to 1983 and 1985 when Social Research Planning Committee on States and Social Structures was set up under the Social Science Research Council (SSRC) and *Bringing the States Back In* was published. This edited book by Evans, Rueschemeyer and Skocpol lays out the main principles of this new statist approach. Skocpol, in her introduction to the book, declares the emergence of the analytical approach that proposes 'to bring the state back in to its proper central place in explanations of social change and politics' (Skocpol 1985: 28). Following the development of the literature viewing the state 'as social actors and society-shaping structures' (ibid: 6), the main focus of the decentralization literature moved towards state institutions and the political agenda of elites. Protagonists of this perspective are widespread, including governments and the international institutions such as the World Bank, Interamerican Bank and United Nations.[4] Similar to the liberal-individualist approach, the statist approach accepts that decentralization can be the route to greater accountability, transparency and participation in governance; it adds that this path should be guided by political elites and institutions. It argues that if local governments have strong institutions with the capacity to assume the newly received functions, decentralization policies could produce efficient governance at the local level; if not, however, decentralization may lead to local authoritarian regimes due to the survival strategies of the political elite.

---

3   See World Bank (1994a, 1994b, 2004); see also Adib et al. (eds) (2008), Blair (2000), Bulki, Perry and Dillinger (1999), Campbell (1997, 2003), Guigale and Webb (eds) (2000), Parker and Serrano (2000), Peterson (1997), Ribot (2004), UN-Habitat 2007.

4   See Bardhan and Mookherjee (eds) (2006), Boone (2003), Dickovick (2007), Eaton, (2003, 2004), Grindle (2009), Interamerican Development Bank (1994), Montero and Samuels (eds) (2004a), O'Neill (2003, 2005), Rodden, Eskeland and Litvack (2003), Rodríguez (1997), Shotton and Winter (2007), Willis, Garman and Haggard (1999), World Bank (2000).

The analyses informed by these two theories are unable to come to terms of dynamics of social transformation in the course of the 1970s and thus fail to explain 'policy change' towards decentralization in many developing as well as developed countries in the particular context of evolving international economic order. These two theories focus mainly on the political transformations that decentralization policies brought about at the local level and understate the extent to which decentralization policies have been implemented lockstep with neoliberalization of national economies. Although these studies provide some insights into the potential effect of decentralization on local political regime (democratization or authoritarianism), they do not explain satisfactorily how the outcome of these policies change social relations and forms of state intervention into the economy at the local level. Thus existing studies leave us without a framework for explaining (1) the relations between decentralization policies and changing class strategies in the face of economic and/or political crises of the late 1970s and (2) various local development patterns have replaced the national development agenda that was disintegrated by decentralization policies. This book therefore distinguishes these two *explananda* that requires further explanation and suggests that an alternative theoretical approach which gives social class an explanatory primacy could fill this gap by providing conceptual and analytic tools.

This book aims to explain policy change towards decentralization in Mexico by examining different class strategies in the face of 'hegemony crisis' in the course of the 1970s. It shows that strategies of northern factions of Mexican bourgeoisie and dominated masses especially in the southern states shaped the particular extent and content of decentralization. The analyses put an emphasis on how and why these class strategies were framed by the specific stage and phase of capitalism. For example the role of International Monetary Fund (IMF) and the World Bank cannot be overlooked in understanding this policy shift towards decentralization. Evolving international economic order privileged certain factions of capital vis-à-vis others and states selectively filter the various class strategies and at a particular conjuncture certain class strategies become more decisive in shaping policy change. Thus transition to neoliberalization may not necessarily imply decentralization yet carries a strong structural tendency towards decentralization. Through a subnational comparison of local development policies in three states of Mexico, this book makes the case that outcome of the decentralization policies is dissemination of 'politics of global competitiveness' (Cammack 2006, 2010) into local level, generating different local development patterns.

This book demonstrates that the nature of the state-economy relationship prevalent with the local social formation is an important *explanans*[5] in making sense of the variations in the impact of decentralization policies on local politics in Mexico. It shows that decentralization led to 'restructuring and

---

5 In the positivist methodology, this is commonly referred to as 'independent variable'. See footnote 8 of this chapter for ontological and epistemological reasons behind this concept preference.

strategic reorientation of state intervention' (Jessop 2002: 177–8) to build local competitiveness for facilitating the articulation of the local economy with the world economy. Local level becomes an important space of competitiveness (Brenner 2000: 321). The market relations and rules of neoliberal competition begin to constrain the strategies and alliance of the actors. The mode of articulation of a local economy with the world economy with its external ties, needs, strengths and weaknesses determines the interests, aspirations, and strategies of policy makers and social classes which in turn shape local development patterns.

This book has three overarching goals. First, by showing that decentralization policies have the effects of diffusing neoliberal rules of competition down to local governments and economies, it challenges optimistic democratization expectations rooted in liberal-individualist and statist approaches. Second, it provides a framework for explaining different local development patterns evolved in the process of decentralization. Finally, it develops a new research agenda for political economy: the study of local development in the process of decentralization.

Subnational Comparison

The book focuses on Mexico – a country where decentralization policies have been implemented gradually since 1983 and produced a range of outcomes in different states. The Mexican state has been described as one of the most centralized in all Latin America. The Revolution (1910–17) represents a turning point in the country's history which brought about new forms of domination and subordination. The goals of the Revolution were articulated in the Constitution of 1917 outlining the essential features of the Mexican state. The centralization of national political power in the federal government culminated in the establishment of a single government party, the Revolutionary National Party (*Partido Nacional Revolucionario* – PNR), in 1929, which eventually became the Institutional Revolutionary Party (*Partido Revolucionario Institucional* – PRI) in 1946 and ruled the country until 2000 when the National Action Party (*Partido Acción Nacional* – PAN) gained the presidency and kept the post in the 2006 elections.[6] Since the early 1980s, decentralization policies appear to be the key elements of the significant changes in the centralized institutional setting. These policies transferred an array of administrative, political and economic responsibilities to state and municipality governments. Concomitantly, the main opposition parties, the PAN and the Party of the Democratic Revolution (*Partido de la Revolución Democrática* – PRD) have started to challenge the PRI in the local as well as the national elections.

---

6   According to the official results of the 2006 presidential elections, the PAN beat the center left opposition party, the Party of the Democratic Revolution (Partido de la Revolución Democrática – PRD) by only 0,58 per cent with over fourth million turnout. For the 2012 elections, the PRD is running with the same candidate, Andrés Manuel López Obrador to whom some polls are giving a big lead.

The book employs a subnational comparative method which proves to be effective in examining the spatially uneven nature of major processes of political and economic transformation (cf. Snyder 2001a) such as the impact of decentralization in different regions of a country. I examine the effects of the Municipal Reform of 1984 and New Federalism Reform of 1994 in three Mexican states: Chihuahua, Guerrero and Tabasco.

The research for this book draws upon the realist methodology which postulates the social world as independent of our thoughts about it – hard and concrete. The realist ontology is based on stratification of distinguished levels of abstraction. Real, actual and empirical constitute three domains of reality. The real refers to structures and mechanism with causal powers which may or may not produce regularities. The actual refers to events which occur when/if the powers of the real structures and mechanisms are activated. The empirical refers to the observed and experienced phenomena, whereas neither real nor actual are necessarily observable. The existence of the unobserved real and actual can be shown by revealing their observable effects on the empirical domain. The analysis therefore would be misleading if it confined itself to the empirical domain, yet it should begin with the description of the empirical (Sayer 2000:10–12).

The starting point of the comparison is the empirical differences observed in each state along a political continuum. Chihuahua is one of the pioneering states where the PAN challenged the PRI rule in local politics; in Tabasco and Guerrero, the PRI has been historically very strong. In Tabasco, the PRI still holds onto the governor's office and important municipalities. In Guerrero, the PRD has become a strong challenge to the PRI and was able to win the governor's office in the 2000 elections. The analysis then inquires into the possible relations between *actual* effects of the decentralization policies in each case and these *empirical* variations across cases. 'Variation-finding comparison' requires delving into specificities of cases (Tilly cited in Pickvance 2001: 16).

The primary source of my understanding of how decentralization policies impacted subnational development in Mexico is the 96 in-depth and open-ended interviews conducted in 2005, 2006 and 2011 with scholars, policy-makers, prominent businessmen and other non-governmental agencies in different regions of the country.[7] The interviews provide a glimpse into explaining policy change towards decentralization. These interviews were also useful in understanding agents' perception of the decentralization policies that have been implemented and in identifying their conflicts and alliances that are necessary to reveal dynamics of social transformation in the process decentralization. Moreover, commercial media, sub-national newspapers, publications of various civil and political associations were reviewed to identify the motives, strategies, choices and networks of specific agents.

---

7 See Appendix A for the list of the interviewees. Because the interview subjects were guaranteed confidentiality to encourage candor, some interviewees are not identified by name; and identifying features, such as official position, have been disguised or omitted.

Based on these information sources, the subnational comparison first constructs/uncovers the variations in each case in the process of decentralization then searches for the underlying *real* structural causal patterns that could explain the *empirical* and *actual* differences among the cases. For that purpose, the analysis should account for the processes of class and state formation at the local level, and historicize the explanation of the variation, while at the same time locating decentralization policies and their impacts in the international economic order, the context that produces them. A substantial requirement of this comparison is to unravel the state-economy relationships in each case study that produce different outcomes by defining and constraining the interests, aspirations and strategies of agents. The *explanans*[8] of this study, the state-economy relationships prevalent with the local social formation, can be operationalized by bringing the nature of the local economy into the fore of the analysis.

The main criterion for selecting the cases of this subnational comparison is the nature of the local economy: Chihuahua has one of the most important *maquiladora* economies;[9] Tabasco is the richest of the Mexican states in terms of oil and natural gas; Guerrero has a significant indigenous peasant population coupled with a valuable tourism sector. The comparison aims to reveal that each local economy defines the relationship of the locality with the rest of the world and the struggles that take place among networks of local, national and global agents.

The nature of the local economy provides a glimpse into both the observed and constructed/uncovered variations in the industrial structure, social composition and political institutions of the locality. Observed variations in the breaks and continuities in party politics are important as they reveal as well as disguise the representational ties between social classes and political parties. Chihuahua and Guerrero witnessed a political opening in the local regime for the PAN and PRD respectively and various local agents have been empowered and new struggles have emerged regarding local development: in Chihuahua, local businessmen behind the PAN have become central agents in local development; in Tabasco, the local policy-makers have held the leash of local politics and led the development programs; and in Guerrero, local indigenous peasants and tourism capitalists have gained strength in determining the pattern of local development. Consequently, each case represents a different pattern of local development: Chihuahua corresponds to entrepreneurial local development; Tabasco to authoritarian state-led local development; and Guerrero to contested local development.

---

8   In realism, social reality is conceived as relational and multi-dimensional whole rather than a set of variables or atomistic objects that could be isolated out as in natural science experiments (Pickvance 2001: 12; Sayer 1984: 3).

9   The term 'maquiladora' is used to describe factories along the US–Mexico border where foreign merchandise – machinery, raw materials, parts, and components – is imported duty-free into Mexico on a temporary basis, assembled or manufactured by Mexican workers and then exported with duties assessed only on the value-added, either to the country of origin or to a third country.

Chihuahua

The main economic activity in the northern border-states of Mexico is the *maquiladora* production, and the state of Chihuahua is one of the most important *maquiladora* industry economies. After decentralization, local capital groups involved in the *maquiladora* industry, which supported the PAN, intervened in the political processes as a united front in order to increase the competitiveness of their locality. Decentralization policies created an opportunity for these groups to pursue their own development agenda in the region. Foreign capital invested in the region to exploit cheap labor reserves engaged in alliances with the local capital. The local and foreign bourgeoisie formed a partnership with the local state; and from then on, this public–private partnership initiated and executed all the local development plans. Nevertheless, the capitalist alliance, in time, curbed the development capacities of the local state and took control of development. In this process, dominated masses have been either marginalized and excluded from local politics or absorbed into capital-funded civil societal organizations. Decentralization led to entrepreneurial local development.

The main factor that explains the emergence of the entrepreneurial local development is the nature of the border economy in Chihuahua which has impact on local social relations and state institutions. Due to partnerships and alliances of the bourgeoisie on both sides of the border, the local capital groups in Chihuahua and their representative organizations have had significant political power vis-à-vis other local agents. Northern bourgeoisie have been among the most organized capitalist groups in Mexico.

Since the Lázaro Cárdenas period (1934–40) until the 1980s, they have had uneasy relations with the central state regulations. While national development was based on inward-looking import substitution (IS), the local economy of Chihuahua was mainly dependent on outward-looking border relations. Hence, the national development programs tied the hands of local state governments and weakened the overall legitimacy of the local state. The lack of political support for the local governments led to weak organizational capacities of the local state institutions.

After the 1982 debt crisis, northern bourgeoisie and their representative organizations became more important for policy-makers because of their close relations with their US peers. With their new strategic position, these local capital groups organized the other social agents around their development agenda and led the entrepreneurial local development.

Tabasco

Decentralization policies did not lead to a decrease in state regulations or to a transfer of power to social agents. Rather, they gave more powers to local policy-makers to re-regulate the local development. The leadership of the local policy-making elite reinforced a kind of corporatism and encapsulated the social dynamics into state-initiated organizations. The hegemony of this local development model was secured by buying off the opposition and containing dissent through state employment as well as using decentralized revenues to reward loyal constituencies and, if necessary, mollify others. Decentralization led to authoritarian state-led local development.

The main difference between the Chihuahua and Tabasco cases is that, in the latter, local policy-makers had the capacity to lead development programs. The strength of the policy-making elite stems from the historical legacy of the local institutions which was shaped by the main characteristics of the local economy: public ownership of the natural resources in the region have strengthened the local state institutionally and bestowed the policy-makers with institutional capacities in leading the development.[10]

In Chihuahua, the *maquiladora* sector relies on local and foreign capital. In Tabasco, on the other hand, the oil industry involves cooperation with large foreign capital. Foreign oil oligarchs extract, refine and ship Tabasco's oil in partnership with the Mexican Petroleum (Petroleos Mexicanos – PEMEX). Since the foreign investments in the region are mediated through the public sector, local bourgeoisie and their representative associations have become the junior partners of development. The local agents, which are overwhelmingly dependent on oil revenues, have ascribed the local state a central role in development. Under these conditions, in alliance with foreign oil companies and local bourgeoisie, local governments have led development by placing the primary focus on bolstering the economic competitiveness of the economy to create a suitable environment for private capital accumulation.

Guerrero[11]

Decentralization policies have weakened the control mechanisms of the traditional PRI elites and increased collaboration between tourism sector bourgeoisie and indigenous peasants in local development programs in Guerrero. Local and foreign tourism bourgeoisie got involved in the local development plans to increase the competitiveness of the tourism sector. They allied with the strong indigenous peasant movement to reduce poverty, encourage indigenous culture and improve the infrastructure: after all, the streets had to look clean for tourists. Nevertheless, inherent interest conflicts between the tourism bourgeoisie and indigenous peasants resulted in contentious local development. The process of decentralization has opened spaces for local agents to establish their own economic and political organizations.

---

10   Mexico is the fifth largest oil-producing country and its oil wealth has generated the largest portion of the country's income for most of the post-war era. The state of Tabasco is the richest of the Mexican states in terms of oil and natural gas.

11   The analysis on Guerrero is confined with the municipalities around the tourism centers, especially Acapulco. The analysis here also leaves out the impact of increasing drug-cartel conflict since President Felipe Calderón took office in 2006.

The main factor that differentiates the case of Guerrero from the other two cases is the agricultural economy based on strong indigenous peasant population coupled with a valuable tourism sector. Until the 1980s, political economic relations based on agricultural production had produced clientelism as an instrument for hegemony. The local policy-makers had often resorted to repressing the opposition groups using military force. Bourgeoisie in Guerrero appear far from being hegemonic.

As the tourism bourgeoisie began to determine the local development programs to increase the competitiveness of the local economy, the power of the agricultural capital had been curtailed. This in turn removed some of the repressive mechanisms and helped dominated yet locally organized, indigenous peasants to mobilize around their own political organizations. These organizations carry the potential to deepen collective struggle of the dominated masses which would forge the unity of their position as class subjects. Thus in Guerrero, local development turned into an open-ended contest among agro-business families, tourism bourgeoisie and dominated masses.

Structure of the Book

Chapter 2 discusses the strengths and weaknesses of the two dominant theoretical approaches to decentralization and builds the theoretical framework of the argument that is offered in this book. The chapter first sets certain criteria against which the liberal-individualist and statists approaches to decentralization can be assessed. After showing that both approaches have important inadequacies, it lays out an alternative theoretical approach which offers explanations for the relations between transition to neoliberalism and decentralization policies and possible outcomes of these policies. The alternative approach developed in this chapter acknowledges and incorporates the relationships among local, national and global levels, theorizes the local state as a part of national statehood and, last but not the least, emphasizes the indispensability of class analysis.

Chapter 3 presents the findings of a historical investigation on how and why Mexican policy-makers have implemented decentralization polices since 1983. This chapter explains this policy shift by examining inter- and intra-class relations. It argues that the first round of decentralization policies were shaped by class strategies in the face of the economic and political crises of the late 1970s; and the second round of decentralization can be understood in the context of the 1994 economic crisis and the NAFTA integration process. The chapter concludes that decentralization policies circulate and extend state power and state intervention to the local level.

Chapters 4 through to 6 analyze the distinct decentralization experiences by focusing on the three Mexican states – Chihuahua, Tabasco and Guerrero. These chapters start with a nuanced analysis of processes of class and state formation in each state prior to the decentralization polices in 1983. The first question that drives these chapters is how the nature of local economy shaped state-society relations at the local level. Then, the chapters turn to an in-depth study of the process of decentralization in each of the three states. They provide an analysis of how the development programs crafted and executed at the state level since the first decentralization policies were put into effect. The focus of each case study chapter is on identifying the alliances and strategies of key local actors.

The concluding chapter lays out a cross-case analysis, comparing the three cases and highlighting the key factors that account for the contrasting effects of decentralization. This chapter highlights several key themes that emerge from each case and underscore a certain underlying uniformity throughout the country in the process of decentralization. This chapter also explores how the framework developed in this book could be extended to other countries and raises questions for future research.

Chapter 2
Toward a Political Economy
Approach to Decentralization

Each theory is built by the theorist's epistemological and methodological commitments. This construction process is not completely free and unstructured because each theory is naturally bounded by the ontological realms of what is. That is to say theory construction does not start out from abstract concepts.

Prior to any evaluation of existing theoretical approaches to decentralization, the indispensable first step of theory-building is to identify certain conditions that hint about the ontology – nature and existence – of the *explanandum*, that is, what is explained. The second step is to evaluate existing theoretical approaches according to the degree to which it meets these conditions. Thus, ontological conditions serve as mutually agreed criteria of validity or litmus tests for theories that make explicit to a large extent the theoretical controversies about the nature of the reality in question. These controversies over the description of social reality usher in rival research traditions. On the basis of the ontological conditions, theories may be adopted, their boundaries redrawn or they may even be abandoned altogether. A powerful critique of a given theory is to show that it is contradictory with some of the conditions and that it is, therefore, not an 'explanatory' theory. Then, the third step of theory formation is to construct an alternative theoretical framework as an abstraction that conforms to these conditions.

This chapter aims to build a theoretical approach to decentralization by following these steps. First, based on the ontological challenges that emerged in the field research for this book, four conditions are identified to assess whether existing theoretical approaches to decentralization could explain the main characteristics of the concrete reality. Then, the main tenets of the dominant theoretical approaches to decentralization will be laid out and assessed in terms of their adequacy according to the conditions provided. The third section provides the theoretical framework of this book, which aims to understand and explain the sources and the outcome of the decentralization process.

Ontological Challenges and Conditions

As I set out to conduct the inquiry, I had encountered four ontological challenges regarding local politics and the decentralization process in the field research for this project. These reveal certain characteristics that set the conditions for the analysis of decentralization right from the beginning. The form in which decentralization and local politics is presented in Mexico represents certain conditions that theoretical approaches to decentralization need to account for.

While preparing the interview questions and analyzing interviewees' responses, I immediately faced the problem of how to isolate local phenomena from national and global ones. Questions that enquire about the effect of the decentralized development projects on the local economy of each state of Mexico forced me to think about the place of each locality in both national and global economic relations. The *maquiladora* sector in Chihuahua, the oil industry in Tabasco and tourism in Guerrero are necessarily embedded in both national and global economic networks. Local agents' perceptions of local economic relations reveal these interrelations among various levels. When local agents are asked to explain the effects of the decentralized development projects in their locality, their response often shifted among national, local and global levels. Furthermore, in their responses, several interviewees often skipped the national level by relating their locality's local issues to global processes. The ontological condition stemming from this setting refers to the question of how to deal with the relationality among local, national and global levels without assuming a hierarchical order among them.

How to conceptualize the local state posed another ontological condition. Responses to the questions about the main characteristics of local state institutions or local elites revealed the fuzzy nature of the relationships between local and central policy-makers. The local governments in each state are understood with reference to how the policy-making elites in Mexico City benefited from the local policy-making elites, or how local elites attempted to resist central control. The informants defined Mexican politics with its internal conflicts and alliances at the local-national nexus. Therefore, state theories should be revisited with a focused framework that accounts for local institutions and agents.

The third condition is related to the various patterns of decentralization policies in the different cases. Most existing studies argue that decentralization policies have various outcomes. Similarly, at the empirical level, the process of decentralization seems to have evolved in different directions in each case study. Therefore, this challenge means that the theoretical approaches to decentralization need to identify various impacts of decentralization and provide an explanation for what produces this variety and reveal the conditions under which local politics evolve toward one pattern versus another.

The last ontological condition is regarding how much capacity the theoretical frame should ascribe to agency. In order to come to terms with the policy change towards decentralization, it is imperative to focus both on the various demands of the social classes without ignoring the evolution of the economic and political structures in the face of the crisis of the late 1970s. Regarding the outcome of decentralization, although local agents are observed to be empowered by decentralization policies, structural factors may continue to shape the perceptions and strategies of the local agents. In the interviews, local agents presented their strategies as if they are shaped solely by their will, power, programs, alliances and so on. Nevertheless, the striking similarities in agents' strategies across different localities underline the necessity to integrate the non-empirical but real tendencies having causal powers into the analysis. How much of the variation is generated by these real tendencies, and how much of it is realized due to agents' strategies should be assessed carefully within a broader framework that looks at the relations between the agents' and processes instituted at the local, national and global levels.

Now, let us identify the four ontological conditions that theoretical approaches to decentralization should satisfy in order to be able to provide a comprehensive understanding of the process.

Condition 1: A Theory of Decentralization should Explicate the Intrinsic Relations among Local, National, and Global Levels without Assuming a Hierarchical Relation among them.

In order to understand the process of decentralization, it is necessary to focus on the social relations that constitute localities without keeping the focus of the analytical lenses locked at the local level. Local relations cannot be confined to the local level. The complexity of decentralization cannot be captured if different levels of relations are regarded as being made up of discrete levels of bounded spaces which fit together neatly, as if different levels could be stacked, one above the other, or fitted together in much the same way as that Russian Matryoshka dolls are contained one within another (Herod and Wright 2002: 8). Therefore, observations and abstractions should be made at different levels of analysis since social relations at different levels of reality can shape the dynamics of the decentralization process. Furthermore, it is not sufficient to investigate the interrelations among various levels, because the relative importance of these levels is not naturally fixed. They operate simultaneously, but not hierarchically (Smith 1984, 1993). Therefore, local and global processes are increasingly articulated in complex patterns that defy resolution into neatly segregated and nested sets of spaces (Sayer 2000: 113).

Condition 2: A Theory of Decentralization should be able to Disaggregate Statehood and Pay Special Attention to its Local and Regional Parts.

This necessity is elevated as the process of decentralization has had considerable effects on the role and structure of the local and regional institutions of the state. As some functions and faculties of the central state are decentralized, statehood is also expected to extend its limits to the local. The circulation of power replaces the condensation of power at the pinnacle. That is, politics can no longer be contained within the capital city. Therefore, local and regional governments should be conceptualized as active agents providing a legal and regulatory framework, despite possible internal conflicts within them. Institutions and personnel in local politics constitute a parcel of the institutional complex of state system.

Condition 3: A Theory of Decentralization should Account for the Multifaceted Nature of the Decentralization Process.

A theoretical approach to decentralization should not set an a priori link between decentralization and a certain type of local regime. Attributing a predetermined trajectory and a telos to the process of decentralization would lead to essentialist explanations, such as fetishizing decentralization and/or local politics for theirs essentially democratic nature. A theory of decentralization should provide a framework that explains various outcomes of this process without ascribing an essential nature to social relations at local, national or global levels.

Condition 4: A Theory of Decentralization should come to Terms with the Dialectic between Structure and Agency in Explaining Various Outcomes of Decentralization.

In order to identify continuities and discontinuities in the policy framework, it is important to focus on the changes in the balance of forces within the society with direct implication for the evolution of the economic and political structures (cf. Yalman 2009: 3). Although the decentralization process puts emphasis on the transformative capacity of local relations for power, struggles of local agents should be combined with larger structural processes and big transformations. Social relations and structural factors are, in a fundamental sense, interrelated entities. As they entail one another, we cannot account fully for the one without invoking the other. Therefore, a theory of decentralization should not regard structure and agent as two poles in explaining various outcomes of the decentralization process but rather, it should give explanatory primacy to social relations and envisage the structures as the phenomenal forms of existence of these social relations (D. Sayer 1987: 34). It should ascribe agents the capacity to make a difference in the process of decentralization.

Two Theoretical Approaches to Decentralization

In the wake of decentralization, two influential theoretical perspectives have dominated the literature on the process and its consequences. These perspectives can be named as liberal-individualist and statist approaches to decentralization. This section will critically evaluate each approach and assess their adequacy in the face of the ontological conditions provided above.

The Liberal-Individualist Approach to Decentralization

Tim Campbell's[1] work (1997, 2003, 2008) provides an overly rosy picture of decentralization. Campbell (2003) suggests that Latin America has been going

---

1   Campbell worked as a lead specialist with the World Bank between 1987 and 2005.

through 'a silent revolution' of democratization with decentralization reforms. These policies reshaped the very nature of governance in the region. Campbell's perspective assumes that decentralization will automatically enhance popular participation at the local level and support local government capacities. The roots of this position go back to the nineteenth-century liberal philosophers and political thinkers John Stuart Mill and Alexis de Tocqueville.

Both Mill and Tocqueville argue that active participation into politics nourishes the public spirit and give individuals collective strength. In his essay, *Considerations on Representative Government*, Mill notes that government's end is to guide communities to educate fellow members and 'gradually train the people to walk alone' (1991: 234). In order for government to serve its end, Mill suggests the central government should transfer some of its tasks to 'local representative bodies' (ibid: 411). While he claims 'that the ideally best form of government is representative government' (ibid: 238), he extends the meaning of representation to mean active participation, stating that '[e]very citizen not only having a voice in the exercise of that ultimate sovereignty, but being, at least occasionally, called on to take an actual part in the government' (ibid: 244). He advocates the centrality of local bodies for politics because, to him, in the case of local bodies, many citizens have the chance of being elected either by selection or by rotation, and also minorities have greater opportunity for representation (ibid: 413–4). Therefore, he concludes, local administrative institutions are the chief instruments for the nourishment of public spirit and the development of intelligence (ibid: 412). Likewise, in his *Democracy in America* what Alexis de Tocqueville admires most in America is the political effects of decentralization (1969: 95). He claims that 'you will never find true power among men except in the free concurrence of their wills' (ibid: 94). Decentralization, according to him, moves society rapidly by shaking and awakening it (ibid: 91). Due to decentralization, 'people are enlightened and alert to their interest' (ibid: 90–91).

Mill and Tocqueville agree that decentralization is effective in producing social well-being. For Mill, the criterion for the state's effectiveness in taking care of the affairs of the communities is its efficiency (Magid 1987: 791). The government should be efficient in its conduct. He is concerned that strong centralized states are inefficient because 'the governing body busies itself far too much with local affairs which 'distracts [parliament members] from the proper occupation of the great council of the nation' (Mill 1991: 411). Consequently, he suggests that '[o]n the principle of division of labor, it is indispensable to share [the duties] ... between central and local authorities' (ibid) to attain efficiency of state conduct. Tocqueville has a reservation on the short-run outcome of decentralized policy making. 'In the short run, individuals may succeed less than if the State took their place', he notes. But in the long run, he adds, the general result of all of these individual undertakings surpasses by a great deal what the government would be able to accomplish (Tocqueville 1969: 95). He also claims that the 'collective force of the citizens will always be better able to achieve social prosperity than the authority of the government' (ibid: 91).

In the context of the crisis of the world economy of the late 1970s, Mill's and Tocqueville's ideas were reformulated by neo-classical orthodoxy blending with 'free market' dogma. The objective of the discussion ceased to be an academic one and turned into drawing a roadmap for policy making. The position that promotes decentralization policies on the premises of efficiency, equity and responsiveness to local demands can be defined as the liberal-individualist approach to decentralization.

In the liberal-individualist theory, the state is assumed to be constituted as an independent entity from economy. This independence is derived from the separation of institutions of state and economy with their own rules and priorities. State institutions have their capacity which could only be attained through 'constitutional constraints' over governments' rule (cf. Callaghy 1989, Buchanan 1991). While 'free market' ideology is placing an emphasis on 'rolling back' of the state from the sphere of economy, state's role in economy in policy design and implementation has been enhanced (Yalman 2009: 34). At this point state–civil society relations have been reformulated. While the centralized state is portrayed as a barrier to economic development and civil society a vehicle for participation and empowerment independent of both the state and the market, the focus of the development paradigm shifted towards local communities.

The liberal-individualist approach advocates that decentralization increases the efficiency of local level politics because the participation of local actors, especially the private sector, in politics 'make necessary public functions more efficient and less subject to bureaucracy, clientelism and administrative corruption' (Campbell 1997: 9). The benefits expected from decentralization stem from improvements in 'allocative efficiency' and in 'productive efficiency' (Prud'homme 1996). Allocative efficiency would be improved because locally elected councils can allocate scarce public resources to better match the local demand. Productive efficiency is expected to be elevated because local bodies would be able to deliver goods at a lower cost than national bodies (ibid: 155).

Liberal-individualists argue that decentralization leads to democratization by bringing decision-making closer to civil society (Campbell 2003, 2008, Kähkönen and Lanyi 2001, Oates 1972, Parker and Serrano 2000, Webster 1992). In the process of decentralization, plural subjects of grassroots movements could increase their control over state power and achieve equity. UN-Habitat *Guidelines on Decentralization and Strengthening of Local Authorities* note that political decentralization is an essential component of democratization, 'good governance' and 'citizen engagement'. The *Guidelines* also claim that 'local authorities should recognize the different constituencies within civil society and should strive to ensure that all are involved in the progressive development of their communities and neighborhoods' (UN-Habitat 2007).

The notion of 'governance' which refers to the inclusion of non-governmental 'actors' in governing became the central theme of development studies. Public and private sector 'cooperation' or 'partnership' was prescribed to build up the capacity of state institutions and to achieve local and national development. The claim was made that the incorporation of civil society and the private sector into local public life could transform the nature and style of local governments (Campbell 1997: 4). The state can facilitate development efficiently only when organized within a partnership with the private sector at the national, regional and local levels. 'Both public and private interests ... gain from improved quality of public management' (ibid: 8). Campbell observes rather accurately that 'active private sector participation in policy and services at the local level' will 'improve public responsiveness to private sector needs' and 'foster local private investment' (ibid: 5). Increasing private investment in the local economy is supported to the extent that it creates new opportunities for self-sustained local growth. Justified on these grounds, international development agencies started to provide the bulk of assistance for public–private partnership projects and governance reforms (International Development Bank 1994, UN-Habitat 2007, World Bank 2000, 2004).

Local politics are neither understood nor explained, but rather idealized within this approach. Through this idealization, efficiency and democracy are assumed to result from decentralization. Local politics and local actors, according to this approach, are accepted as consensual, democratic and homogeneous in nature. Mill states that 'there are local interests peculiar to every town ... [T]he different quarters of the same town have seldom or never any material diversities of local interest' (1991: 415). Similarly, Tocqueville claims that in a decentralized country, 'the inhabitants care about each of their country's interests as if it were their own' (1966: 95). Eventually, he adds, 'each man has much the same feeling for his country as one has for one's family ...' (ibid.: 95). The notion of 'social capital' is often employed by the World Bank to indicate how decentralization policies can unite local communities around common goals and build trust bonds among community members (Fine 1999, Fox 1997).

The liberal-individualist approach to decentralization fails to fulfill satisfactorily any of the four conditions provided above. In this theoretical approach, the liberal order is assumed to evolve as a 'kind of spontaneous mutation' (Barry 1988: 73). Due to this emphasis on 'unpredictable, unplanned, undersigned' nature of order, these explanations fail to come to terms with the significant changes in the social reality in general and policy framework in particular. Since local politics is not understood in the context of ongoing economic and social transformations which are national and global, important factors in explaining the determinants of decentralization are left out of the framework. The clearest implication of these problems is their insufficiency in explaining the timing of the decentralization policies. The following quotation from the back of Campbell's book is a good example revealing this limitation: 'As if by an *unseen signal* toward the end of the 1980s, many Latin American governments *suddenly* transferred money and decision-making power to local municipalities' (2003, italics mine). Due to the under-theorization of the links between local, national and global levels of relations, the national and global 'signals' for decentralization are left 'unseen' by the liberal-individualist framework. There are attempts to explain policy change towards decentralization, yet as liberal-individualist theory rejects a general theory of history they rely on explanatory pluralism (Yalman 2009: 29). In each case of decentralization the causal primacy changes.

The argument regarding the necessary relationship between delegating power to local governments and strengthening democratic relations is implicitly accepted as a mutation towards a liberal state based on a basic principle of limited government. There should be constitutional constraint on the arbitrary exercise of the governmental authority (Gray 1995: 71). One way to constraint the government is to minimize the concentration of its power and authority in any one center through fragmentation and diffusion. Liberal-individualist theory adopts a zero-sum approach in explaining the distribution of power within the state. The amount of governmental 'power' is fixed. Thus, if the local level gets more power, it must do so at the expense of central state institutions. Decentralization, therefore, will reduce the dangers of absolutism and corruption which would curtail the individual liberties.

Liberal-individualist students of decentralization do not attempt to theorize the range of possible outcomes of decentralization policies, because the normative stands of the liberal-individualist approach overwhelm its explanatory capacity. To the extent that contextual differences – such as local economy, institutions and local social relations – are underplayed, this approach fails to explain the cases where decentralization policies reinforce authoritarian local state regulations or entrepreneurial local regimes marginalizing large sections of local communities. By essentializing and romanticizing local level politics, the liberal-individualist approach fails to theorize the internal power relations, 'class divisions and structural forces operating on individuals at the local level, constraining their actions in significant respects and ways' (Veltmeyer 2001: 27–8).

In the 1990s, accumulated research concerning the outcomes of the decentralization policies, especially in Latin America, revealed that there was no direct link between decentralization and democratization in practice. These research findings suggested that the optimistic assumptions of the liberal-individualist theories did not hold and an alternative theoretical approach should be developed to understand how the diverse ranges of interests in local politics interact and bring about various alliances that may change the trajectory of decentralization in each locality.

The Statist Approach to Decentralization

The second approach that chooses state institutions as privileged entry points in explaining social change and politics can be defined as the statist approach to decentralization. First settlement of this approach in the US academia was in 1983 when Research Planning Committee on States and Social Structures was set up under SSRC. The public manifesto of this approach was released in 1985 with the publication of *Bringing the States Back In* edited by Evans, Rueschemeyer and Skocpol. In the early 1990s, these ideas were assimilated by the World Bank following successful development and industrialization strategies of the Asian Tigers which reinforced the focus on governing coalition of elites capable of implementing the market friendly reforms and healthy state institutions (Haggard and Webb (eds) 1994, World Bank 1997).

Following the general current, the proponents of the liberal-individualist approach to decentralization felt the urge 'to bring state institutions back in' to their analysis. The advocates of the statist approach to decentralization, who are widespread, including governments, the international financial institutions and academics, do not speak with a single voice. There are certain differences between the proponents of this approach as they state that no single theoretical approach can be adequate to explain the complexity of concrete historical development (Skocpol 1984: 375). Despite their differences, what these analyses have in common is an assumption that the state, with its 'actors' and institutions, is essentially autonomous in its actions. From this methodological standpoint, two leading statist scholars state that 'political choices and political institutions have played a major role in explaining the variation in the form, degree, and success of decentralization in Latin America' (Montero and Samuels 2004b: 5).

From this framework, the decentralization process appears to be primarily a political, and more precisely, a change in the institutional rules that divide political authority and governing capacity between levels of government (Eaton 2004). '[D]emocratization and neoliberal reforms are neither necessary nor sufficient to explain decentralization' note, Montero and Samuels (2004b: 29). The exhaustion of the central state model is linked with the legitimacy crisis that major political parties were faced with in the 1970s (Montero and Samuel (eds) 2004a) or even the collapse of the Soviet Union (Campbell 2008). Yet, the material sources of the legitimacy crisis have not been adequately examined in these studies.[2]

The statist approach emphasizes the key role played by the higher levels policy-makers termed 'state elites' as self-interest maximizers in the formulation of decentralization policies (Skocpol 1979: 32). O'Neill (2003, 2004, 2005) and Rodríguez (1997) argue that decentralization policies have been implemented as survival strategies of national and subnational politicians. Through decentralization, 'state elites' at the center attempted to control local politics more closely while cultivating legitimacy from local communities with improved channels of participation and representation.

When we evaluate the statist approach from the viewpoint of the four empirical conditions, we observe that it has greater leverage than the liberal-individualist approach. Compared to the liberal-individualist approach, which fails to conceptualize local level politics within the reach of the state, statist scholars incorporate local level institutions within the state system. Although the statists are aware of the fact that local governments are part and parcel of the state system, their conceptualization of the state seems to neglect how institutions at different

---

2   There were some attempts within the statist camp to pull the theory away from this trajectory by focusing on the links among the demise of the developmental state, neoliberal economic policies and decentralization; such views could not become as influential within the statist theory. See for instance Falletti (2004, 2010).

levels interact with each other. According to statist approach, political relations radiate from a center (Mann 1985: 187). The natural level of politics is the national one, and the other levels are simply shaped by the policies designed centrally by the 'political elite'. The proposition that ascribes the central position to national level politicians in designing decentralization reforms tacitly ignores the global level dynamics and allocates a marginal position to the subnational level. The majority of statist theorists adopt the metaphor of 'top-to-bottom' which not only corresponds to state-to-society, but also refers to the pinnacle of the state to lower tiers (Manor 1999, Montero 2001, Willis, Garman and Haggard 1999). The local level is regarded as a passive recipient of the policy designs by the center.

The statist approach claims that decentralization is potentially democratic (Bardhan and Mookherjee 2006, Cheema and Rondinelli 1997, Grindle 2009, Wilson et al. 2008). As three notable statist scholars, Willis, Garman and Haggard (1999: 8), claim '[d]ecentralization has been championed as the route to greater accountability and transparency in governance, an avenue towards increased participation by ethnic minorities and social groups excluded under semi-democratic or authoritarian rule'.

Analyses informed by the statist approach provide a more nuanced analysis of various outcomes of the decentralization policies. Although there are various interpretations within the statist camp, it would not be unfair to generalize that statists do not presuppose a direct link between decentralization and democratization. Instead of an automatic transition to democratization, these scholars placed an emphasis on the potentials of decentralization which could only be unleashed by 'healthy'/'strong' institutions', those which can open up new channels for local groups to participate in the policy process. This will increase the 'capacity' of the state to penetrate civil society. Thus, the local regimes that result from decentralization policies are described as a function of the qualities of institutions within them (Connerly, Eaton and Smoke 2010, Falletti 2010, Montero and Samuels (eds) 2004a, Rodden, Eskeland and Litvack (eds) 2003). Decentralization 'will make citizens better off only if local governments are capable ... of delivering services effectively' (Peterson 1997: 22). That is, *once the institutions are fortified, they will be more open to citizen involvement.* On the other hand, as some scholars warn, due to low-level institutionalization and to the clientelistic nature of local politics, decentralization may proceed by strengthening authoritarian elites in the periphery (Cornelius 1999: 4, Fox and Aranda 1996, Rodríguez 1997). These scholars address the risk that local institutions might reproduce long-standing patterns of top-down, exclusionary policy-making, leading to a further tightening of the control of central governments over sub-national politics.

In statist analyses, state institutions are taken as 'independent variables'. They are regarded as autonomous from processes of social formation. This characterization of institutions stems from the compartmentalization of the political, economic and social spheres and ascribing the political one a determinant position vis-à-vis the other two. It is assumed that the strategies and choices of the agents are predetermined by the institutional settings of local and national politics. Therefore, state institutions turn out to be the *explanans* in explaining specific features of the decentralization process without being considered as *explananda* themselves. Internal dynamics of state institutions remain as enigma.

Treating state institutions as independent factors creates a void. The interrelations and interdependence between state institutions and social forces are dealt with in a rather unsatisfactory manner. This framework overlooks possible economic and societal determinants of the decentralization process. Moreover, statist approach to decentralization fail to explain the question of what shapes institutional arrangements at the local level and what kind of social relationships bring about the institutional changes in the process of decentralization. While state institutions play a critical role in producing certain patterns of decentralization, the 'local' is not simply determined by the nature of institutions. Institutions can be examined by looking at the balance of forces within the wider society as well as with the state's institutional ensemble (cf. Jessop 2002: 6).

An Assessment of the Existing Theoretical Approaches to Decentralization

The above literature contributes valuable theoretical insights concerning political and economic transformations, yet none of the available theoretical approaches to decentralization proves to be adequate. In one way or another, they are inconsistent with at least some of the ontological constraints of local politics and decentralization.

Both the liberal-individualist and the statist approaches fail to explain the policy-change towards decentralization. Both approaches are insufficiently sensitive to the fact that the decentralization process has evolved parallel with significant transformations of the international economic system which shape struggles and conflicts of interests involved in actual processes of policy-making. Thus competing political strategies of social agents at a particular conjuncture of the world economy should be examined neither liberal-individualist nor statist approach to decentralization undertake.

Both approaches are misleading in crucial respects. The liberal-individualist approach recognizes the importance of decentralization for democratization. However, it makes the mistake of insisting – with very little evidence – that local politics is essentially democratic. The statist approach correctly observes that decentralization may lead to various trajectories. But this approach ignores the fact that these trajectories cannot be defined simply by institutional settings of the political regime and that they are also shaped and reshaped in social relationships.

These analyses could be challenged by providing a framework that explains various outcomes of decentralization with reference to changing balance of social forces in the process of decentralization. In sum, at the present stage of research, they do not provide a satisfactory framework for the determinants and various outcomes of decentralization.

Theoretical Framework: A Political Economy Approach to Decentralization

This section, drawing upon the literature on state theory, globalization and urban politics, attempts to build an alternative approach to decentralization. It first identifies the relationship between evolving international economic order and decentralization. Then it examines the state debates since the late 1970s with a particular focus on the local state. Finally, the main characteristics of local politics are laid out and the conditions under which decentralization evolves in a certain direction are identified.

Towards the late 1970s and early 1980s, developing countries were faced with problems exacerbated by the economic shocks and the recession in the developed countries. As capital accumulation faced a bottleneck, changing imperatives of capital accumulation required changes in the field of intervention as well as in the field of representation. The profound transition in the functioning of capitalism originated in the developed world, precisely in the UK and the USA, then gradually influenced the developing countries. The crisis and the transition, however, cannot be explained solely with reference to structural factors or processes as if they represent coherent forces with distinctive projects. Neoliberalism, 'a universal class project to reassert the hegemony of capital over labor on the global scale', is not simply a trend (Cammack 2010). Although it stemmed from the developed world, the neoliberal policy framework was shaped to a great extent by diverse social and economic alliances in each country. The new forms of intervention and representation were to be shaped by the changing balance of forces in this conjuncture.

In the context of the decreasing rates of profits of the late 1970s, the deepening of the internationalization of the economy appeared as a viable strategy to overcome the crisis which would enhance the capacity of nationally based multinational corporations to exploit the unevenness of natural and social environment. The internationalization tendency of the world economy is not new (Wood 2002: 35). As Harvey (1999, 2000) notes, the capitalist law of motion based on geographic expansion has produced a differentiated world of uneven social environments and different labor regimes. While investments and subcontracting activities tend to flow to regions that are closer to profitable markets, cheap labor reserves and raw materials, the majority of workers are only able to move within national borders in search of jobs. Multinational companies and banks sought to relocate their activities in the countries where they could escape from restrictive regulations and militant labor unions.

That these international actors do not have direct influence in shaping national agendas, brings the Bretton Woods institutions – the World Bank and the IMF – into the scene. The growth in foreign exchange transactions, the international mobility of capital and the expansion of multinational corporations created a new role for the Bretton Woods institutions. These institutions turned into important agents in regulating the global economy (Wood 2002). In the context of the late 1970s, when many developing countries had already built up large foreign debts and could not get new credits anywhere else, stand-by agreements and structural adjustment programs tailored by the IMF appeared as the only way out of the debt crisis. The tenacity of the economic reforms and the healthy articulation of national economies to the world market were to be restored through the transformation of the social relation which also involved fundamental institutional restructuring of the state. The key running theme in the World Bank and IMF reforms was the pursuit and promotion of capitalist competition on a global scale by accelerating the increasing interconnectedness of national economies and toppling the administrative and legal barriers to capital (Cammack 2010: 271; Jessop 2002: 81–3).

These reforms and adjustment packages were not imposed against the will of dominant coalitions in the countries. The International Financial Institutions (IFIs) could make an impact on policies only if dominant domestic actors had a vested interest in those transformations. After the world recession of the late 1970s hit and was felt in every country to a varying extent, the capitalist classes in the developing countries began to search for solutions similar to their peers in the developed world. In that context, each country's internationalized capitalist classes, backed the stand-by agreements and structural adjustment packages of the IFIs perceiving that further integration into the world market would be advantageous for them.

The states of the developing world are not subordinated to the impersonal dynamics of globalized capital. Rather than withering away, the shift to the neoliberal model organizes and rationalizes state intervention in different ways (Peck 2001: 447). The changes in the state's role are re-imagined, redesigned and reoriented in response to the need for mediating and supporting the *competitiveness* of the national economy (Jessop 2002). The pursuit and promotion of capitalist competitivess, which Cammack calls 'the spirit of competitiveness', signals a turning point in world politics (Cammack 2006).

In order to account for the changing nature and role of the nation state and understand historically specific dimensions of the shift to neoliberalism, one needs to examine its restructuring of the different levels of polity without fixing the analytical focus at the national level (Brenner 2004, Harvey 2000, Jessop 2002, Peck 2001, 2002, Taylor 1996, Sassen 2006, Swyngedouw 1997). There have been significant changes in the roles of national, regional and local governments not only in the economy but, more widely, in social regulation (Brenner 2004, Jessop 2002, Peck 2004, Peck and Tickell 1992). The main implication of the changing social relations for the nation state is the 'scale question' which means that the national scale is no longer the natural level of politics (Peck 2001, Taylor 1996). Uneven development coupled with the effect of the flow of mobile capital tended towards territorial fragmentation of space and political authority.

The transition to neoliberalism has a tendency to bring about decentralization policies but it does not necessitate a specific extent and content of decentralization. In many developing countries as well as in advanced capitalist countries, decentralization policies took various forms which were introduced in lockstep with neoliberal policies. A wide variety of decentralization policies underlines the importance of the interplay of global, national and local agents within their specific institutional settings.

Within the framework developed here the decentralization policies implemented under these conditions are described as neoliberal.[3] These policies were implemented as mechanisms for reducing state deficits and cutting public-sector expenditures by transferring these services to local level authorities. At the same time, they aimed to strengthen the local governments' capacity to raise their own financial resources through fiscal policies, privatizations and public–private partnerships. Foreign borrowing could be used as a last resort which could not be expected to be bailed out by the central government. Thus the local governments are expected to employ 'hard-budget constraints' in undertaking their new assumed responsibilities (Rodden, Eskeland and Litvack (eds) 2003). These policies were justified on the grounds of democracy. In 1973, in Chile, the Pinochet regime implemented the first extensive neoliberal decentralization reforms accompanied by the World Bank reforms (Veltmeyer 2001: 24). In the early 1980s, the World Bank became the pioneer advocate of decentralization policies with reference to Chile's neoliberal experiment. Decentralization policies became more acceptable for local communities via offers of participation. Even the military regime of Pinochet proposed 'to teach the world a lesson in democracy' with these policies (cited in Veltmeyer 2001: 24). 'Since the 1990s, the World Bank has devoted an increasing share of its financing to support its clients countries' decentralization efforts' (World Bank 2008: ix).

Neoliberal decentralization policies carry two structural tendencies which constrain their outcome. Firstly, these decentralization policies tend to extend the disciplinary force of neoliberal rules of competitiveness into local governments and economies. Decentralization policies appeared as an effective mechanism to stimulate and tap the energies of dynamic regions. With increasing interconnectedness among regions, capital mobility turns out to be one of the strongest structural constraints on local political economic relations. Since mobility seems to be a less viable option for territorially-rooted local agents, they would rather ally with the globally mobile foreign capital. Attracting capital investments would become the main motivation behind the actions of local agents. This strategy would put them in competition against other localities to show their

---

3   These decentralization policies as described as neoliberal to be able to differentiate them from a different sort of decentralization. A sort leads to abolishing the state as we know it. One important experience of 'decentralization' was experienced in Paris in 1871. A workers' uprising led to self-government of workers through elected councils in the Paris Commune. Other sorts of non-neoliberal decentralization policies were implemented in Yugoslavia in mid 1952 which aimed at reaching communal/social ownership of the means of production and management of production by direct participation of workers at the workplace level. In this practice of planning, decentralization has been implemented parallel to centralized planning which regulates and overlooks plans shaped by the representative local bodies of the country (Neal 1958: 21–5).

commitment to a good business climate and attract the mobile foreign capital (Danson 1998, Harding 1996). Therefore, mobility of capital could force locally based agents to pursue policies that are in accordance with the neoliberal policy framework (Gottdiner 1986, Logan and Molotch 1987). Within these constraints, local governments tend to adopt a pro-business stance in order to create a 'business-friendly environment'. This process could naturalize market logics on the grounds of efficiency (Peck and Tickell 2002).

Secondly, with decentralization policies, the class bias inscribed on the terrain of the state is diffused into its local institutions. These policies have a tendency to bring the market-oriented groups closer to political decisions. Decentralization policies increased the role of the local state in relation to local development. That is to say the local state assumes an increased role in the state system in organizing a balance of forces favorable to capital accumulation. Paraphrasing Woodrow Wilson's remark, 'when the [local] government becomes important, it becomes important to control the [local] government' (Wilson cited in Dowd 2004: 7). This newly assumed role of the local governments could cause the bourgeoisie gain the upper-hand in local politics. The capacity of the local bourgeoisie to pursue their interest is enhanced, since they are likely to be able to make the case that their self-interests correspond to higher tax revenues for local governments which could lead to better public services, boosted investment and growth rates (Lindblom 1977). In response, to hold on to their political power, local policy-makers privilege the strategies, access and interest of the bourgeoisie over others and cultivate closer relations with capital groups. For that purpose, businessmen with a vested interest in local economy would be invited to cooperate with the local state in pursuit of development strategies and become co-opted into local advisory and executive institutions (Keating 1997: 21–2).

At this point, there is a need to revisit briefly the theories of local state which flourished in the 1970s in the urban politics literature taking these two structural tendencies into account. While the theoretical approach to the local state developed by Cockburn (1977) is characterized as the 'instrumentalist' and Castells' (1977) as 'structuralist', they both regard the local state as part of the state system. Cockburn takes the state as 'a basic unity' all part of which 'work *fundamentally* as one' (1977: 47 original emphasis). Castells (1977), on the other hand, underlines internal contradictions and conflicts within the state apparatuses whose role is to facilitate capital accumulation and reproduce labor power. Therefore, Castells' perspective is open to conceptualize the local state as subject to contradictory pressures. Similarly, Cockburn acknowledges that non-dominant classes may be able to win power in local politics (Pickvance 1995: 261).[4] These scholars, therefore, agreed that the local state could pose an obstacle to reproduction of capitalist relations. Different

---

4   In his comment on the local state, Ralph Miliband himself appears to be in conflict with the so-called 'instrumentalist' premises as he sees the local state 'both an instrument of central control and an obstacle to it' (Miliband cited in Duncan and Goodwin 1988: 251). These general agreements in the Marxist theories of urban politics suggests that differences

interests from those of the nationally dominant groups can dominate particular localities. The classes which are locally but not nationally dominant could be factions of the capitalist class as well as dominated class forces. According to the conflicts and alliances between these local elements and nationally and globally dominant classes, the local state can be vulnerable to transformation.

Although, these local state theories explain various favorable outcomes of local democracy, it should be emphasized that neoliberal decentralization policies have a tendency to increase political class domination inscribed in the material organization and institutions of the [local] state (Poulantzas 1978: 14). This potential power of class domination at the local level becomes actualized in the development goals and shifts in the direction of the policies. As bolstering economic competitiveness of the region becomes the main motivation behind policy making and market-oriented actors gain the upper hand in local politics, the meaning of development may be narrowed down to the potential to bring private economic returns. Resources would be allocated to those which promote economic development, growth and competitiveness. For example, convention centers or mega-projects like highways, international airports and harbors, may be presented as development projects (Keating 1997: 30–31).

It is important to note that structural tendencies and constraints do not strictly determine a particular outcome, but shape the range of outcomes. Confirming this proposition, previous research shows that a wide range of possible outcomes have emerged from decentralization policies in different countries. Looking at the range of outcomes, classified according to which agents are empowered and which are disempowered, one extreme would be where bourgeoisie or certain factions of it dominate local politics and marginalize other classes. At the other extreme, decentralization would empower local dominated masses and open up democratic and participatory local politics. Nevertheless, the theoretical framework offered here, which places an emphasis on how neoliberal decentralization policies could diffuse the rules of competitiveness into localities and increase the strategic importance of local bourgeoisie and mobile capital, limits the possibility of the extreme of the spectrum where dominated masses see their influence increase substantially. Instead of absolute empowerment of dominated classes, this framework proposes the likelihood of an outcome in which the local state becomes a center of resistance used to oppose the power of the dominant classes and local politics turns into a locus of an open-ended struggle between social classes.

Whether neoliberal decentralization leads to the domination of bourgeoisie or an open-ended struggle between social classes depends on the state-economy relationships prevalent with the local social formation and how these relationships evolve as local economies incorporate into the world economy. The mode of integration shapes which social agents are empowered and which are disempowered.

---

between so-called instrumentalist and structuralist Marxist theories are largely due to differences of 'vantage point' in abstraction (see Ollman 2003: 110–12).

Conclusion

The framework drawn in this chapter offers an explanation for policy change towards decentralization and possible outcomes of the decentralization process. The rest of the book applies this theoretical framework to Mexico to explore the determinants and outcomes of the decentralization policies implemented since the 1980s.

Chapter 3
Decentralization Policies in Mexico: Reshaping Forms of Interest Representation and State Intervention

The Mexican Revolution (1910–17) represents a turning point in the country's history. The Revolution generated a national political force that aimed to diminish the power of local and regional authorities and allies of the dictatorship of Porfirio Díaz (Leal 1986: 22). The goals of the Revolution were articulated in the Constitution of 1917 which set the legal ground for centralized state capacity that was concentrated in the federal executive branch and exercised mainly through the presidency. With this institutional structure, the Mexican state has been described as one of the most centralized countries in all Latin America.

However, in the early 1980s, as the country moved to a new period of economic restructuring with neoliberal policies, there have been significant changes in the centralized institutional setting. Decentralization policies appear to be the key elements of the major changes that the country has experienced since the early 1980s. In this process, top-down control corporatist organizations have weakened; regional organizations of the dominated classes have started to emerge; local governments (state and municipality) were given fiscal autonomy and authority to initiate socioeconomic development programs; the local governments' own independent assemblies and law-making powers were boosted in order to increase their administrative capacity; and the role of local state authorities in policy-making processes has increased. These changes have reshaped the forms of interest representation and state intervention.

The main purpose of this chapter is twofold. First, it aims to lay out the material basis that brought decentralization policies into the political agenda in the early 1980s in Mexico. It explains why decentralization policies were implemented hand-in-hand with the neoliberalization policies in Mexico. To answer this question, the chapter examines the inter- and intra-class relations that made decentralization part and parcel of the Mexican transition to neoliberalism. Second, it aims to examine the main characteristics of decentralization policies since the early 1980s.

The main argument of this chapter is that the decentralization policies in Mexico can best be understood within the context of the hegemony crisis of post-war economic development. Within this context, the decentralization policies were shaped as a result of collective pressures and struggles of certain key agents in Mexican politics: dominant fractions of capital, the dominated classes and the

IFIs such as IMF and the World Bank. While certain factions of capital asked for a reorganization of the state which would allow neoliberal market forces to operate at the local level, the dominated classes stepped up their demand for more participatory and democratic local politics. To respond to these demands, the crisis of hegemony required a restructuring in the representational ties between the classes and the political party in power. On top of these pressures, when the debt crisis hit the country in 1982, the IFIs 'advised' the policy-makers 'structural reforms' as a mechanism for reducing state deficits and cutting public expenditures. These restructuring reforms were filtered through the institutional settings and class relations of the country and took the form of decentralization policies which represent a further restoration of the state-economy and state-society relations in line with the deepening neoliberal policies. Through the decentralization policies, the capacity of local governments to initiate social and economic development programs has been significantly strengthened and bottom-up participation channels for local communities in decision-making were generated.

This chapter is organized in four sections. The first section provides a brief historical overview of the process of Mexican state formation and consolidation following the Mexican Revolution. The second section examines the crisis of the late 1970s and maps out how class relations were shaped by development policies and centralized interest representation mechanisms of the import substitution (IS) strategy. The third section focuses on demands for decentralization. The fourth section maps out the major decentralization reforms since the early 1980s.

The Revolution and Establishment of a New State

The pre-revolutionary history as well as new forces, alliances and conflicts emerging from the Revolution shaped state institutions in Mexico thereafter (Hamilton 1982: 3). The 35-year reign of Porfirio Díaz (1876–1911), known as the *Porfiriato*, had resulted in the economic and political domination of a small oligarchic clique at the national, regional and local levels.[1] The Díaz regime maintained close relations with the successful merchants and industrialists of the north, and the owners of large estates (*hacienda*) in the center and south, all of whom had strong links to foreign capital (Hamilton 1982: 45, Katz 1981: 7). The common motive behind the uprising of dispersed revolutionary forces was to destroy the liberal oligarchical state and to diminish the power of local and regional allies of the dictatorship of Porfirio Díaz (Leal 1986: 22).

The Revolution, however, brought about new forms of domination and subordination. After the defeat of the Díaz regime, confrontations arose among the revolutionary forces. As the Díaz bourgeoisie was losing its power neither the

---

1   In 1910, 97 per cent of Mexico's lands was owned by just 830 people or corporations (Wynia 1990:153) and an estimated 97 per cent of the rural population was landless (Hamilton 1986a: 74).

peasants nor the industrial proletariat was capable of controlling the establishment of the regime. Rural and urban petty-bourgeois leaders of the Revolution took the lead in structuring the new state (ibid: 23). These leaders aimed to bring together and discipline the local and regional revolutionary elements. The Constitution of 1917 outlined the essential features of the Mexican state by uniting a multiplicity of local, regional and national electoral organisms (ibid: 27). Despite the constitutional framework, local oligarchies and regional military leaders knows as *caudillo*s, many with their own armies, threatened the hegemony of the centralist coalitions in the 1920s by seeking to build their own political bases among the peasants, workers and the unemployed (Cockroft 1983: 63, Hamilton 1982: 74–9). First caudillos were the military generals leading local and regional private armies during the independence and used their military power to achieve economic power in the newly independent regions. In order to contain these local and regional powers, the central policy makers gradually took legal responsibility for agrarian reform and the implementation of labor legislation that had previously been performed by the state governors. Centralization of national political power in the federal government culminated in the establishment of a single government party, PNR, in 1929, which eventually became PRI in 1946 and ruled the country until 2000 (González Casanova 1970: 33–5). While the party was projected as a loose confederation of regionally based small parties formed during and after the revolution, in practice the party structure was centralized and authoritarian. The organizational base shifted to emphasize individual membership, reducing the influence of political groups and ultimately eliminating local and regional parties (Middlebrook 1995: 25–9).

During the presidency of Lázaro Cárdenas (1934–40), the dominant coalition sought to legitimize the state's power vis-à-vis the peasantry and the working classes, and organized Mexican politics into a corporatist model that was already to be found in the Constitutions of 1917. The legitimation function was fulfilled for the peasantry through a relatively large land reform which was indeed a land distribution program focused upon the small-holding, with the communal holding, or *ejido*. For the working class, the state offered the new labor law that protected the right to unionize and the right to a 'living' wage (Cypher 1990: 11). According to Schmitter (1974: 93–4), corporatism is defined 'as a system of interest representation in which the constituent units are organized into a limited number of singular compulsory, noncompetitive, hierarchically ordered and functionally differentiated categories, recognized (if not created) by the state respective categories in exchange for observing certain controls on the selection of leaders and articulation of demands and support'.

Schmitter (1974: 103–4) further differentiates two forms of corporatism: state and societal corporatism. State corporatism is characterized by monopolies of interest representation that are imposed from above by the government. Societal corporatism differs from state corporatism in terms of the degree of autonomy of interest associations from the state and their bottom-up evolution. Although Schmitter's definition of state corporatism describes the observed characteristics of interest mediation in Mexico which remained intact until the 1980s (Camp 2003: 145–8), the inadequacies of his theorization of corporatist state need to be set out to provide a more comprehensive explanation of the post-revolutionary Mexico.

In Schmitter's framework, the state is treated as being outside conflicts rooted in the economy and civil society (Jessop 1990: 112). It is true that this framework 'recognises the existence of the classes of a capitalist society and proposes an institutional method for regulating the class struggle' (Leal 1986: 30). However, the inadequacy of Schmitter's perspective concerns the state's particular role in regulating class struggle. The delegation of state power to certain interest associations articulates state and non-state institutions in the overall reproduction of capital accumulation and political domination. Therefore, it should be underlined that the corporatist state has an unequal and asymmetrical effect on the interest representation of different social classes.

The corporatist form of state is distinguished by particular forms of political representation and forms of state intervention. Political representation is mediated through a system of public 'corporations'. In 1936, the Confederation of Mexican Workers (*Confederación de Trabajadores de México* – CTM), and in 1938, the National Peasants' Confederation (*Confederación Nacional Campesinos* – CNC) became pillars of the state party (Hamilton 1982: 142–83, Leal 1986: 31).[2] In this way, both workers and peasants are absorbed into and subordinated to these corporatist associations. The direct political control over workers and peasants was established through the authoritarian and top-down control of union bureaucrats (Cockroft 1983: 156). The interest representation of the private sector was regulated through four national business organizations which the Chamber Law defined as the 'consulting organizations'. The Confederation of National Chambers of Commerce (*Confederación de Cámaras Nacionales de Comercio*-CONCANACO) and the National Confederation of Chambers of Industry (*Confederacion Nacional de Camaras Industriales* – CONCAMIN) were united under the umbrella of the National Chamber of Commerce and Industry (*Cámaras Nacionales de Comercio y Industria* – CANACOMIN). The National Chamber of Manufacturers (*Cámara Nacional de la Industria de Transformación* – CANACINTRA) was designed as a mixed-activity catch-all chamber for new and emerging manufacturing sectors that lacked chambers of their own (Shadlen 2000: 77). Although, Article 27 gave the president of the Republic the authority to act as a 'neutral mediator' between opposing interests in society making him the 'supreme arbiter', state intervention occurred through these corporatist associations. Therefore, in corporatism intervention and representation are institutionally fused (Jessop 1990: 120).

Although the Mexican Revolution added certain peculiarities, it is important to note that this corporatist state form was developing in the context of the evolving

---

2   In 1943, the National Confederation of Popular Organizations (*Confederación Nacional de Organizaciones Populares* – CNOP) was founded to incorporate a 'third section' of the society called the 'popular sector' into the party. The popular sector included teachers, public employees, small farmers, and the military.

international economic order. The impact of the world depression of 1929 and the requirements of the post-war world economy shaped the changing imperatives of capital accumulation which entail redefinition of the state intervention and interest representation. The hegemonic strategy of capitalist development in the countries that were highly dependent on foreign trade was adherence to a process of rapid industrialization instituted with the purpose of catching up with the 'developed' countries. This aim forged the idea of a 'mixed economy' which should be guided by the state (Cypher 1990: 11). The guiding role of the state complied with the IS strategy that many countries of the periphery adopted after World War II. This model called upon the 'state elites' to plan and implement development policies, mostly financed by foreign loans, for the construction of the 'national economy' (Cockroft 1983: 184; Hamilton 1982: 121).

The strategies of economic development and the corporatist social formation shaped in the aftermath of the revolution functioned as a hegemonic apparatus as these policies were promoted to aim at the improvement of the living conditions whilst, at the same time achieving industrialization. The revolutionaries promised to liberate the people from the exploitation of foreign capital and the oligarchies of Díaz and construct the national economy. Nevertheless, it was claimed that only through cooperation and, if necessary, short-term sacrifices could the dual objectives of industrialization and social justice be attained. Although Mexico has managed to maintain a high rate of growth for a longer period, social justice remained as a distant dream. The concentration of capital, the monopolization of key industrial sectors by foreign capital and increasing regional disparities triggered a latent conflicts of the 1960s, later became more manifest through the 1970s, and aggravated a crisis of hegemony finally leading to a major transformation in the relations between classes and the state as well as in the integration of the Mexican economy to the world economy in the early 1980s.

The Crisis of Hegemony

The student protests of 1968 constituted a major political earthquake challenging the dominance of the PRI (Álvarez 1987: 17–29). The bloody repression of these student protests on the eve of the 1968 Olympic Games revealed the undemocratic and authoritarian nature of the post-revolutionary order, and ignited further protests. Peasants and workers joined the students in their struggle for a democratic regime (Delarbe 1986: 197). The union leaders attempted to pacify these uprisings and, consequently lost their remaining credibility among peasants and workers.

In the 1970s, the dominated masses started to scrutinize the state's role as neutral arbiter among social classes as well as the centralized interest representation by state-orchestrated corporatist association (Carr 1986). The insurgent workers struggled within the CTM to take control of the union leadership. Upon the failure of this attempt, several worker groups led by automotive workers left the CTM and formed their own unions (Middlebrook 1995: 232–6).[3] Local and regional agrarian and urban social movements that emerged in the 1970s constituted further pressure on the government to introduce limited political liberalization (Otero 1996: 10). The peasants in Puebla, Oaxaca, Chiapas, Morelos, Hidalgo and Guerrero refused to join the CNC and mobilized to establish alternative organizations in the south to represent their interests. Among those, the attention of the central government was concentrated in Guerrero, due to its persistent and intense popular armed resistance (Álvarez 1987: 25). Having lost the consent of these masses, the government applied rigorous military coercion to repress these peasant uprisings.

The restlessness of various social classes triggered a slow political change via the formation of opposition parties. The system needed a 'safety valve' to release the increasing pressure. For this purpose, in 1977, José López Portillo's political reforms legalized the Mexican Communist Party (*Partido Comunista de México* – PCM) and allowed one quarter of the congressional seats – 100 seats – to be allocated to the opposition parties. Following PCM, numerous political parties – mostly of the left – were founded by the dissident groups: the Mexican Unified Socialist Party (*Partido Socialista Unificado de México* – PSUM), the Socialist Workers' Party (*Partido Socialista de los Trabajadores* – PST), the Social Democratic Party (*Partido Social Demócrata* – PSD), and the Revolutionary Workers' Party (*Partido Revolucionario de los Trabajadores* – PRT). These political reforms permitted opposition groups to raise demands through electoral politics. Although the opposition parties 'had a foot in the door', they were still unable to bring about a political opening in the regime (Rodríguez and Ward 1995: 5).

This period of intensified social conflict had significant ramifications for the relations between bourgeoisie and the government. Meanwhile, as the PRI cared more about their relations with the masses, in the 1970s, the Mexican economy began to show declining levels of profitability due to which state-bourgeoisie relations would come under increasing strain (Soederberg 2001: 65). The growing paralysis of the bureaucracy and other institutions of the state partly due to intensified struggles of workers and peasants reduced the effectiveness of the state's intervention to promote private capital accumulation which increased discontent among the capital groups (Cypher 1990: 97, Tirado 1987: 491–2). The Mexican foreign debt was growing at an unsustainable level, from $842 million in 1960 to $3.5 billion in 1969 to $50 billion in 1976 and to $100 billion in 1980 (Barkin 1986: 17–42, Cockroft 1983: 259, Otero 1996: 6). In the first half of the 1970s, as various representative associations of bourgeoisie frequently complained

---

3   Álvarez (1987: 22) identifies four important trade unions founded in 1971 challenging the CTM were as follows: Union of Electricity Workers of Mexico (*Sindicato de Trabajadores Electricistas de la República Mexicana* – STERM), Trade Union Movement of Railroad Workers (*Movimiento Sindical Ferrocarrilero* – MFS), Authentic Front of Labor (*Frente Auténtico de Trabajo* – FAT), and Independent Front of Trade Unions (*Frente Sindical Independiente* – FSI).

about the political instability and inconsistent government policies, they attempted to become a united front to control policy formulation more closely. They felt that they had lost their representative connection with the PRI. To resolve this representation crisis, different sections of the bourgeoisie came together around the Private Sector Council (*Consejo Coordinador Empresarial* – CCE) in May 1975.

The availability of foreign loans and the large supply of 'petro-pesos' provided a breathing space for the economy and gave the regime a certain stability. Despite the huge debt, after new discoveries of rich oil reserves in Chiapas and along the Caribbean coast, the US and other foreign creditors poured US$3 billion worth of new credits into the country between 1976 and 1979 (Cockroft 1983: 260). In order to rein in the social discontent, the policy-makers allocated new credit funds from revenues brought in by the increasing oil price and foreign borrowings. However, falling oil prices and dried up foreign loans in the early 1980s came as a final punch to the regime. The government had little or nothing to deliver in terms of material benefit.

In 1981 and 1982, Mexico witnessed what was then generally considered as the gravest economic crisis in its history. Due to the increasing debt burden, the crisis was primarily one of balance of payments that had the effect of raising inflation and aggravating foreign exchange difficulties. In August 1982, the government declared a moratorium on payments to service its foreign debt. In September 1982, as a last resort, the government announced the nationalization of the banking system.

After the nationalization, the relations between bourgeoisie and the government took a turn for the worse (Cypher 1990: 124). Leading business circles had no tolerance for the government whose unilateral decision would choke the inflow of the foreign credits. The nationalization decision created infighting within the PRI as well. Some groups within the party were apparently critical of the decision, claiming that the government was unable to provide the necessary foreign exchange resources both to maintain the import requirements of manufacturing industry and to service the growing foreign debt. As some PRI members continued to back nationalization, arguing that it was in agreement with the spirit of the Mexican Revolution, the bourgeoisie felt the urge to exert stronger pressure on the political process by becoming actively involved in politics (Luna 2004). In becoming a 'class for itself', the CCE called for a general strike of business 'to bring the economy to its knees' (Cypher 1990: 125). On the day Miguel de la Madrid assumed the Presidency, the press declaration made by the CCE in the semi-official newspaper of the PRI, *Excelsior*, illustrated the attitude of the capitalist classes. The CCE also underlined that 'the time has changed and so should the rules of the game'. With this declaration they announced that, 'productive sectors would not accept unconditional state authority' and they asked for 'a government that govern only what is necessary'.[4]

---

4 *Excelsior*, 1 December 1982.

The combined impact of the debt burden, growing social unrest and a paralysis of the bureaucracy and other institutions of the state due to political infighting led to a crisis of hegemony. To use Gramscian terminology, in the late 1970s 'the ruling class lost its consensus', and 'the great masses became detached from their traditional ideologies, and no longer believed what they used to believe previously'. During this period, Mexico experienced a 'crisis of authority' which was 'precisely [a] crisis of hegemony, or general crisis of the state' (Gramsci 1971: 210). The 'old [was] … dying and the new [could not] … be born' (ibid: 275–6).

At this historical juncture, a new social order had to be born to secure the economic power of the dominant coalitions of the capitalist class and ensure the legitimacy of the state. As Valdés Ugalde notes (1997: 203), the period between September and December 1982 and the presidency of Miguel de la Madrid (1982–88) marked the opening of a new period that was clearly distinguished from the post-revolutionary period. The crisis of hegemony led to two parallel processes: a shift in economic development policies and an institutional restructuring which would reform the representational ties between the classes and political parties. Collective pressures and struggles of certain key actors placed the decentralization policies at the conjunction of these two processes.

Demands for Decentralization

In order to lay out the dynamics that brought the processes of neoliberalization and decentralization together in the Mexican context, we need to trace the inter- and intra-class relations back to the late 1960s, when the 'hegemony crisis' originated and the basic components of the regime stated to crumble. Certain factions of the Mexican bourgeoisie as well as the dominated classes particularly from the south started to show discontent with the post-revolutionary planning and development policies as well as various institutional arrangement that accompanied the IS strategies.

Higher productivity and profits generated between 1940 and 1960 (the 'Mexican miracle') resulted in the worsening of regional disparities. In spite of repeated declarations that the construction of a centrally planned 'national economy' would mitigate and correct imbalances in regional development, capitalist growth and Mexico's integration into world market had widened the disparities among regions (Barkin 1986: 111; Garza 2003: 487–8). IS strategies facilitated the concentration of capital in three major regions in the country: the center, the west and the north. The central region refers to the Valley of Mexico which includes Mexico City and the contiguous State of Mexico; Guadalajara became the west's main pole of economic and political activity, and Monterrey became that of the north (Valdés Ugalde 1996: 132). More broadly, the country was divided into three regions: industrial zones (Valley of Mexico, Guadalajara and Monterrey); the semi-industrial states (Coahcuila, Chihuahua, Jalisco, Puebla and Veracruz) and the rest of the country (Barkin 1986: 111). While the industrial and semi-industrial states were favored by public investments, the agricultural regions of the south were left relatively backward.

The industrial, commercial and financial bourgeoisie based in the Valley of Mexico were especially privileged in receiving IS subsidies, fiscal incentives and credits (Cordero, Santin and Tirado 1983: 83; Tirado 1987: 485). The concentration of capital reinforced the concentration of economic activity around Mexico City. Mexico is often referred to as the archetype of the 'macrocephalic' state, where national political-economic life is dominated by an oversized center (Campbell 2003: 40). Mexico City was the largest city in the entire Western Hemisphere at the beginning of the nineteenth century. It gained more economic importance in the 1930s. In 1930, Mexico City had a 28.5 per cent share of the total manufacturing production of Mexico; in 1940, 32.1 per cent; in 1950, 40 per cent; in 1960, 46.5 per cent, in 1970, 46.8 per cent; and in 1980, 48.0 per cent (Ward 1990: 20). The manufacturing firms – small and medium ones are represented in CANACINTRA, larger firms in CONCAMIN – are referred to as 'the faction of the forties', since they started to develop with the process of industrialization protected by the state from that decade (Gaspar and Valdés 1987: 503). These businessmen had close ties with the PRI; even a considerable number of businessmen became high-level civil functionaries in government (ibid: 504). Some of the more powerful firms were negotiating with the president directly bypassing the 'consultation organization' (Leal 1986: 37).

Although northern bourgeoisie – usually called 'the Monterrey Group' – can be traced back to the pre-revolutionary period, they were also the beneficiaries of the centralized state policies (Gaspar and Valdés 1987: 502). These groups were ideologically opposed to state intervention and argued that the best way to promote the industrial development of the country was to lure foreign investment and produce for foreign markets, mainly the US, rather than producing for the internal market (Chand 2001: 20–21).[5] In the early 1960s, the representatives of these capital groups approached the federal government with concerns about rising unemployment and social unrest in the region.[6] In order to promote the border economy by attracting foreign capital, alleviate unemployment and address the demands of the capital groups, the federal government implemented the Border Industrialization (*Maquiladora*) Program in 1965 (Gereffi 1996: 85; Schmidt 2000). As a result of the expansion of export assembly production, both public investments and the private banking sector gave preferential treatment to the north (Appendini et al. 1972).

---

5 Since the northern economy depends largely on the border with the US, the northerners saw their interest not in the inward-looking industrialization policies but in adopting a 'free-market-led' development allowing a greater integration with the world economy. The emphasis on 'laissez faire liberalism' was brought up by the businessmen from Chihuahua in the interviews.

6 In 1922 and 1942, the US and Mexican governments signed a Contract Workers' Program, known as Bracero. Yet when the Bracero Program was unilaterally terminated by the US, many workers and peasants employed in the US firms and farms were sent back to Mexico in 1964. This created an estimate loss of 185,000 jobs especially in the north of Mexico. See Baerresen (1971).

Integration into the world economy through *maquiladoras* made the northern bourgeoisie less tolerant of central policy-making processes. The representative associations of these capital groups considered that their influence and as well as direct representation in policy making was becoming weaker compared to business leaders in Mexico City (Gaspar and Valdés 1987: 516–7). The interests of the northern bourgeoisie were represented in the Confederation (*Confederación Patronal de la República Mexicana* – COPARMEX) and the corporatist structure left all associations of regional bourgeoisie outside of the dominant power networks (Shadlen 2000: 91; cf. Gaspar and Valdés 1987: 516). The COPARMEX was founded in 1929 by oligopolistic commercial bourgeoisie and industrialists from Monterrey and other northern states, big land owners who had been a strong economic force before the land reform of the Cárdenas government, with finance bourgeoisie that had been effective before the foundation of the state banks. COPARMEX, which attacked the Cárdenas scheme for its 'socialist' objectives (Cypher 1990: 47), has not been accepted as one of the officially accredited voluntary organizations and suffered from a lack of representation.

In the late 1970s, decentralization of economic development became one of the strongest demands of the various bourgeois associations in northern Mexico.[7] The 'unilateral decision' of bank nationalization in 1982, which would drastically injure the *maquiladora* industry, became the tipping point of the discontent about authoritarian central government (Luna 2004). These groups responded to the economic crisis by demanding the restructuring of state-economy relations towards a more open and liberal economy with more local state involvement. They claimed that the usual national macroeconomic policies and standardized industrial and/or regional policies formulated at the center were inadequate to tap the energies of the dynamic regions.[8] This was, arguably, because the transfer of authority to local governments would divert credit in their favor and increase the economic dynamism of their region.

The position of the northern bourgeoisie became stronger vis-à-vis other factions both politically and economically. Within the context of the economic crisis, alienated by their lack of representation, the northern groups looked to developing their own political resources rather than relying on their traditional alliance with the PRI. Since the Revolution, the PNR and its successors had not been able to harness the northern bourgeoisie to its development project. Although

---

7   Interview with Miguel de la Madrid, former president of Mexico between 1983 and 1989.

8   Most of these business groups were indeed offspring of the central governments' development policies. However, in the interviews with the leading *maquiladora* businessmen from Chihuahua, they emphasized that their region was economically self-sufficient and their prosperity was not so much dependent on central governments' protection, concession, contracts, credits or subsidies. For a similar argument, see also President of CANACO in Chihuahua, Rodrigo Legarreta Soto 'La Geografía nos ha Favorecido', *El Heraldo de Chihuahua*, 16 December 1982.

the northern bourgeoisie did not overtly challenge the regime, they have tended to support the PAN since its foundation in 1939 (Tirado 1987: 487). The PAN defined central state planning in Mexico as socialist, and demanded more autonomy for the northern states and municipalities (Valdés Ugalde 1987: 439). Allegedly, some former PRI supporters among these groups shifted their support to the PAN, which forced the PRI leaders respond to the demands of the northern bourgeoisie (Tirado 1987: 491–5). Economically, the devaluations of the peso and the decline of real wages in the 1970s stimulated tremendous growth in the *maquiladora* industry. For example, while Mexico's share of US imports was less than 1 per cent in the late 1960s, it became almost 20 per cent in 1976 (Sklair 1989: 12).

Foreign bourgeoisie joined the domestic bourgeoisie demanding a reorganization of the institutional infrastructure through which neoliberal market forces would operate in the local markets. The *Maquiladora* Program provided the foreign – mostly US – capital with cheap labor and tax exemptions (Sklair 1989). In the 1970s, however, faced with decreasing profits, these companies, in search of more fiscal concessions and easier and more practical bureaucratic procedures, started to challenge the Mexican state by threatening to relocate their business to other countries.[9] Foreign bourgeoisie in the *maquiladora* industry demanded local state regulation in the *maquiladora* sector, because localized or regionalized development policies would enable them to exploit further the unevenness of natural and social environment and demographic structure of Mexico.

While the concentration of capital created a representation crisis among bourgeoisie, authoritarian decision-making through the corporatist organizations triggered discontent among the students and dominated classes. To maintain order, the links between the PRI and the leaders of each sector became so strong that they had developed entrenched interests: patron-client relations formed an intricate web that acted as a filter against demands from groups located at the base (Dresser 1994a: 128) As a result, the CTM and CNC lost their credibility among the bottom rungs. Given the failure of their attempts to capture the corporatist organizations, a large number of workers and peasants detached from their organizations and formed alternative unions at the local level (Delarbe 1986). They started to establish their own grassroots organizations which later became the mobilizing force of the struggle for democratization and participation at the local level (Otero 1996:1).[10]

---

9   In an interview with the chairman of the board and CEO of an American company investing in the *maquiladora* sector in Chihuahua, he mentioned that the foreign investors were not content about the centralized administrative and fiscal structure. He claimed that these foreign investors voiced their demands for administrative and fiscal decentralization in the late 1970s.

10   In the 'Federalism and the Decentralization of the National Life' meeting, held in Mexico City in May 1982, representatives of local labor and peasant organizations claimed that the federal government should delegate most of its political, economic and social functions to state and municipal level governments to better include local communities in the system. *El Heraldo de Chihuahua*, 31 May 1982.

As Carr rightly observes, the economic crisis displaced the center of the conflict away from the capital-labor relationships at the point of production to the distribution of resources (1986: 222–3). Valdés-Ugalde (1987) and Luna (1987) claim that the northern bourgeoisie was effective in defining the terms of crisis and shaping the demands of the working classes. Once the crisis was defined with reference to distribution, the demands of the working classes could be easily crafted around how to 'deliver the goods' more efficiently. Housing problems, transport problems, the deterioration in urban living conditions and maldistribution of food became the main points of struggle (Carr 1986: 222). The solution to these problems was seen as being to make public service more efficient and enhance participation in local development programs. Popular discontent in the relatively deprived regions was transformed into local movements with regional identities which, in turn, triggered pressures for participation in development.[11]

By the early 1970s, widespread poverty in the marginalized regions of the south had become politically unsustainable. Responding to participation and democratization demands of the working classes was urgent owing to their potential to deepen the crisis by elevating public resistance. Therefore, the struggle of the dominated masses for egalitarian social justice was central in determining the democratization emphasis of the decentralization policies which will be laid out in the next section.

Decentralization Policies

The Spanish crown aimed to establish a centralized state as an effective means of controlling and optimizing the extraction of resources. At the same time, the colonists wanted to keep the remnants of the old ruling classes to help in the organization of the labor force. Most former nobles and high bureaucrats who cooperated with the colonists became known as *caciques*.[12] Some of these *caciques* became governors of the Indian communities and maintained a degree of autonomy over their internal affairs. In order to find a middle way between the centralized colonial bureaucracy and power of the *caciques*, the Spanish created the concept of the *Municipio Libre* (Free Municipality), as the basic unit of government. Each community – that is, municipality – had its own town council, to which it elected five to ten councilors from the old ruling class. Although the town council had a degree of guaranteed autonomy vis-à-vis the colonial authorities, this autonomy of local

---

11   In 1981, the PRI organized several meetings as part of the election campaign of Miguel de la Madrid. The meetings, which were called *consultas populares*, were held in each state with the invited representatives of the social groups. In 1982, the PRI published the booklets of these meetings. The demand for local democracy and participation was voiced in every meeting by various agents (*Consulta Popular* 1982).

12   The term *cacique* is imported from the Caribbean to define co-opted Indian authorities. The term comes from the Taíno word '*cacike*' or the Arawak word '*kassiquan*' both meaning to have or maintain a house.

authorities was very limited and the main political structure was centralized (Véliz 1980: 170; Gamas-Torruco 1975: 157–76). After the revolution, although *pueblos* (local communities) remained as the basic constitutive elements of the society and the sovereign nucleus of the regime (Loveman 1993), these diversified local and regional interests were forced to take part within the centralized institutions.

Despite this federalist institutional structure, the local governments were not granted any real autonomy and independent authority. The 1917 Constitution accepted the federalist structure with 31 states. The states were to be led by governors who would be elected for six-year periods and could not be re-elected for two consecutive terms. Article 115 of the Constitution kept the legacy of the *Municipio Libre* by designating the municipalities as autonomous administrative units. Every municipality would be governed by the town council (ayuntamiento), made up of both elected and appointed officials. The *ayuntamiento* would be comprised of a mayor, council members (*regidor*), and other public officials, assisted by professionals, technicians and administrative personnel. The municipal presidents, council members would be elected for three-year terms, and could not be re-elected for two consecutive terms. This institutional structure resembled more a unitary polity than a constitutional federal system (Edmonds-Poli 2006: 388).

Besides, the PRI dealt with local affairs by extending itself to the localities through local level party committees and informal domination of the local party bosses. Rather than incorporating local communities, party committees functioned as a control mechanism of the PRI. Rural areas were dominated by the local party bosses. The old term *cacique* is used for these local party bosses. The imposition of the *caciques* was absolute and proceeded unmolested, as long as these bosses delivered political support for the PRI. Although *caciques* were strong in their localities, the hierarchical lines were neither substantially broken nor weakened. The central party organization could always intervene in and take control of local politics. With this institutional and social structure, post-revolutionary Mexico is considered as the most centralized country in Latin America.

There are two significant phases of decentralization in Mexico. The first phase was initiated by the de la Madrid government (1982–88). These decentralization policies were significant in setting the agenda for further decentralization. The second phase of decentralization policies was implemented during the Ernesto Zedillo government (1994–2000). This period also corresponds to the 1995 economic crisis and Mexico's integration into the world market through NAFTA. In what follows, I will lay out these phases of decentralization as well as the decentralization attempts of the Carlos Salinas de Gortari government (1988–94) and of the post-2000 period when the PAN defeated the PRI and put an end to the single party domination with two consecutive presidents, Vicente Fox (2000–06) and Felipe Carderón (2006–12).

The Miguel de la Madrid Government (1982–1988): 'Decentralization of National Life'

On 3 December 1982, only two days following his inauguration, President Miguel de la Madrid got together with 31 governors and presented his forthcoming decentralization reforms.[13] On 6 December, he proposed amendments to Articles 26 and 115 of the Constitution, which set the legal frame for the first extensive decentralization policies in Mexico. With the amendments to Article 26, the federal governments' major responsibilities with regard to social and economic development were transferred to municipal and state authorities. For this purpose, an Under-Secretary of Regional Development was created under the Ministry of Programming and Budget (Secretaría de Programación y Presupuesto – SPP) as an entity responsible for overseeing the regional development programs and as a liaison with states and municipalities. The amendments to Article 115, known as the Municipal Reform, expanded municipalities' authority over their budgets and extended proportional representation in municipalities by making it easier for opposition parties to compete.[14]

The new model of development was called the National System of Democratic Planning (Sistema Nacional de Planeación Democrática – SNPD) which was crafted around the following four principles (de la Madrid 1982: 96):

1. To support the development of productive activities in various regions.
2. To encourage social development at the municipal and state levels.
3. To improve and expand regional infrastructure construction and development projects.
4. To promote economic activities and public services of the states.

While the federal government kept the right to regulate and supervise the planning of development projects, the right to make operative decisions concerning design and implementation of these development programs and services was passed on to subnational governments. The Development Agreements (Convenio Único de Desarrollo – CUD) became the fundamental instruments to coordinate the investment at both federal and state levels (SPP 1983: 5). These treaty-like agreements would bring together the president, governors, and the SPP representatives to stipulate the size, terms, and conditions of investment projects financed jointly by federal, state and municipality governments. All the development programs were financed from one regular budget line (*Ramo*) 26 or Regional Development. Budget line 26 was largely disbursed through the CUDs. By the late 1980s, about a fifth of the public sector investment budget was channeled through this program (Campbell 2003: 43).

---

13   *El Heraldo de Chihuahua*, 'Mayor Apoyo Federal a los Gobiernos Estatales', 4 December 1982.

14   The Municipal Reform allowed municipalities under 300, 000 inhabitants to have city council members of minority parties, including a *síndico*, who countersigns executive measures. For *síndico*s, see Rodríguez (1997: 31–2).

To qualify for Budget Line 26, local governments were obliged to implement a planning process that involved the participation of interest groups, agencies, and organizations in decisions over public spending. Decision-making processes at state and municipality levels would be facilitated through State Development Planning Committees (Comités de Planeación para el Desarrollo del Estado – COPLADEs) and Municipal Development Planning Committes (Comités de Planeación para el Desarrollo Municipal – COPLADEMs). These committees were to decide on annual investment projects and rank the development projects in order of priority to be negotiated with the federal level at the CUDs. 'The COPLADEs were chaired by the governor and consisted of permanent technical staff and an elaborate array of sectoral and regional authorities as well as representatives of the civil society'. Similar to COPLADEs, 'COPLADEMs were formed in each municipality to facilitate the participation of civil society, government representatives and state bureaucrats at the municipal level' (SPP 1983).

In addition to the development programs, state governments were authorized to handle state auctions for subcontracting the infrastructure services as well as construction and lightening of roads and bridges. The responsibility to provide basic public services, including water, street lighting, street cleaning, markets, cemeteries, slaughterhouses, road construction and maintenance, parks and gardens, public security and local transportation was transferred to municipalities. To handle these responsibilities, the reform assigned new revenues to state and municipality budgets from the federal government.[15] The financial responsibilities of the states and municipalities also included levying property taxes and charging fees for public services (Bertran and Portilla 1986).

The Salinas Government (1988–1994): National Solidarity Program

Despite the efforts of the Miguel de la Madrid government, the hegemony crisis of 1982 left its deep mark on the 1988 presidential elections. The PRI candidate Carlos Salinas de Gortari was faced with a real opposition in this election. Southern dominated masses demanding democratization and participation and northern bourgeoisie demanding more neoliberalization and autonomy got organized around their respective candidates, Cuahtémoc Cárdenas and Manuel Clouthier. Cárdenas, who had resigned from the PRI protesting the economic policies of the Miguel de la Madrid government, gathered the left coalition opposition. The

---

15   According to the new *Ley de Coordinación Fiscal*, the federal government allocated revenue to the states through three separate mechanisms: the General Fund of Participations (*Fondo General de Participaciones* – aka *participaciones*), the Complementary Finacial Fund (*Fondo Financiero Complementario*) and the Municipal Strenghtening Fund (*Fondo de Fomento Municipal*). Federal law also requires that states pass on at least 20 per cent of their receipt from the *participaciones*, complementary funds and all receipt from municipal strengthening funds to the municipal governments.

electoral competition became fiercer when the PAN nominated a leading northern businessman, Clouthier, as its presidential candidate.

The 1988 elections turned out to be the most controversial elections in Mexican history. On election night, the first results showed Cárdenas with a significant lead. However, the Secretary of Interior announced that the electoral results could not be officialized, due to a suspicious collapse in the central computer system. When the system was recovered, Salinas was declared the official winner. The elections were followed by massive rallies organized by Cuauhtémoc Cárdenas to protest 'the stolen elections'. In this process, the legitimacy of the newly installed president, Carlos Salinas de Gortari was severely challenged.

On his first day in office, the President Salinas outlined 123 new social programs knows as the National Solidarity Program (*Program Nacional de Solidaridad* – PRONASOL). The stated goal of the 1989–94 National Development Plan, which lays out the main tenets of the PRONASOL, was to combine economic growth with social development (Poder Ejecutivo Federal 1989: 16). However, the PRONASOL is viewed as an attempt to overcome the legitimacy crisis of the presidency of Salinas by aiming to offset the social cost of the 1982 economic crisis and subsequent neoliberal policies (cf. Cornelius, Craig, and Fox eds. 1994). It was an effort by the federal government and the PRI to win back support of low-income urban populations (Campbell 2003: 44, Dresser 1994a).

Although Salinas claimed that the PRONASOL aimed to create a new relationship between the state and citizens based on participatory democracy, as Selee (2011: 53) notes, the program was an ambiguous decentralization attempt because it did not entail transfers of decision-making authority to lower levels of government. Kaufman and Trejo (1997: 717) note that PRONASOL marked the highest point of the President's efforts to augment their control over local power structures. Similarly, Cabrero (2000) calls the PRONASOL as centralized decentralization. The only change in the legal framework of the development and planning programs was relabeling the CUD as Social Development Agreements (*Convenios de Desarrollo Social* – CDSs). These development agreements were highly centralized and decisions were taken at the discretion of the federal office of the President (Rodríguez 1997: 76–83).

The centralist character of the PRONASOL is closely related to Salinas's aim of destroying the Cardenista opposition in the states and municipalities of the south. The program deliberately bypassed state and municipal governments in social development. Therefore, the PRONASOL was a strategy to buy off dissent and weaken their political organizations through tightly controlled central government-run development programs.

The Zedillo Government (1994–2000): New Federalism

At the end of the Salinas government, Mexico witnessed serious economic and political crises which did not lead to a crisis of authority as in 1983 but paved the way for deepening of neoliberalism. Assassinations of high-level politicians and scandals of various forms of corruption strengthen the claims about increasing institutional capacities of the state. The largest peso devaluation since the early 1980s gave more power to the IMF and World Bank in restructuring the national economy. The economic crisis remained within the financial sector and the discontent coming from the dominated masses was confined to indigenous communities in the south.

Mexico's full integration into NAFTA came into effect on 1 January 1994, and aimed to increase the level of integration of the Mexican economy with the North American economy. The NAFTA agreement required extensive tariff elimination which opened the Mexican economy for more foreign direct investments in the profitable sectors and regions. With the integration, foreign direct investment started to concentrate in the *maquiladora* sector of the northern states and some tourist enclaves in the south. The NAFTA integration increased the parcellization of the national economy into regions which stimulated more decentralization to increase the competitiveness of the dynamic regions (Griswold 2002, Warner and Gerbasi 2004).[16]

Between 1983 and 1995, due to insufficient financial resources, subnational governments accumulated heavy debt burdens and huge payment obligations (Hernández Trillo, Diaz Cayeros and Gamboa González 2002). The decentralization reforms of the de la Madrid government authorized state and municipal governments to borrow, in the event that both Budget Line 26 and federal transfers failed to cover expenditure. The 1995 financial crisis came after a period of reckless credit expansion, a sharp increase in interest rates, and big budget deficits among subnational governments. The federal government had to ease the credit burden of the subnational governments through extraordinary transfers and debt rescheduling programs (ibid: 370). Therefore, the second wave of the decentralization reforms was also necessitated as part of the recovery plan for the 1995 economic crisis (Rodríguez 1997: 247).

The New Federalism project of the Ernesto Zedillo government led to a clear definition of the distribution of administrative functions across federal, state and municipal levels (Selee 2011: 56–57). There were three objectives of the New Federalism: far-reaching decentralization of the federal public administration; a national system of budget coordination and raised revenue-sharing allocations to the states; and renewal of the municipal governments (Poder Ejecutivo Federal 2000: 125). The new faculties and functions of the subnational governments had to be financed by increased funds. Two main strategies were devised to strengthen them: to transfer more federal funds to the states and municipalities; and to expand opportunities to raise revenue locally through taxation and other mechanisms. The

---

16 Zapatista rebels started on the day that the NAFTA agreement went into effect and demanded respect for their indigenous traditions and customs (*usos y costumbres*) with decentralization of power to the community level. These demands of Zapatistas strengthen the arguments regarding achieving local participation and democratization through decentralization.

federal transfers to states and municipalities were increased gradually as new funds were assigned for regional and social development through Budget Line 26. The New Federalism also marked conceptual and operative changes in the development policies by attempting to establish closer relations between public and private sectors. In order to raise revenues, subnational governments were advised to appeal to the private sector for their support in the development programs.

The 1997 midterm elections changed the configuration of the Chamber of Deputies, showing that the opposition parties especially the PRD proved itself as an important political actor in national politics.[17] For the first time in history, the PRI lost its majority in the Chamber of Deputies. Encouraged by these results, the PAN initiated a municipal reform backed by the PRD. The Congress passed an amendment to Article 115 of the Constitution with a large majority. This amendment, aimed to improve some of the deficiencies of the 1983 amendment, designated municipalities as political entities which could set policy for local affairs within their jurisdiction like states and the federal government (Guillén and Ziccardi 2004: 5–48). The reform also gave municipalities the faculty to assume new powers and functions through agreements with state governments. City councils assumed the faculty to make long-term planning commitments without the approval of the state legislator. Crafting and implementing regional development plans became one of the responsibilities of the municipalities. In the negotiations over the federal budget in 1998, Budget Line 26 was converted into Budget Line 33 which meant an automatic transfer to states and municipalities. Budget Line 33 was made up of several funds to combat problems associated with poverty such as improving the health services, social infrastructure, education and security. These transfers became one of the most significant sources of revenue for the local governments. With this change, the annual CUD meeting was abolished and federal government transferred the right to regulate and supervise the planning of development projects to the state governments. State revenues increased to an average of 28 per cent of the national budget between 1998 and 2000 (Edmonds-Poli 2006: 398). The financial decentralization policies implemented between 1980 and 2000 resulted in a significant increase in decentralized spending, from 20.3 per cent in 1980, to 47.3 per cent in 1984 and 60.3 per cent in 2000 of all public expenditure (Poder Ejecutivo Federal 2000: 3, 13).

The PAN Governments: Fox (2000–2006) and Calderón (2006–2012)

As the 2000 elections were approaching, the PAN candidate for presidency, former governor of Guanajuato, Vicente Fox, promised to strengthen the autonomy of subnational governments as part of his election campaign. When he assumed

---

17   The PRD gained 60 new seats in the Chamber of Deputies, while PAN gained 2. The Green Ecologist Party of Mexico (*Partido Verde Ecologista de México* – PVEM) was also an emerging new party which gained 8 seats. As opposed to these, the PRI lost 59 seats of the Chamber of Deputies in these elections.

the presidency, it was expected that decentralization would be at the top of this policy agenda. Despite these expectations, neither of the PAN presidents – Fox or Calderón – implemented extensive decentralization policies compared to the previous three consecutive PRI governments. These two governments pursued the decentralization path that had been on track since 1983. While the volume of transfer revenues given to the local governments has continued to increase since 2000, both Fox and Calderón consistently put emphasis on fiscal discipline and hard budget constraints at subnational levels. The subnational governments have been reminded that seeking new revenue-raising powers is one important responsibility that governors have to accomplish.

As PAN replaced the 71-year-old rule of PRI, an important transformation took place in the intergovernmental relations. Since 2000, the governors of PRD and PRI as well as the mayors have lobbied to increase their capacities and financial resources. To pressure the federal government, the National Governors' Conference (*Conferencia Nacional de Gobernadores* – CONAGO) was founded in July 2002 in Cancun with the participation of PRI and PRD governors.[18] On February 2003, the PAN governors joined the CONAGO. The stated aim of CONAGO was to strengthen and promote the process of decentralization.[19] More precisely, the foundation of this Conference presents a strong effort towards fiscal federalism. With similar intentions, the National Conference of Mexican Municipalities (*Conferencia Nacional de Municipios de México*-CONAMM) gathering 2000 municipalities under its umbrella, was established in 2005. The federal government agreed with the intentions of the CONAGO and CONAMM and showed its approval of these efforts with the Special Program for an Authentic Federalism (2002–2006) which expresses the government's aim to achieve 'enhance just, efficient, transparent, and responsible federalism' (Fox 2002: 564).

CONAGO has become an active agency to increase competitiveness of the country. Under CONAGO, various subcommittees have been formed to deal with improving the main functions and tasks of local governments. One of the most effective subcommittees has been the one on competitiveness. In March 2008, the Secretary of Economy initiated the Process to Strengthen the Regulatory Framework for Competitiveness (*Proceso para el Fortalecimiento del Marco Regulatorio para la Competitividad* – a.k.a. *Proceso Marco*). The CONAGO was also invited to be in this process together with the representatives of the private sector, academia and OECD.[20] In January 2012, the president of CONAGO, José Calzada Roviroza makes the case that CONAGO should have closer relations

---

18   *The Economist,* 'Redrawing the Federal Map', 29 March 2003.

19   For more information on CONAGO see, http://www.conago.org.mx/Sobre/QueEs. aspx.

20   Acuerda CONAGO participar en Proceso Marco de Competitividad Impulsado por SE, Secretaría de Economía, [Online]. Available at http://www.apps1.economic.gob. mx/webportal/boletin/html/BoletinsD.asp?NumBoletin=991&Cveldiome=1 [Accessed: 10 November 2011].

with their North American counterparts to increase their competitiveness.[21] Soon enough, towards the end of February 2012, Calzada Roviroza paid a visit to Washington for a series of meetings with North American governors, business circles and the U.S. President Barack Obama. [22]

Conclusion

This chapter suggests that in order to explain how and why decentralization policies were implemented since 1983 in Mexico, the analysis should focus on the inter- and intra-class relations within the context of the hegemony crisis of the post-war economic development. The decentralization policies were advised by the IFIs, yet these policies took their particular shape within the dynamics of class relations. Corporatist interest representation and increasing regional disparities during the post-war era shaped the inter- and intra-class relations which eventually expanded the economic crisis towards a hegemony crisis. The decentralization policies were implemented by the policy-makers a strategy to restore business confidence and popular consent in the regime with a promise of an alternative form of interest representation and participation. In addition to building consensus on the neoliberal project, the transfer of political and policy issues to subnational states reshaped state intervention. The following chapters inquire how decentralization policies led to different outcomes in each state of Mexico, corresponding to distinctive forms of interest representation and state intervention at the local level.

---

21   *El Economista*, 'Conago Busca Nuevo Modo de Competir' 30 January 2012.
22   El Federalista, 'Gira el Gobernador Calzada por Washington como presidente de CONAGO', 22 February 2012.

Chapter 4

Public–Private Partnership Leads Local Development: Entrepreneurialism in Chihuahua

In Chihuahua, the decentralization policies unleashed an opportunity for local bourgeoisie to pursue their own development agenda in the region. Local capital groups and their representative associations involved in the *maquiladora* industry intervened in the political processes as a united front in order to increase the competitiveness of their locality. Local and foreign capital investing in the *maquiladora* industry formed a partnership with the local state; and from then on, this public–private partnership initiated and executed all the local development plans. This business alliance, in time, took control of local development.

In this process, dominated masses have been either marginalized and excluded from local politics or absorbed into business-funded civil societal organizations. Joint ventures between domestic and foreign firms strengthened the position of the local-global coalition of the private sector in Chihuahua vis-à-vis other local social agents. Although the decentralization policies facilitated a move towards electoral democratization in Chihuahua, they failed to pave the way for equal participation of different local groups in political processes. Local bourgeoisie organized civil societal organization and controlled the social movements according to their interest. Both local policy-makers and social agents adopted an entrepreneurial discourse, narrate their cities as entrepreneurial, and market them as entrepreneurial (cf. Jessop and Sum 2000: 2289). Local development pattern in Chihuahua has evolved towards entrepreneurial.

This chapter examines the formation of Chihuahua's entrepreneurial form of local development in the process of decentralization. It analyses how and why local firms' business connections – subcontracting and/or joint-ventures – with foreign firms gave them relative strength vis-à-vis other social classes. The analysis shows that the main factor that explains the emergence of entrepreneurial local development is the strategies and alliances of local bourgeoisie.

The argument is laid out in six sections. The first section of this chapter explores how the formation of the local state institutions and social structures are rooted in the historical development of states' local political economy which has been shaped by its geographical location and underground resources. The second section focuses on the *maquiladora* industry and examines this new breed of bourgeoisie's increasing regionalist sentiments and discomfort with the corporatist relations. The third section traces the design process of the decentralized local development programs. The fourth and the fifth sections examine the ramifications of the decentralization process on social formation and on the political institutions respectively. They show that both civil society organizations and local political institutions have been encroached on by the market rationale and that local politics has become entrepreneurial. The final section concludes the chapter by overviewing the findings from the case of Chihuahua.

Formation of the Local Social Relations and State Institutions

Local political economy of Chihuahua has been shaped by its geographical location and underground resources. Chihuahua is located in the north-western region of Mexico bordering the United States with several border crossings that link Ciudad Juárez with the state of New Mexico and El Paso. Since the late nineteenth century, the state's bonanza of metal and mineral mines has attracted businessmen across the border to the region. They allied with local landowners to launch their businesses. Parallel to the new business partnerships, a financial sector also developed in the region. The regional banks, *Banco Mexicano, Banco Minera de Chihuahua*, became the largest banks in Mexico.

Mineral and metal mining business stimulated development of communications and transportation networks in the region. In 1881, telephone services were introduced in Chihuahua by the manager of *Banco Mexicano* and a local merchant. Using the telephone infrastructure, Enrique C. Creel[1] installed the *Compañía Telefónica de Chihuahua* in 1887. Establishment of the communication network was followed by transportation. Making Chihuahua a transnational railway connection point was the main objective behind the railway construction that both Enrique C. Creel and his partner across the border, Albert Kinsey Owen, undertook in 1897. The Copper Canyon railroad connected different regions of Chihuahua to each other. It also built a strong bond between Chihuahua and its neighboring cities in the US.

Although these investments in the telephone and railway systems were primarily to facilitate the transportation of raw materials, they fueled the rapid growth of the local economy and helped support the industrial development of the region. While communication networks and railways allowed the domestic markets to greatly expand, they also enhanced the integration of people along the Mexico–US border. In the beginning of the twentieth century, Chihuahua was already a significant center of business with industry, finance, mining and cattle breeding sectors.

The strengthening of the local economy further increased the interaction between local businessmen and various US and British companies investing in Chihuahua.

---

1   Enrique C. Creel was Mexico's leading banker, industrialist, and a representative of country's largest land and cattle owner. He was the governor of Chihuahua between 1905 and 1910.

When Enrique C. Creel became governor of Chihuahua in 1905, he enacted a law that allowed the selling of community land to foreigners. Small landowners (*rancheros*), feeling threatened by the centralization of land ownership, sold their land to these newcomers (Wasserman 1984: 48).[2] With this law, the US and the British companies managed to hold over 20 per cent of the state's land (ibid: 188).

The ability of local businessmen to forge successful and relatively independent relations with foreign businessmen brought the former dominance over other factions of bourgeoisie and society in general. This class alliance was proved to be an important factor backing the Díaz regime (1876–1911) and as well as the post-revolutionary governments until 1934. Ironically enough, it was also this class alliance which motivated the forces of Pancho Villa during the revolutionary years (1910–17) and made Chihuahua the center of the revolutionary movement (ibid: 48). The selling of community lands to foreign investors drastically increased the number of landless unemployed laborers. Increasing unemployment, the dispossession of small businessmen, and the monopoly of a few families led to a rebellion of small landowners, workers and elements of the middle class. When the revolutionaries led by Pancho Villa took over control of Ciudad Juárez, General Díaz resigned from his position. They expropriated strong families' landholdings, banks and mines. After the revolution however, these families negotiated power shares with the new revolutionary leaders and were able to control local politics until 1934 (Williams 1990: 302). Álvaro Obregón's accession to power in 1920 signaled a fresh start of an alliance between center and north which was so successful that 'the Northern Dynasty' reigned in Mexico City until Cárdenas came to power (ibid).

During the Cárdenas government (1934–40), the north's representation went into relative decline. As Chand notes, northerners were alienated by the central government's imposition of political leaders on the state without even a semblance of popular support. Moreover, he adds, when those candidates failed to win a popular mandate, the PRI resorted to fraud (2001: 29). Motivated by these impositions, there have always been attempts to challenge the central powers with struggles to nominate their candidates in local elections.

The decline of the north's power in the capital city led to the foundation of the PAN in 1939. Since its foundation, the party has attracted significant support from the northern bourgeoisie with its strong emphasis on the need for decentralization of the central powers. The party leaders targeted the municipal level electoral politics in the north and demanded more independence for municipalities.[3] Support for the PAN increased in the 1950s, when most of the capital groups realized that they would not have any influence on the federal government. They supported the failed gubernatorial and presidential campaigns of Luis H. Álvarez

---

2   The effects of the economic depression of 1907 and three years of drought (1907–1909) exacerbated these conditions.

3   Interview with Trevizo Gutiérrez.

in 1956 and 1958 respectively.[4] Despite this local appeal, the PAN was never able to successfully challenge the rule of the PRI in Chihuahua arguably due to the centralist structure of policy making. As a local businessman from Chihuahua noted, 'in those years [referring to pre-1980], the local governments had only symbolic power. They were not functional to solve our problems. So, we used to support the PAN in local elections only under the table.'

The Mexican state was not able to harness the northern bourgeoisie to its development project. The state of Chihuahua had a distinct development pattern which was primarily led by investments from foreign corporations. Various capital groups in this region benefited from the growth of the economy due to the direct foreign investment entering through the US border. Although COPARMEX was very influential among the northern capital groups, the corporatist institutions left this association outside the dominant power networks.

The local networks of the PRI were never tight in Chihuahua. The dependence of social classes on the border economy weakened the corporatist unions and associations that provided support to the PRI at the local level. The relative strength of the PAN further curtailed the effectiveness of corporatist power relations. Although the PAN was not able to pose a challenge to the PRI until the 1980s, its strong presence with a prominent capital group's support created unrest among the PRI leaders. This uneasiness fortified the strategy of imposition of outsiders nominated by the central government to fill the posts of mayors and governors.

The outcome with respect to state 'capacity' in Chihuahua depended crucially on the balance of social forces. The organizational capacities of the PRI in Chihuahua have become rather ineffective at sustaining the legitimacy of the local system. The imposition of the local state governments by Mexico City has weakened the consolidation of political support of various social agents. Due to weak social support, the local policy-makers have not been effective in providing solutions to regional problems. The lack of organizational capacity of the local state in effectively mobilizing social support attempted to be rectified by closer relations with the central government which reinforced the local discontent. Therefore, as a result of the historical evolution of the local political economy, the state of Chihuahua lacked both the strategies for organizing an adequate social base and the organizational capacity to collect the necessary information to craft effective development projects.

The *Maquiladora* Industry

In 1917, as a result of its own wartime labor shortages, the US campaigned for a more open immigration policy. The US and Mexican governments signed a

---

4   Luis H. Álvarez was a major textile industrialist from Chihuahua. Almost 30 years after his first attempt, he was elected as the mayor of Chihuahua City in 1983. Later, he became the leader of the PAN in 1987.

Contract Workers' Program, known as *Bracero*.[5] The program was ended in 1922, when the need for guest workers dropped. In 1942, faced with the necessity of employing cheap labor in agriculture, the US government signed the second *Bracero* Program with its Mexican counterpart.[6] Between 1942 and 1964, 3 million Mexican workers entered the US under this program (Craig 1971: 21). The greatest number of workers sent to the US was from Chihuahua (Hancock 1959). In 1964, the second *Bracero* Program was unilaterally terminated by the US. The US government claimed that the Program created a large movement of undocumented labor into the US economy, since most of the workers and peasants stayed in the US after their contract was over (Zolberg 2006: 310–311). Upon termination of the program, workers and peasants employed in US firms and farms were sent back to Mexico which created an estimated loss of 185, 000 jobs (Baerresen 1971). In 1965, this unemployed reserve army attracted a new form of production, called the Border Industrialization Program, which was the origin of the *maquiladora* industry.

Since the 1970s, the *maquiladora* industry has become the main economic activity along the US–Mexico border. The *Maquiladora* Program provided foreign corporations with a low-waged and disorganized labor force as well as access to the comparatively unregulated conditions in Mexico without trade barriers. Since the 1970s, devaluations and the decline of real wages stimulated tremendous growth in the *maquiladora* industry. By the mid 1980s, it had displaced tourism as Mexico's second largest source of foreign exchange after petroleum, generating approximately 370, 000 jobs (South 1990: 549).

As a result of the growth of the *maquiladora* industry, the economy of Chihuahua became increasingly linked to the US economy and the world market. The establishment of *maquiladora* plants has promoted the development of regional production centers. Initially, the *Maquiladora* Program was restricted to an area 20 km from the US border. In 1972, the federal government relaxed the 20 km zone regulation to allow *maquiladora* plants to locate in most urban places; however, due to the transportation costs, the *maquiladora* industry did not expand to the inland regions.[7] The industry became the most dynamic sector of the economy in the northern border states. The state of Chihuahua ranked in

---

5   The *Bracero* Program allowed Mexican workers (*braceros*) to cross the border for a limited term to work in a variety of US private and public enterprises. The sectors where Mexican workers were employed were railroads, aluminum factories, shipbuilding and other construction operations, fish-packing plants, rice and sugar plantations and even government military camps. For a detailed study on the Bracero Program, see Alanís Enciso (1999).

6   This time, the program was designed to bring farm workers to harvest cotton, sugar beets and other crops throughout the US. Mexican workers were also employed in the mining industry, light industry and the railroad construction.

7   The only geographic limitation on establishing *maquiladora* plants is that they are not permitted in Mexico City, Guadalajara or Monterrey urban areas due to the industrial concentration already present in those areas.

the top third of all Mexican states in terms of its contribution to the nation's gross domestic product. The *maquiladora* industry replaced agriculture, mining and cattle breeding as the fundamental economic activity in the state. Ciudad Juárez, in particular, has become one of the largest *maquila* cities in the border region. By 1974, there were 89 *maquiladora*s in Ciudad Juárez employing 17, 484 people (Martínez 1982: 179).

The growth of the *maquiladora* industry in the late 1970s and early 1980s has shaped the composition of the social classes in Chihuahua. To begin with, it represents both the internalization of foreign capital and the internationalization of domestic capital. Although the origin of the capital invested in the first *maquiladora*s was 100 per cent foreign, in the 1970s foreign investors viewed *maquiladora*s as a partnership. By the 1980s, the capital invested in the *maquiladora*s became almost evenly divided between US and Mexican firms (Gereffi 1996, 2003). As Mizrahi (1994: 85) argues, 'the *maquiladora* industry led to a formation of new type of entrepreneurs who are related to the *maquiladora* industry as … subcontractors'. A number of enterprises servicing the *maquiladora* plants flourished in the industrial, construction, commercial, and service sector. Businessmen who belong to this new generation of the northern capitalist class regard themselves as 'self-made men', and their success is attributed to individual drive, vision and ability, not to advantages of social background, corporatism or institutional position.[8] However, these businessmen were depended upon their networks with mostly US-originated foreign capitalists who needed local partners to better conduct their business in the border region. The *maquiladora* industry also led to emergence of a new middle class. Although the *maquiladora* industry is based on non-unionized and inexperienced labor, it also necessitated and attracted technically trained and highly skilled workers, managers and administrators (ibid).

Alongside the impact of integration into the world economy through the *maquiladora* industry, the local economy of Chihuahua started to have its own problems that revived anti-centralist feelings. Incoming problems of the border region made northern capitalists less tolerant of the excessive centralization of Mexico's political system. Antonio Jaime, the president of the CONACO of Ciudad Juárez, argued that 'as a frontier region, the situation of Ciudad Juárez is very special with its very different problems from other cities of the country'.[9] Local business groups argued that their regional problems could not be solved by the policies formulated at the center (López Ochoa 1987: 123). They claimed that regional development plans should be designed locally according to the specific priorities of the region. These capitalists argued that centralization had been an obstacle to the development of the northern region because regional development plans were not designed with consideration of the characteristics specific to the region.[10]

---

8   Interviews with Villalobos, Reyes López. See also Mizrahi (1994: 86) for a similar interview with Emilio Goicochea Luna.

9   *El Heraldo de Chihuahua*, 7 January 1983.

10   Interviews with Kalisch, Trevizo Gutiérrez and Ramos Vaka.

There emerged a strong sense of regionalism among the northern states as they differentiated themselves culturally, politically and economically from the other regions of the country. The overriding discourse of this regionalism was that the north is a productive and indeed a self-sufficient region, yet the value created in the north is transferred by the central state to the business groups in Mexico City and to the corporatist networks in the south.[11] As a businessman from Chihuahua puts it, 'the rest of the country has been milking the profits of the northern business groups without providing any solutions to our regionally specific problems'. This discourse stemming from the local capital groups has had an effect on other social classes. In comparison with the south and center, northerners started to describe themselves as middle class, individualistic, honest, open, hardworking, and business oriented (Williams 1990: 307).

In the late 1970s, *maquiladora* bourgeoisie started to voice their discontent with the inward-looking industrialization policies of the IS. The concentration of capital in Mexico City generated resentment among small and medium size enterprises of Chihuahua, which were increasingly squeezed by their lack of access to subsidies, fiscal exemption, and credits (Mizrahi 2003: 70). They argued that the federal state's subsidy and credit policies had been benefiting certain groups in Mexico City. The northern capital had a vested interest in adopting a new export-led model of development based on greater integration with the US.

However, integrating small and medium size bourgeoisie into the world market would not be achieved simply by opening up the markets. Their integration into the export sector would require a significant supply of credits to expand and modernize their plants. Therefore, in order to change the form of the state's allocation of resources, the representative associations of these capital groups started to demand a restructuring of state-economy relations towards a more open and liberal economy whose property relations, the rule of law, is still regulated by the state but with more local state involvement, that is decentralization. They claimed political and economic decentralization could facilitate the economic integration of the northern region into the world market, which would benefit the Mexican economy as a whole.[12]

The nationalization of the banking system in 1983 increased the discontent of these capital groups and their demands for decentralization. Three of these banks were owned by financial groups from Chihuahua: *Grupo COMERMEX, Banco BCH* and *Credito Mexicano*. The owner of the COMERMEX was the Chihuahua Group, one of the most important capital groups in Mexico. These financial groups and the industrialists who were getting credits from these banks perceived nationalization as a threat to their existence.[13] As a reaction to the nationalization

---

11 Interview with Riquelme. For the statements of the president of the CANACO, Rodrigo Legarreta Soto in the same line, see *El Heraldo de Chihuahua*, 'La Geografía nos ha Favorecido', 16 December 1982.

12 Interviews with Ramos Vaka, Riquelme, and Kalisch.

13 Interviews with Kalisch and Ramos Vaka.

of the banks, the representatives of the capital groups in Chihuahua amplified their demands for decentralization, decided to form an organized opposition to the PRI and became actively involved in politics.[14]

In the 1970s, the local capital groups in Chihuahua began to organize. The COPARMEX started to become a more active organization in local politics. The Confederation attempted to increase its influence in policy making by establishing closer relations with local branches of the CANACINTRA. In 1973, the Chihuahua Group founded a private economic development organization, the Economic Development of Chihuahua (*Desarrollo Económico del Estado de Chihuahua, A.C* – DESEC), for regulating the *maquiladora* industry in Chihuahua. Both local chapters of COPARMEX and the DESEC played an active role 'in defining the development priorities of the region during the 1970s when the local government did not have a corresponding office for economic development' (Ramos Vaka 2006). In order to be able to attract more investments in the region, these local capital groups were aware that they had to restore a 'business-friendly environment'. The local development programs appear to be the main strategic means to increase the competitiveness of the region through resolving environmental and infrastructure problems as well as improving labor quality. However for effective local development plans financed by the local state, decentralization was necessary. For that purpose, COPARMEX and DESEC voiced the decentralization demands of local bourgeoisie in an organized fashion.

Evaluating the economic success of the region, the central state became more aware of the potential benefits that *maquiladora* activities could bring. The relative economic success and prosperity of the northern states strengthened the impact of these decentralization demands, particularly between 1980 and 1982, when the rest of the country was confronted with a severe economic crisis. However, the border-states recovered more rapidly than the rest of the country due to increasing foreign investments in the region (Williams 1990: 312). Responding to the demands of the northern bourgeoisie became crucial for the central state as the north's economic strength vital to the economy of the country as a whole.

Local Development Programs

Until the 1980s, a fundamental concern of the capital groups in Chihuahua was the lack of communication between the central government and northern bourgeoisie. They felt they did not have a powerful enough voice within the federal state apparatus. In 1982, during the election campaign of Miguel de la Madrid, the need for a 'state-business dialog' in Chihuahua was one of the most important issues brought by various local businessmen. At the *Consulta Popular* meeting held in Ciudad Juárez on 28 November 1981, the president of the State Center for Entrepreneurial Promotion (*Centro Estatal de Promoción Empresarial* – CEPE),

---

14   Interview with Kalisch.

Julio Ornelas Gil, asked for more collaboration between the public and private sectors in the development planning process.[15] Ornelas Gil claimed that 'such harmonic development will be achieved only if the public and private sectors agree on a set of goals common to both of them'.[16] Ornelas Gil's statement reflects the general strategy of the Chihuahua bourgeoisie in the process of decentralization.

In this section, I trace the process of decentralization with a focus on local and foreign capital groups' initiatives in participating in the development plans. While between 1983 and 1988, the capital groups were active within the COPLADE, in the 1990s, these groups took the lead in determining the development projects independent from the COPLADE. The projects initiated by domestic and foreign bourgeoisie and their representative associations determined the regional priorities for the development programs.

Beginning of the Decentralization Process: Local Capital Groups Assisting the Local Development Agency in the 1980s

An influential businessman, Samuel Kalisch notes 'we welcomed the decentralization policies of the de la Madrid government by assisting the foundation of the COPLADE'.[17] The COPLADE of the state of Chihuahua was established soon after amendments of Article 26 and Article 115 were ratified in the Congress. The COPLADE was initially dependent on the DESEC. DESEC assisted the COPLADE in providing staff and economic information about the state (Ramos Vaka 2006).

According to the SPP Report, the decentralization policies between 1983 and 1988 reactivated the economy of the state of Chihuahua converting it into an important source of employment that contributed to the recovery recuperation of the national economy. The decentralized development projects 'reduced the economic vulnerability of the state's medium size entrepreneurs by increasing their competitiveness in the foreign goods and services markets'. The decentralization policies 'favored the growing integration of the frontier cities in national and global markets' (SPP 1988: 125). The expansion of the interstate and interregional road network of the northern border constituted the theme of the decentralized development programs to stimulate the commercial activities (SPP 1988: 125). This also literally paved the way for the emergence of new development areas into which the *maquiladora* industry could expand.

15　Consulta popular en las reuniones estatales, Chihuahua, vol. 1, PRI: 13–14.
16　Ibid: 14.
17　Interview with Kalisch.

Birth of the Public–Private Partnership: Century 21 Chihuahua

The economy of Chihuahua grew 5 per cent on average between 1970 and 1985 under the impact of growing *maquiladora* industry. However, in the late 1980s, the local economy witnessed a relative slow down as a result of decreasing investments in the region. The annual growth rate between 1985 and 1988 was on average 1.6 per cent (Ruíz Durán 2000: 5). This decrease was an indication of the strengthening regional competition for mobile capital. The representatives of the Chihuahua Group were motivated to seek new ways to compete for new investments. The decentralized development programs provided them with a suitable channel to transmit their pressures. As the role of the local governments became important with decentralization policies, local business groups started to become PAN candidates for public offices, to take initiatives in determining the candidates, to provide generous financial contributions to the party and to design the election campaigns (Chand 2001, Mizrahi 1996). Almost all of the PAN's candidates who won mayoral races in Chihuahua had business backgrounds. Eventually, the party won the governorships and state congressional majority in the 1992 elections. The local government became very receptive to the development projects initiated by the *Maquiladora* bourgeoisie.

Leading local capital groups and their representative associations intended to supervise the design and implementation of development plans and strategic actions that would mark the path of the economic development of Chihuahua into the new century. The twenty-first century Chihuahua was an economic development project initiated by the DESEC in March 1991, then adopted by the state government in 1992 and constituted the basic framework of the State Plan of Development between 1993 and 1999.[18]

The development program was well received by policy-makers due to the ability of the DESEC to work closely with the universities especially the Technical University of Monterrey and international research agencies. In the initial phase of the design of the project local capital groups collaborated with the professionals from the University. Leonel Guerra, the director of the Center for International Competitiveness at the Technical University of Monterrey at Chihuahua, was appointed as the director and supervisor of the project in August 1993. A group of researchers working for the Center for International Competitiveness prepared the report of the diagnosis of the development problems, and identified a set of concrete action initiatives on trade, investment, education, infrastructure and finance. This report also prescribed the development of industrial clusters in Chihuahua to increase the competitiveness and productivity of the local economy.[19]

The state of Chihuahua and the DESEC hired an international development consultancy company, DRI/McGraw Hill, for the project in 1993 which can be

---

18   Interview with Ramos Vaka.

19   Clusters are geographical concentration of interconnected businesses, suppliers, and associated institutions.

noted as the first sign of public–private partnership. The state of Chihuahua and the private sector shared the cost of the study equally (Ruíz Dúran 2000: 6). The consultancy agency, the Economic Competitiveness Group (ECG), a unit of DRI/McGraw Hill, studied the region's features to prepare a report on possible development strategies for Chihuahua. The ECG developed 'a vision of a new kind of economy to guide the decisions of policy makers and leaders in the private sector and developed strategies and tactics for moving the economy in new directions'.[20]

The twenty-first century Chihuahua Project was effective in setting the groundwork for public–private partnership. ECG consultants also conducted interviews with local government agencies in order set the framework for a public–private partnership. The ECG report indicated that 'the local state government should facilitate the project together with the private sector to achieve healthy economic development'.[21]

In 1997, one of the leading local businessmen, Gustavo Enrique Madero Muños, was appointed as the General Coordinator of the COPLADE of Chihuahua.[22] The same year in November, the World Bank organized a conference in Chihuahua City. The World Bank's Vice President of Finance for the Private Sector, Elkyn Chaparro said, 'we are going to give a "Bravo Chihuahua" because they managed to change the history attained through a virtuous cycle translated to a better level of life for Chihuahuans, a confidence in the future, and a culture of social capital' (Chaparro 1997: 4). The Bank supported the twenty-first century Chihuahua Project as 'the ideal model of regional development' (ibid.). It is mentioned that 'the collaboration between the government and the private sector attained by the twenty-first century Chihuahua Project attracted $240 million of foreign direct investment in the region as well as generated 140 thousand jobs [between 1992 and 1997] in Chihuahua City and Ciudad Juárez'.[23]

---

20   The ECG is a group of professional economists, planners, and management consultants who design economic development strategies to help their clients achieve sustainable economic competitiveness. The ECG particularly specializes in assisting regions (metropolitan areas, states, countries, and cross-border regions) develop and implement action-oriented economic development strategies. ECG clients are state and local governments, business leadership groups, public–private consortia, partnerships between national and local governments, international agencies, and private sponsors. For more information on the company, see www.ecgroup.com.

21   [Online]. Available at: www.ecgroup.com/proj_1.htm.

22   Madero Muños had served as the vice-president of the Chihuahua chapter of the COPARMEX in 1993, the general secretary of the DESEC, and he was also one of the promoters of the 21st Century Chihuahua Project.

23   *El Diario de Chihuahua*, 'Congreso empresarial asisten 1500', 18 November 1997.

Continuation of the Partnership under the PRI Administration: The Plan Juárez,
CODECH, Nuevo Millenio

Although, the initial phase of the public–private partnership was started during the
PAN government, the partnership was essentially non-partisan. The PRI was able
to counter the appeal of the PAN by selecting local businessmen as its candidates,
which consequently diminished the differences between these two parties in terms
of candidate profile, party organization and policy priorities (Alba Vega and Aziz
Nassif 2000: 99).

In 1998, the PRI won the gubernatorial elections but the new government
accepted a line of continuity in including local capital groups in the decision-
making processes of the development plans as partners. The continuation of the
public–private partnership was presented as a substantial element that had to
remain manifest in the State Plan of Development of the new government (Ruíz
Durán 2000: 12). In the 2004 elections, when PRI candidate José Reyes Baeza
Terrazas was elected the governor of Chihuahua, he aimed to intensify the public–
private partnership by creating quasi-governmental development agencies that
would hamper the functions of the COPLADE.

As a local businessman from Ciudad Juárez noted, 'decentralization policies
facilitated cross-border regional collaboration' which further strengthened the
public–private partnership in Chihuahua.[24] As the control of the central state over
local governments weakened, decentralization policies opened the borders for
joint development plans. Concentration of the economic activities on the border
municipalities brought about various problems on both sides of the border (Alfie
1996). In 1999, to solve these problems, the capital groups from Ciudad Juárez
sought greater cooperation in proposing planning and implementing infrastructure
development.[25] An executive committee was formed to promote strategic
development and progress throughout the city. In May 2001, the Juárez Strategic
Plan Civil Association was formally established. The board of directors of this
association was made up of the governor of Chihuahua, the mayor of Ciudad
Juárez, the President of the University of Ciudad Juárez, and the CEOs of some
23 *maquiladora* corporations.[26] Each private sector member of the association
makes an annual contribution of 20,000 dollars each to the association to support
the Plan.[27] In 2005, the Mayor of Ciudad Juárez, named the chairman of Juárez
Strategic Plan Civil Association as the new Municipal Technical Secretary, a
position that directs urban planning and infrastructure development (Camp 2005).
An international management consultancy firm, the SOCINTEC, was integrated

---

24   Interview with Carlos Riguelme.

25   Interviews with Osbaldo and Murgia.

26   Most of these corporations are foreign corporations invested in the *maquiladora*
industry in the region. The rest are the Mexican contractor companies of the *maquiladora*
industry.

27   [Online]. Available at: www.planjuarez.org/press_coverage.ssp.

into the organization in 2001.[28] The Juárez Strategic Plan combined the strategies 'to attain healthy decentralization and transparency of the local authorities with a new city planning' (SOCINTEC 2003).

With the Juárez Strategic Plan, both foreign and domestic *maquiladora* capital groups became effective in determining the development programs in Chihuahua. It is a development strategy for Ciudad Juárez, yet its scope was not confined to it. The plan suggests a reorganization of the economic activities within the state of Chihuahua. Its detailed development plans for several municipalities with *maquiladora* plants constituted the essence of the State Plan of Development 1999–2005 (Camp 2005).

In 2004, the Baeza Terrazas government (PRI) aimed to intensify the public–private partnership, thus giving rise to new quasi-governmental development agencies and new development projects. On 9 December 2004, the Council for Economic Development of the State of Chihuahua (*Consejo Para el Desarrollo Económico del Estado de Chihuahua* – CODECH) was installed by the DESEC, and the Economic Development of Ciudad Juárez (*Desarrollo Económico de Ciudad Juárez* – DECJ). The governor also participated in this initial meeting and addressed the founders of the CODECH as the keynote speaker, demonstrating the close relationship between the governor and these capital groups.[29] The Council was established as a private organization for planning, executing and following up on the strategic development plans. The head of the Council is a leading businessman, and the governor is appointed as the honorary chairman of the Council. The executive committee of the Council is composed of six secretaries of the state of Chihuahua, presidents of the DESEC and DECJ, three representatives of universities and a representative of the Economic Transformation Group.[30]

Like the previous local public–private development agencies, the CODECH hired international economic consultancy firms, the Economic Transformation Group (ETG) and Economic Competitiveness Groups (ECG).[31] The ECG researchers visited several municipalities of Chihuahua, had meetings with local policy-makers and capital groups investing in the clusters to get in-depth knowledge of economic development priorities. As a result of these diagnoses, the CODECH presented a development plan that is in essence a continuation of the Chihuahua twenty-first century. This new project called *Chihuahua Nuevo Millenio* constituted the essence of the economic and regional development policies implemented between 2004 and 2010. Therefore in this period, the

---

28 The SOCINTEC specialized in fostering economic development and improving the competitiveness of enterprises through management of innovation and technology. The majority of SOCINTEC is owned by a joint venture of a Spanish electric utility company, Iberdrola and a Spanish bank, BBVA.

29 Meeting minutes of the Installation of the CODECH, 9 December 2004.

30 Meeting minutes of the Executive Committee of the CODECH, 17 March 2005.

31 Between January and April of 2004, Economic Competitiveness Groups (ECG) assisted the ETG in conducting the research.

public–private partnership under CODECH designed and closed executed the development projects. Baeza Terrazas conveys this idea with different wording. According to him (2010: 5, 87, 113), these policies were a 'synthetic product' of a 'dialogue' and 'interinstitutional collaboration' between the political and social actors' in Chihuahua.

Social Development Programs: FECHAC

A severe storm and flooding devastated parts of Chihuahua City in 1990, causing significant physical damage in the *maquiladora* workers' neighborhoods. As a safe and clean environment has increasingly become a factor of new investment decisions, the necessity to take an active role in social development was deemed crucial by the capital groups. In the aftermath of the storm, a group of 18 local investors, led by Samuel Kalisch Valdez, then the president of the DESEC, successfully lobbied the state government to levy a voluntary tax amounting to 10 per cent above the required payroll tax to pay for housing and flood reconstruction. Subsequently in 1992, capital groups requested that the local government keep collecting this self-imposed tax to fund social development programs. A trust was established by the state government and Samuel Kalisch Valdez was appointed as the president of the committee that would manage this trust. The amount of funds collected in this trust exceeded the projected expenses of the damage that the storm and flood left. In 1994, the Chihuahua Business Foundation (*Fundación del Empresariado Chihuahua*, A.C. – FECHAC) was created by local capitalists who invested in the *maquiladora* industry to manage this fund in trust.

The FECHAC united the private sector, civil society and the public sector to develop social programs 'to meet the critical needs of the community in basic education, preventive health and social capital formation, with the aim of improving the quality of life Chihuahua by promoting corporate social responsibility, citizen participation, strengthening of civil society organizations in the arduous effort to continue building and strengthening retention and altruistic work'.[32] It has also established a strategic alliance with international organizations that have economic concerns in the region: the Association of *Maquiladoras* and Exporting Companies in Chihuahua (*Asociación de Maquiladoras y Exportadoras de Chihuahua, A.C.* – AMEAC) and the International Women's Group (IWG).[33]

Since its foundation the FECHAC has become a permanent member of the COPLADE meetings. The organization is playing an increasingly important part in setting agendas for urban development. Most of the social development programs of the COPLADE were crafted by the FECHAC and then presented to the state government. Since 1994, the FECHAC initiated more than 1,500 activities

---

32   [Online].Available at:www.charity-charities.org/Mexico-charities/Chihuahua-1562973. html.

33   The IWG is an international organization that works in the Mexico–US border region through the collective efforts of the wives of the *maquiladora* managers.

and programs through the state of Chihuahua, such as building, rebuilding and refurbishing healthcare institutions and schools, providing care for the elderly and training for microenterprise owners (Aguirre 2006: 1).

Entrepreneurial Civil Society

A local newspaper clip from 1983 notes that 'wide segments of the population in Chihuahua view the decentralization policies as an important step towards local participation and democratization'.[34] In agreement with this view, some scholars claim that since the 1980s, Chihuahua has experienced a 'political awakening of society' referring to 'an explosion of activities by a wide variety of civic associations dedicated to the promotion of democracy, clean elections, and human rights' (Chand 2001: 205). The notion of social capital is often employed in the World Bank reports on Chihuahua to indicate how local communities are united around common goals and build trust bonds among community members (cf. Chaparro 1997: 4).

For local capital groups, strengthening civil society also became an issue of public–private partnership. The president of the Chihuahua chapter of the CANACINTRA declared that 'the only formula to end centralism is to strengthen the society and the civil societal organizations. We have to fight against centralism for federalism and democracy. This fight needs all our hands, not only the government's.'[35] Local capital groups defined their struggle for power as a fight for democracy which could only be attained through regional autonomy and decentralization. The election campaign of the PAN candidate for governor, Francisco Barrio, was particularly crafted around this message and received significant support from various other social classes.

Local businessmen, particularly those affiliated with the COPARMEX, relied on awakening their civil society to create 'entrepreneurial culture' in Chihuahua.[36] Entrepreneurial culture is defined as opposed to traditional culture that is said to be represented by the 'old PRI'. As Samuel Kalisch explains, 'entrepreneurial culture needs democracy that is compatible with free-market. Entrepreneurial culture is also based on human rights, citizenship rights, transparency, and efficiency in the use of resources.' According to Fernando Álvarez Monje, 'entrepreneurial culture is like the US culture that promotes competitive, productive and conscience citizenship'. Jesús Trevizo Gutiérrez provides that 'the PAN and the private sector

---

34   'Democratización de la Planeación', *El Heraldo de Chihuahua*, 13 December 1983.
35   Convoca a fortalecer federalismo, *Diario de Chihuahua*, 16 November 1996.
36   The term 'entrepreneurial culture' was mentioned in the interviews by several businessmen in Chihuahua.

are leading civil society in Chihuahua to fight against the traditional culture based on statization, corruption and inefficiency'.[37]

One of the first civil associations in Chihuahua that worked for local participation was the Civic Front of Citizen Participation (*Frente Cívico de Participación Ciudadana*). This association was formed in 1983 by several local businessmen to support the candidacy of Francisco Barrio as a PAN candidate for the municipality of Ciudad Juárez (Mizrahi 1992: 13). The Civic Front continued to organize the local agents after the elections and defined their struggle for power as a fight for democracy which could only be attained through regional autonomy and decentralized citizen participation.

When Barrio became the president of the municipality of Ciudad Juárez, the party increased its links with civil society association. The PAN supported several associations such as Committees of Neighborhood Coalition (*Coalición de Comités de Vecinos* – COCOVE), United Traders and Democracy (*Comerciantes Unidos y Democracia* – CUDE), Youth for Democracy (*Jóvenes para la Democracia*) and Civic Action of Maquila Employers (*Acción Cívica de Empleados de Maquilas*). Following the 1986 elections, when authorities ignored the accusations of fraud lodged against them by international observers, the PAN organized and led a civil resistance movement. These groups formed the Fight for Democracy Coordination (*Coordinadora de Lucha por la Democracia* – COLUDE), which coordinated this civil resistance movement. The democratization and participation rhetoric embraced various local groups who had been suffering from authoritarianism within PRI's corporatist structure. This movement mobilized various social actors and formed a broad alliance among otherwise irreconcilable political interests.[38] The PSUM and progressive teachers' and peasants' unions for instance, actively worked for the organization of the civil resistance movement of the PAN.[39] The weakness of these democratization requests was that they limited the sphere of struggle within the electoral processes. Through this movement, the local capital groups organized in the PAN were able to expand its scope of influence among dominated masses.

In 1994, an umbrella organization was founded by the COPARMEX. The State Committee of Citizen Participation (*Comité Estatal de Participación Cuidadana* – CEPAC) was presented as an alliance of civil associations, business groups, academics and professionals to generate civic consciousness in the community of Chihuahua to promote actions to develop and sustain democratic principles. The organization aims to 'install municipal transparency and citizen participation in coordination with other associations and state government' (CEPAC 2005). There are 10 civil associations integrated in the CEPAC, 5 of which are directly related

---

37   Interviews with Samuel Kalisch, Fernando Álvarez Monje and Jesús Trevizo Gutíerrez.

38   Interview with Alma Gómez.

39   López Ríos, Bernardo, 'El Partido Acción Nacional en la historia de México' [Online]. Available at: www.pan.org.mx.

to local capitalists.[40] Since 1994, the CEPAC has organized a seminar series called 'Constructing Citizenship' in order 'to foster a culture of citizen participation in different sectors of society'. These seminars were also supported by the state government and included in the COPLADE agenda.

As Valdés Ugalde (1996: 139) rightly observes, the civil associations that emerged since the 1990s have had a strong emphasis on '"citizenship" which had not been a prominent category in Mexico's political culture'. Capital groups aimed to transmit the message that 'by virtue of simply being citizens, they belong by definition to the so-called private initiative' (ibid). Therefore, a significant factor in understanding the explosion of civil associations is the leadership of local bourgeoisie and their financial support for shaping civil society independently of the corporatist ties of the PRI. Bourgeois-funded local civil associations emerged as central agents in the public–private partnership supervising social development programs with the state government.

The emergence of entrepreneurial civil society and the rhetoric of democratization explain partly why entrepreneurial domination in Chihuahua has persisted so far. Through civil associations, local businessmen managed to co-opt non-capitalist interests in the region. Entrepreneurial civil society served to seal conflicts and portrayed local politics as more consensual. Once the entrepreneurial vision became the hegemonic view, local businessmen could easily be portrayed as 'maverick', as 'catalysts for change'.[41] Therefore, the local bourgeoisie could become self-appointed spokesmen who speak for Chihuahua.

Although entrepreneurial domination is continuing, there are significant challenges to entrepreneurial local development: the state of Chihuahua, especially Ciudad Juárez, is notorious for urban insecurity, violence and fear.[42] Since the early 1990s, hundreds of women, mostly working in the *maquiladoras*, were murdered and drug cartels' control of one of the busiest trafficking routes translated into thousands of killings (Ronquillo 1999). It can be argued that high levels of violence

---

40 These civil associations are Citizenship Coordination (*Coordinadora Ciudadana*), COPARMEX, the Social Union of Mexican Businessmen (*Union Social de Empresarios Mexicanos* – USEM), the Association of ITESM Alumni (*Asociación de Exalumnos del ITESM* – EXATAC), the Centre of Leadership and Human Development (*Centro de Liderazgo y Desarrollo Humano* – COCENTRO), National Chamber of Graphic Arts Industry (*Camara Nacional de la Industria de Artes Grafica* – CANAGRAF), Primer México, Commission of Young Businessmen (*Comisión de Empresarios Jovenes*), the National College of Industrial Engineers (*Colegio Nacional de Ingenieros Industriales* (CONAII), Mexican Business Development (*Desarrollo Empresarial Mexicana* – IMPULSA), The Institute and College of Public Accountants (*Instituto y Colegio de Contadores Públicos* – IMCP).

41 This definition of the capital groups is adopted from Jamie Peck (1995). He uses these terms to define a new breed of British capital groups burgeoning in the 1980s with Thatcherism.

42 'Ciudad Juárez, Mexico: The world's most dangerous place?' *Toronto Star*, 21 May 2010. Available at: www.thestar.com/news/world/article/812757. [Accessed: 11 November 2011.]

and drug trafficking in the region have the effect of challenging and destabilizing the entrepreneurial local development. As Koonings and Kruijt (2006: 7) suggest 'the absence or failure of governance opens the ways for a variety of armed actors and violence brokers who carve out alternative, informal spheres of power on the basis of coercion'. Increasing insecurity and violence in the region raise doubts about the level of corruption, the quality of basic public services and spaces for community participation in local governance.[43]

Party Politics

Entrepreneurial local development in Chihuahua has transformed local politics substantially. Foreign and domestic capital groups have become involved in every stage of policy-making which empowered most of the local businessmen politically. The majority of the local capital groups that were involved in the *maquiladora* industry gave their support to the PAN to flex their muscle against the PRI and local politics spun out of the PRI's control. In order to regain the trust of the local capital groups, the PRI selected local businessmen as its candidates. Although this strategy enabled the PRI to win in the 1999 gubernatorial elections, it further undermined the traditional corporatist base of the party. In this process, the major differences between the PRI and the PAN have diminished. Through the public–private partnership, local capital groups have been able to control the local chapters of the political parties.

The decentralization policies have increased the strategic importance of local politics that would be used to challenge the central state. The local bourgeoisie's increasing disapproval both of the PRI policies and of the central state's regulations were the major sources of PAN's increasing electoral strength in Chihuahua in the 1980s. Following the bank nationalization, various groups of capital, particularly those invested in the *maquiladora* industry started to approach the PAN which served as 'the dominant political vehicle of the north's regionalistic resurgence' (Williams 1990: 314). Francisco Barrio's candidacy for the municipality of the Ciudad Juárez epitomized this private initiative in intervening in local politics. In the 1980s, the major municipalities of Chihuahua and the majority of the local congress developed into one of the most important bases of the PAN. In 1983, Francisco Barrio became the first opposition mayor elected on the PAN ticket, in Ciudad Juárez, the state's largest city. Later, in 1992, Barrio won the gubernatorial elections, and Chihuahua became the second state to elect a non-PRI governor.

The public–private partnership strengthened the local capital groups as they became involved in every stage of policy making. The political and administrative power that they assumed gave them a stronger position vis-à-vis the political

---

43   'Chihuahua: corrupción=pobreza= violencia,' *Mediodrama* 16, 25 October 2009. [Online]. Available at: http://mediorama.uacm.edu.mx/spip.php?article129. [Accessed: 11 November 2011.]

parties. Leading business groups started to become party candidates for public offices, to take initiatives in selecting the candidates, to provide generous financial contributions to the party and to design the election campaigns (Chand 2001: 116; Mizrahi 1996). In 1983, most of the party's candidates who won mayoral races in Chihuahua had business backgrounds. In 1983, the PAN swept to victory in all major cities of Chihuahua, thus governing more than 70 per cent of the state's population. The PAN was supported by various groups with 'great expectations'.[44]

Although the PAN has historically been a significant opposition party in Chihuahua, prior to the involvement of local bourgeoisie in the PAN, the party was electorally weak and poorly organized (Mizhari 1996). The role of bourgeoisie was therefore critical in tipping the balance in favor of the party. Although local capital groups became involved in the party structure, they lacked the institutional memory and loyalty of long-time members (Chand 2001: 143). After all, 'business groups did not necessarily need the PAN but the PAN needed them'.[45] Their intention was to challenge the central PRI authorities through the PAN.

However, the strategy differences between the traditional PANistas and the capitalist groups intervening in the party led to internal party conflicts during the 1980s and 1990s (Chand: 143). The businessmen clashed with traditionalist PAN members who were not willing to shed their own agendas, old ways of thinking and acting, and cede power to new groups (ibid). As a result of the conflicts between these two groups, the PAN in Chihuahua remained organizationally weak as a political institution. It had difficulty in redefining its missions and reorienting its practices as a party in power eventually lost its organizational capacity to respond to the demands of various social groups that had supported the party in the elections.

The PRI selected local businessmen as its candidates that enabled the party to win back the governor's office in the 1999 gubernatorial elections. At the same time, this strategy undermined the corporatist base of the party since the new candidates of the party had not been from within the party organization. The PRI experienced an internal conflict similar to the PAN's with the contest between business-oriented PRI candidates and the party's traditional corporatist networks. Consequently, the differences between the PRI and PAN lessened drastically in terms of party organization and policy priorities.[46] The style of governance under the PRI was not different from the PAN period (Alba-Vega and Aziz-Nassif 2000: 99). Behind the apparent electoral interplay between the PAN and the PRI lies a very elitist regime in Chihuahua. A small group of businessmen actually rule and mass participation and decision-making is confined to the selection of leaders in elections. The political party system is no longer strong in Chihuahua.

---

44   Interviews with Gabino Gómez, Alma Gómez, and Quintana.

45   Vikram Chand's interview with José Angel Conchello, PAN national president 1972–75 and the President of the PAN in Mexico City 1987 to 1990 (Chand 2001: 94n67).

46   This view is expressed in many of my interviews with various local actors in the state of Chihuahua.

Conclusion

The case of Chihuahua illustrates the importance of decentralization policies for cross-border regions. The characteristics of the local economy differentiate Chihuahua from other states in Mexico. In order to explain the particular pattern of local participation in Chihuahua in the process of decentralization, this chapter examined the strategies and alliances of the key agents in Chihuahua. It is the contention in this chapter that the implications of decentralization for Chihuahua should be studied, focusing on the networks linking local bourgeoisie with foreign bourgeoisie. For the border regions, the possibility to integrate in the world economy shaped the expectations, strategies and alliances of the agents in the process of decentralization.

The case of Chihuahua also shows that via the decentralized development, internationalized local capital groups and their foreign partners orchestrated the local development plans directly through their own organizations and indirectly through the civil society that they organized and political parties that they captured. Proponents of decentralization in Latin America and elsewhere have argued that strengthening local and regional governments would improve the efficiency of governments and contribute to better democratic governance. However, in the regions where the internationalized capital groups are well organized and other social classes are relatively weaker, decentralization policies favor local capital groups. In Chihuahua, *maquiladora* bourgeoisie became stronger in political contests in the early 1980s. As opposed to the PRI, the *maquiladora* bourgeoisie actively supported and funded the PAN in order to influence the design and implementation of decentralization policies. The new breed of bourgeoisie, *maquiladora* capital, seems to have taken over the local development programs. In Chihuahua, the process of decentralization led to a public–private partnership. Eventually, this partnership evolved towards a resurgence of entrepreneurial local governance by domestic bourgeoisie allied with foreign capital. This model of local development weakened the organizational capacities of local political parties and state institutions.

The findings from the case of Chihuahua suggest that although decentralization brings political power to local communities, the access to power by different local groups is uneven, such that some segments of society may find themselves excluded or marginalized, while others enjoy more favorable terms. Where the local and foreign bourgeoisie have a vested interest in the local economy, decentralization policies favor the local capital groups as these groups become the most effective participants in the development and planning meetings. The development programs crafted in these meetings marginalized the dominated masses in the policy-making processes. Therefore, local capital groups' strategies and relative strength vis-à-vis other social classes shape the trajectory of the decentralization policies.

Local capital groups' relative independence from the central state regulations and their dependence on the regional economy motivate them to get involved in the decentralized development programs. The foreign agents with interests in the local economy joined with the domestic bourgeoisie and became involved in the planning of the local development programs. Thus, the decentralization process did not bring about the localization of decisions. Instead it led to an inclusion of foreign agents in the local politics in Chihuahua. Under the rubric of public–private partnership, the bourgeois interests and values became the interest of society and of the state. The leading businessmen increasingly appear to be the modernizers of the traditional relations.

If the case of Chihuahua suggests an intriguing affinity between decentralization policies and the weakening of local political institutions, paralleled to increasing involvement of the local bourgeoisie in local politics, the case of Tabasco, which is analyzed in the next chapter, shows how the dominance of oligarchs in development policies brings about authoritarian state-led local development.

Chapter 5

Oil Production as the Dominant Force: Authoritarian State-Led Local Development in Tabasco

While the decentralization policies have enabled local bourgeoisie and their foreign partners to play the central role in local development in Chihuahua, the decentralized development programs in Tabasco have been crafted by the PRI-dominated policy-makers and implemented in the municipalities under close supervision by these elites. Unlike in Chihuahua, decentralization in Tabasco did not lead to a transfer of the development capacities and regulatory mechanisms of the state to the private sector. Instead, the local state employed strong organizational capacities to design and implement decentralized development programs. Policy makers in Tabasco took the initiative to re-regulate the local economy to increase its competitiveness through development programs.

Whereas Chihuahua witnessed a clear political opening in the local regime with the process of decentralization, the political regime of the state of Tabasco has not changed drastically. Local policy-makers hold on to authoritarian state power and have not opened political space for social actors. Although some peasants have organized around the PRD and the opposition has had a significant presence in some municipalities since the late 1980s, the PRI is still the governing party in the state government. Local governments have managed to control the newly emerging social associations and aimed to minimize local participation in policy-making processes. Neoliberal decentralization policies have strengthened the role of the state of Tabasco in local development, reinforced corporatism, encapsulated the social dynamics into state-initiated organizations and led an evolution towards *authoritarian state-led local development.*

This chapter sets out to explain the formation of the authoritarian state-led local development in Tabasco. For this purpose, it examines how the growing oil industry shapes local social relations and how those relations translate into the institutional structure of the local state. It argues that the main factor that explains the emergence of authoritarian state-led local development is the nature of the local economy which brings the relations among foreign oil companies, local bourgeoisie and policy-makers to the fore. As the oil industry had taken over the position of the agricultural production in the state, the strategies and alliances of the big landowners and peasants are also important in explaining the formation of authoritarian state-led local development. In the process of decentralization, the PEMEX, also decentralized its structure, which gave more scope for the local state of Tabasco to regulate PEMEX's activities and its relations with national and foreign oil companies as contractors and suppliers. Since foreign investments in the region were mediated through the public sector via the local state, local bourgeoisie have assumed the role of junior partners in crafting and executing local development programs.

Despite the optimistic premise that decentralization reforms are a way to improve opportunities for local communities, in the localities that assume an energy-feeder role for the world economy, alliances between large foreign companies and the public sector increase direct state interventions at the local level and prevent other social classes from having equal participation in the decentralized development programs. In Tabasco, therefore, decentralization refers not to deregulation but to re-regulation of local affairs through the local state.

This chapter is composed of five sections. The first section looks briefly at the formation of local state institutions and social relations in Tabasco, exploring how such institutions and relations have been shaped within the state's geographical location and natural resources. The second section focuses on the emergence and boom of the oil industry and the changing dynamics of local social relations in the early 1970s. In the third section, an analysis of the local development programs illustrates how the decentralized development programs have been regulated by the state of Tabasco. It traces the evolution of the development programs from the early 1980s and shows that the decentralization of PEMEX and an increase in foreign contractors and suppliers in the petrochemical sector shaped the role of the local governments in boosting the competitiveness of the local economy and creating a business-friendly environment for these investments. The fourth section examines the inherent contradictory dynamics of authoritarian local development. This section also traces the impact of the changing power relations on local party politics. The final section outlines the main findings from the case of Tabasco.

Formation of Class Relations and Local State Institutions

The geographic characteristics of Tabasco have been an important determinant of the formation of local class relations and local political institutions. The state is bordered by the Gulf of Mexico and Campeche in the north, Campeche and the Republic of Guatemala in the east; Chiapas and the Republic of Guatemala in the south; and Veracruz in the west. The determining geographical characteristic is not Tabasco's borders with Guatemala, but its natural resources. Tabasco contains a third of the water resources of Mexico which has made its agricultural sector more productive than the rest of the country. Since the 1970s, Tabasco has been called 'the energy state'. It has acquired a prominent role in national economic development due to hydro-electric power and rich under-soil resources with extensive exploitation of oil in both gas and crude form.[1] Oil took over the position of agriculture as the leading industry in the state.

Tabasco region's fertility and the richness of its nature astonished the Spanish rulers who attempted to control the resisting local communities by allying with local *cacique*s in the area (Prescott 2001: 200–211; Ruz 1989). Later, as the Spanish crown weakened, these families became regional leaders in the movement for independence (Assad 1996: 42). In the aftermath of independence, the *cacique* families and regional *caudillos* of Tabasco with equal power in their sub-region could not reach a consensus on the local regime. In 1825, the first constitution of Tabasco was promulgated to restore order as a result of fierce negotiations among the *cacique* families. Nevertheless, Tabasco has had 150 governors during the period between Independence and 1877, when Díaz triumphed over the other groups to declare his government (ibid: 81).

Díaz aimed to weaken the influence of competing *cacique*s and *caudillo*s in order to restore order. He had a particular interest in promoting the administrative structure of the local state which would enable local policy-makers to keep the immense natural wealth of the region under control.[2] Oil reserves in Tabasco were discovered in the 1830s, but the influence of this discovery on the state economy was felt gradually during the Porfiriato period as the demand for petroleum rose (Brown 2002: 2). Díaz prioritized the establishment of transportation and communication services in the state. In 1881, the first telegraphy service was established between Mexico City and Tabasco. A contract was co-signed by the central state and North American railway companies to connect Tabasco and Chiapas by railway. The first kilometers of the railway connected the major municipalities with oil reserves to the capital of the state, Villahermosa. From the late 1870s, a US company, Standard Oil and its major sales company, Waters-Pierce Oil, had a monopoly in the Mexican oil market. The new discoveries of oil deposits in 1902 and improved infrastructure attracted British companies to the region. In 1906, the government signed a contract with a London-based firm Pearson & Son for the drilling the wells and extensive explorations in the area (Celis Salgado 1988: 56). In 1908 and 1909, another British company, Anglo-Mexican Oil, was authorized to work in the region (ibid: 59). This move of the Díaz regime converted the Mexican oil market from monopolistic ownership of northern Americans to oligopolistic ownership (Brown 2002: 7–8).

---

1   Mexico is the fifth largest oil-producing country and its oil wealth has generated the largest portion of the country's income for most of the post-war era.

2   For this purpose, Díaz appointed a governor from Veracruz, in 1887, who had arrived in Tabasco in 1885 as the chief of the security forces and had weak links with the local families but could mediate among them (Assad 1996: 94).

Although the Díaz regime allied with these foreign companies to divide and repress petroleum workers (cf. Hamilton 1982: 219), since the local economy of Tabasco was predominantly agricultural the first signs of unrest preceding the revolution came from small landholders and peasants. The repressive rule of Díaz's governors and the regime's alliance with big local landowners increased tension in the region which had a booming economy based on the export of agricultural products and precious timber (Arias Gómez 1987: 293–6, 307). While the living conditions of small holders and peasants were becoming intolerable, the local policy-makers supported the big local landowners at the expense of the resentful rest. This resentment eventually transformed into local revolts of small landholders and peasants, who joined with the revolutionary groups of other regions. Although the Tabasco region did not have a strong influence on the armed struggle (Rico Medina 1993, Scherr 1985: 40), the ideals of the Revolution were so strong that Lázaro Cárdenas considered the state of Tabasco to be one of the 'laboratories of the Revolution' (Canudas Sandoval 1989: 280).

Tabasco was also a 'laboratory' of the corporatist state form at the local level. The Radical Socialist Party of Tabasco (*Partido Socialista Radical Tabasqueño* – PRST) was the organizing force behind the revolutionary forces in Tabasco. After the Revolution, the leader of the party, Tomás Garrido Canabál, assumed the governorship in 1920. The Garrido Canabál governments (1920–24 and 1931–34) successfully mobilized the social forces under the state control (Balcázar Antonio 2003: 116). The foundation of the state-run workers' union, the Central League of Resistance (*Liga Central de Resistencia*) organized the workers (González Calzada 1940: 130–31). Farmers and peasants officially gathered under cooperatives: in total, 176 cooperatives – 115 producer, 58 consumer and 3 mixed, most of which had remained active until the 1990s (Assad 1996: 140). The rank-and-file of these organizations were closely tied to the local state and the local communities received benefits in return for their loyalty to the local regime (Canudas Sandoval 1989, González Calzada 1940: 130–136). First and foremost, jobs in the state enterprises were the main basis of patronage with workers. In 1934, when Lázaro Cárdenas visited Tabasco as the presidential candidate, he expressed his praise for the form of local state-society relations in Tabasco (Assad 1996: 145). The same year, Garrido Canabál was named the Secretary of Agriculture by President Lázaro Cárdenas. These two political leaders maintained close relations during the formation of national level state corporatist structures. Several informants I interviewed emphasized that both Tomás Garrido Canabál and Lázaro Cárdenas left strong marks on state-society relations in Tabasco.

The regulative capacity of the local state originating in Garrido Canabál's corporatist attempts was later consolidated by the nationalization of the oil resources by the Cárdenas government. The mobilization of the petroleum workers led to the formation of the Mexican Petroleum Workers' Union of the Mexican Republic (*Sindicato de Trabajadores Petroleros de la República Mexicana* – STPRM) in 1936. The national petroleum union put significant pressure on the Cárdenas government as well as on foreign oil companies. The Union brought together some 21 separate unions (Brown 2002: 25). STPRM joined also with the CTM and went on strike to obtain a collective contract for better wages and social benefits. When the oil companies rejected these demands, the struggle between the Mexican workers and the foreign oil companies forced the Cárdenas government to expropriate foreign-owned petroleum resources in 1938 and establish Mexican Petroleum (PEMEX).

The oil sector started to become a significant industry for the region with the discovery of new deposits with very high quality crude oil in 1940, 1949 and 1950. In 1951, an industrial town with a gas absorption plant with 300 employees, called Pemex City, was set up in Macuspana which was the first sign of the localization of the oil industry in Tabasco (CODEZPET 1985, Scherr 1985: 43). The same year, the installation of new gas pipelines and a refinery paved the way for an increase in the oil supply to other regions.

The growing oil sector strengthened the regulative capacity of the state in Tabasco both by providing an institutional channel for state intervention in the sector and producing consent in the region (West, Psuty and Thom 1976: 178). The public ownership of the rich natural resources in the region has enlarged the administrative apparatus of the local state and bestowed local policy-makers with enhanced capacities in leading development programs. The local state has played a relatively central role in the construction of the road and railway networks in the region which have stimulated local socio-economic development. Unlike in Chihuahua, in Tabasco the local state has been able to gradually incorporate the different classes into its policy agenda and render them dependent.[3] On the one hand, the construction of road and railway networks helped the big agricultural producers to reach national markets, and on the other hand the growing oil industry started to attract peasants to the oil-rich municipalities. Through these mechanisms, the PRI became a hegemonic power in local politics and did not face significant challenges from local social classes until the late 1980s. The anniversary of the expropriation, 18 March, is nowhere celebrated more enthusiastically than in Tabasco.

The nationalization of oil resources, the foundation of PEMEX and the discovery of rich deposits began to define Tabasco as an area of exploitation of oil and gas. In 1940, the industrial sector contributed with 6.1 per cent to the Gross National Product from the state of Tabasco. This figure has accelerated from 1950 to reach 47.4 per cent in 1970. In contrast, the trend was reversed for the primary sector – agriculture, animal husbandry, forestry and fishing – which fell from 70 per cent in 1940 to 13.8 per cent in 1970 (CODEZPET 1985: 15). Despite these significant changes during the period 1940–73, the gradual development of the oil industry had a very limited impact on the livelihood of dominated masses which had been characterized by predominantly rural and dispersed communities dedicated to subsistence-agriculture (CODEZPET 1985: 12, 14). The next section

---

3   For instance, the PRI integrated the leaders of the Community Party of Tabasco and the Revolutionary Social Action Movement into the party.

looks at how local social relations evolved as the oil industry became the dominant economic activity in the region during the 1973–82 boom.

1973–1982 Period: The Oil Boom and Consolidation of the Institutional Structure of the Local State

The oil boom in 1973 produced profound changes in Tabasco. It became the crossroad of important national and international economic relations due to its precious natural resources. Large revenues from the oil industry started to become available to the state government and led to the foundation of various development agencies as new intervention channels.

High international oil prices stimulated more exploration and exploitation in the region. PEMEX accelerated its drilling activities exploiting newly discovered oil sites (Díaz Serrano 1992). The number of drilling teams increased from 8 in 1973 to 40 in 1974, to 60 in 1977, to 90 in 1980 and to 100 in 1981 (CODEZPET 1985: 18). As a result, the number of productive wells rose from 114 in seven fields in 1976 to 160 in 14 fields in 1978 (Tirado 1987: 10–11). The vibrant oil industry provided employment opportunities in PEMEX for peasants from all over the country (Tuleda 1989: 278). Small producers and peasants began to migrate towards the municipalities and localities with growing oil industry: the number of PEMEX workers rose from 6,345 in 1974 to 20,065 in 1981 (CODEZPET 1985: 24).

The oil boom increased public investments in the region as well as bringing federal transfers to the state government. In 1977, the federal government defined the oil industry as national priority for development and the main axis of economic growth. Since 1977, major share of public investments has been channeled towards the development of this industry (CODEZPET 1985: 18). In addition to public investments, with a new Law of Fiscal Coordination in 1976, the state of Tabasco and its municipalities started to receive revenue shares proportional to the international oil prices and the volume of oil exportation (Ruíz and Fabregas 2009: 239–41). To put it differently, PEMEX became the most important taxpayer. The total budget of the state of Tabasco increased from 1.5 million pesos in 1973, to 234 million in 1974 to 650 million in 1977, 3,130 million in 1979 and to 19,906 million in 1982 (COPRODET 1979: 1, Tuleda 1989: 262).[4]

This enormous increase in financial capacity permitted the local state to transcend the traditional political-administrative limits of its actions and start assuming an effective 'guiding role' in regulating the local and regional economy (Tuleda 1989: 262–3). The Committee for the Promotion of Socioeconomic Development of Tabasco (*Comité Promotor de Desarrollo Socioeconómico de Tabasco* – COPRODET) was established in 1975 as a result of this increased

---

4 By taking 1973 as the base year, the real budget increased from 1.5 million pesos in 1973, to 194 million in 1974 to318 million in 1977, 1,106 million in 1979 and to 2,124 million in 1982.

financial capacity. The COPRODET was the most well-established local development agency in Mexico and received more professional, logistical and political support for planning than any other state (Wilson Salinas 1983). The central state ordained that PEMEX collaborate with the COPRODET and with the governor of Tabasco to resolve issues of mutual concern, such as material bottlenecks and transport difficulties, and to inform the agency of its planned activities (Scherr 1985: 60). The establishment of the COPRODET provided the state institutions with a coherent perspective on development and enabled the state to regulate the development programs more effectively, even before the decentralization policies were introduced.

Local Development Programs

During the presidential campaign of Miguel de la Madrid, in the *Consulta Popular* meeting held in Villahermosa, two groups of local agents raised demands for decentralization: representatives of local bourgeoisie and local policy-makers both called for financial decentralization and more fiscal autonomy from the federal government.[5] Due to its oil revenues, the debt crisis of 1982 had relatively less impact on the local economy of Tabasco.[6] However, decreasing oil prices were the biggest concern of the local state policy-makers and local bourgeoisie. They attempted to compensate the loss of the financial privileges due to decreasing oil prices with new financial resources that would be transferred from the central state with decentralization. In these meetings, the Secretary of Finance of the Government of Tabasco, Arturo González Marín pointed out that the principal problem of the state of Tabasco was the issue of public spending management.[7] He added that 'decentralization of the funds would enable a healthier insertion of financial resources into the circuits of the local economy'.[8] Both local policy-makers and bourgeoisie representatives underlined that the public sector in Tabasco had become a massive source of jobs for growing the local economy. They claimed that if the revenue shares transferred from the federal state fell parallel to the price of oil, the capacity of the local state to implement development programs would be curtailed overwhelmingly.[9] It was also argued that the state economic enterprises increased the administrative burden on the federal state and PEMEX particularly had to decentralize its structure (Pazos 1983: 106).

---

5   Interviews with González Pedrero, Chablé and Priego.

6   *Rumbo Nuevo*, 'Independientemente del problema típico de Tabasco que es controlar el agua', 1 October 1982.

7   *Rumbo Nuevo*, 'El Diario de la Vida Tabasqueña', 7 October 1982.

8   *Rumbo Nuevo*, 'Reunión de prioridades estatales que sobre Administración Pública y Fortalecimiento Municipal', 7 October 1982.

9   Ibid.

In this section, I trace the process of decentralization with a focus on the main social and economic development programs and local policy-makers' initiatives and objectives in designing these programs. Parallel to the decentralization of PEMEX, foreign oil companies play an indirect role in shaping the local development of the oil-dependent economy. The local policy-makers have strategically selected the development programs that would increase the competitiveness of the region.

Early Attempts at Regulating Development

The first decentralization policies were hailed by the governor and the local chapter of the PRI. In his various public speeches, the governor of the time, Enrique González Pedrero (1982–87), underlined the importance of decentralization and its impact on local democratization and development.[10] His government attempted to make 'the PRI in Tabasco penetrate into the conscience of the citizens and be an efficient motor for socioeconomic development'.[11] He claims that development is the primary responsibility of the state within its federal, state and municipality levels.[12]

In April 1983, the state government established Development Planning Committee of Tabasco (Planeación para el Desarrollo del Estado de Tabasco – COPRODET). In addition to the COPLADET, in May 1983, the governor sent another proposal to the state congress to establish another planning agency, State System of Democratic Planning (*Sistema Estatal de Planeación Democrática* – SIESPLADE). In his speeches, González Pedrero noted that the COPLADET coupled with the SIESPLADE would strengthen the 'rector' role of the state, increase the sovereignty of the state government, and stimulate a 'mixed economy' for socioeconomic development (González Pedrero 1987a: 37, 46). Several national politicians celebrated the state development agencies in Tabasco as the most efficient institutional structure in the country.[13]

In 1984, the state government launched a course for the personnel of the municipalities in order to provide COPLADEM teams with high technical qualifications as well as training about political, economic and social problems

10   These ideas came up several times in the interview with him. For some of his statements on this line, see *Rumbo Nuevo*, 'Para el descentralización fortalecer el municipio es la solución', 10 October 1984; González Pedrero 1987a: 90–91.

11   Interview with González Pedrero. Also see *Rumbo Nuevo*, the editorial article by Bartolo Jimenez Mendez, 2 September 1982.

12   *Rumbo Nuevo*, 'Reunión de Presentación del Plan Municipal de Desarrollo y Programa Operativo Anual', 8 December 1983.

13   By Secretary of Planning and Budget, Carlos Salinas de Gortari, *Rumbo Nuevo*, 'Reunión de Presentación del Plan Municipal de Desarrollo y Programa Operativo Anual', 8 December 1983; by Senator Acever Saucedo, in *Rumbo Nuevo*, 'Muestra clara del funcionamiento del sistema nacional de Planeación', 3 February 1984; and by Undersecretary of Regional Development 1984–88, Manuel Camacho Solis, in the interview with him.

of the country and the region.[14] In all 17 municipalities of the state, the COPLADEM agencies were established to implement the development programs. However, the state government did not transfer development responsibilities to the municipalities.[15] In the interview with him, González Pedrero defended his methods, by claiming that 'Tabasco needed an enlightened despot for development at that moment in its history'.

The Increasing Influence of PEMEX in Local Development

In the National Development Plan of 1983–88, the Miguel de la Madrid government included the 'restructuring' of PEMEX. It was claimed that the new oil reserves found in 1971 were very expensive to obtain because in one of the fields very deep wells were needed while the other fields were offshore and thus demanded special technology for production (Cypher 1990: 109; Díaz Serrano 1992). Furthermore, it was argued that PEMEX was suffering from a declining level of competitiveness, low productivity and poor management (cf. Székely 1983: 240). The Miguel de la Madrid government made certain changes in Article 28 which had outlawed private concessions in 'strategic areas' including oil and solid, liquid or gas hydrocarbons in the exploration and exploitation of deposits. With these changes, the oil and basic petrochemicals were reserved for the state yet could be undertaken through joint-ventures with the private sector.

As a result of the liberalization of the Petroleum Law in the 1980s, the petroleum and petrochemical industries started to attract new oil companies. The oil and gas industry was largely privatized in the 1990s by way of contracting and special agreements between PEMEX and big oil companies. By 1997, the petrochemical industry – pharmaceuticals, paints, and synthetics – accounted for almost 30 per cent of US industrial investments in Mexico (Cockroft 1983: 262). Foreign oil companies like Halliburton, Shell, Exxon and BP started providing technical assistance to PEMEX exploratory work. The oil industry also attracted finance capital to Mexico. Foreign finance banks provided loans for most of the technology and equipment investments in the sector (Martínez Laguna 2004: 2035). Eximbank, Chase Manhattan and West Germany's Commerzbank advanced billions of dollars in credit for Mexico's oil-development plans (Martínez Laguna 2004).

In Tabasco, decentralization primarily meant decentralization of the PEMEX administration. With decentralization, the local state of Tabasco has earned a strategic position in terms of energy production. When the design and implementation of local development projects were decentralized, the local governments of Tabasco became more involved in the oil production sector. Although the oil industry is primarily controlled by the public sector, since it is a capital-intensive sector requiring highly skilled workers and technology, foreign

---

14 *Rumbo Nuevo*, 'Indispensable Capacitar Cuadros Políticos Para el Apoyo Municipal', 9 October 1984.

15 Interviews with Abardía Hernandez and Torpey Andrede.

oil companies get involved in the sector through public–private partnerships. With decentralization, the state of Tabasco assumed the role of key agent in this partnership. Villahermosa was accepted as the regional center of PEMEX. New PEMEX offices were followed by new branches of the foreign companies which opened in Villahermosa. Foreign oil companies developed closer relations with the local governments either through PEMEX or directly with their branches.[16]

Between 1983 and 1988, PEMEX started to become an important local agent in the region. Governor González Pedrero acknowledged that 'we defended the interest of PEMEX, because development in Tabasco depends on oil'.[17] It was expected that social well-being in Tabasco would be dependent on oil revenues. González Pedrero added that 'since most of the state income was gained through the energy sector, PEMEX administration started to get involved in the local development programs'.[18] The government used state-owned enterprises as its key instruments of development. This structural dependence on PEMEX revenues shaped the local development plans (González Pedrero 1987b: 54, 149). In 1983, the COPLADET launched the Development Program of the Coast of Tabasco (*Programa de Desarrollo de Costa de Tabasco* – PRODECOT) for the oil areas to which PEMEX contributed over one billion pesos (Arias Rodríguez and Gusmán Hugo 2004: 6).

Unlike the *maquiladora* industry in Chihuahua, the foreign companies investing in Tabasco were not in direct partnership with local bourgeoisie. Instead, they had 'partnership' relations with PEMEX as contractors and suppliers. With decentralization policies, the state policy-makers were constrained to craft the development programs with the supervision of PEMEX to provide a business-friendly environment and easier market entry for its foreign partners.[19] This tendency, which started in the mid 1990s still continues today.

Re-Regulation of Development and Local Competitiveness

The governor Roberto Madrazo Pintado (1994–2000) made an accurate observation on the impact of neoliberal globalization. He notes '[n]owadays as the phenomenon of globalization reached countries, regions and subnational governments, they started to compete for the attraction of capital' (Madrazo Pintado 2000a: 64). The main objective of the Madrazo Pintado government was defined as 'establishing the necessary conditions' to push the local economy (ibid). For this objective, the government crafted the Strategic Program for Economic Promotion in 1998, as an 'aggressive strategy of diffusion and promotion of the local economy' and created

---

16   Two interviewees who served in key positions in the state of Tabasco during the 1980s noted that, a series of formal and informal meetings were arranged with the representatives of state government, PEMEX and foreign oil companies.

17   *Rumbo Nuevo*, 'Por contener una parte importante de la riqueza petrolera nacional', 12 December 1983.

18   Interview with González Pedrero.

19   Interview with Hernandez Hernandez.

'instruments and mechanisms that would enable us [Tabasco] to compete in better conditions with other states and regions of the Mexican Republic' (ibid). The local state has led local development by placing the primary focus on bolstering the economic competitiveness of the local economy (Madrazo Pintado 2000b).

The local state mediated the relations between local and global private companies. The local policy-makers took the initiative to join an international organization, World Energy Cities Partnership, which aims to increase the collaborations of 'energy cities' around the world. To increase foreign investment in the region, the government initiated new partnerships with the US states of the Gulf of Mexico. In 1995, regional development meetings were held with the participation of the US and Mexican governors of the states in the Gulf of Mexico.[20] These meetings aimed to form partnerships between Mexican and US companies in oil production which would promote the region as a zone of opportunity for investment and trade.[21] During these meetings, the Roberto Madrazo government cultivated relations with the Texas governor, George Bush, Jr., to launch new business partnerships in the agro-industry, cattle breeding, tourism and energy sectors between Texas and Tabasco.[22] In 1997, the state government initiated the launch of Tabasco House (*la Casa Tabasco*) in Houston to open new markets for local bourgeoisie (Madrazo Pintado 2000a: 65). Roberto Madrazo mentioned that 'the new connections would consolidate business relations and generate major flux of investments between Texas and Tabasco and strengthen the nexus that sustains the member states of the meetings of governors of the basin of the Gulf'.[23] According to the government report, as a result of these visits investments in Tabasco increased drastically in 1998 which contributed to the improvement of local socio-economic development (Madrazo Pintado 2000b).

Business finance was an important aspect of the development strategy of the Madrazo government. The local policy-makers channeled the financial resources to support the competitiveness of the local bourgeoisie by launching new credit mechanisms.[24] In March 2000, the state government established the Regional Center for Business Competitiveness (*Centro Regional para la Competitividad Empresarial* – CRECE). The state government also launched the Trust for Business of Tabasco (*Fideocomiso para el Apoyo Empresarial de Tabasco* – FIDETAB) with the objective of complementing national sources of credit for local bourgeoisie.

---

20 The Mexican members of the group are composed of the governors of Campeche, Quintana Roo, Tabasco, Tamaulipas, Veracruz and Yucatán. The American part of the group is Alabama, Florida, Louisiana, Mississippi and Texas.

21 *Novedades de Tabasco*, 'Impulsa George Bush Jr. Comercio Texas–Tabasco', 15 November 1996.

22 *Novedades de Tabasco*, 'Abordan Agenda Comercial Bush y Madrazo', 16 November 1996.

23 Ibid.

24 Interviews with Llergo Latournerie.

Local state investments in socio-economic development in the period from 1994 to 2000 were predominantly allocated to the commerce and industry: In 1995, the Madrazo government and the General Director of PEMEX co-signed a 'Special Coordination Agreement', which ascribed to the local government the central role in managing the PEMEX-funded development programs. The percentages of the state investments in commerce is 38.9 per cent, industry is 28.2 per cent respectively. In this period the agriculture sector received 1.8 per cent and tourism 8 per cent (Madrazo Pintado 2000b: 65).

The Grand Vision of Tabasco XXI Century: Sub- and Supra-National Regional Partnerships

The State Development Plan of the Manuel Andrade Díaz government (2002–2006), also known as the Grand Vision of Tabasco XXI Century, aims 'to promote the comparative advantage and competitiveness of the entity' (Andrade Díaz 2005: 236). The Grand Vision reveals the evolving development strategies: the state government assumed the role of integrating the local economy into the supra-regional – Central America – markets. Concomitantly, sub-national regional – south and south-east Mexico – cooperation to boost economic development was another important development strategy that this state plan reveals.

Although the Grand Vision aimed 'to take advantage of the increased commercial relations between Mexico, Canada and the US which brought more opportunities to Tabasco', the main emphasis of the development program was integration with Central America. The Grand Vision contained development projects to better integrate Tabasco into the Puebla Panama Plan (PPP). The PPP is a development plan officially launched in 2001 by President Vicente Fox with credits provided by the Inter-American Development Bank. Its objective was presented as 'to promote the regional integration and development' of nine southern Mexican states of Puebla, Guerrero, Veracruz, Oaxaca, Chiapas, Tabasco, Campeche, Yucatan and Quintana Roo, through the most southern Central American country of Panama.[25] The same year, the governors of these nine states formed the Trust for Regional Development of South-Southeast (*Fideicomiso Para el Desarrollo Sur-Sureste* – FIDESUR). At the federal level, the Secretary of Social Development participates in the FIDESUR which aims to channel financial and technical support for projects to augment social and economic development of the region.[26] Later in 2004, the Secretaries for the Economic Development of these nine states agreed to form the Economic Group of the South-Southeast Region of Mexico (*Grupo Económico*

25   In 2001, Puebla Panama Plan (PPP) is a project which seeks to open up the southern half of Mexico and Central America to private foreign investment and establishing the foundation for the Free Trade Area of the Americas (FTAA). The plan depends upon multi-lateral development bank support and private investment to create infrastructure that will attract industry and expand natural resource extraction.

26   [Online]. Available at: www.sursureste.org/gersse_grupo_economico.html.

de la Región Sur-Sureste de México – GERSSE). 'The mission of the GERSSE is to increase the competitiveness of the businesses of the states and of the region through the coordination, negotiation and consolidation of the strategic regional projects and initiatives'.[27] GERSSE worked with FIDESUR in financing a report to search for opportunities to boost the competitiveness of the south-southeast region prepared by the Monterrey Institute of Technology and Higher Education.

The state of Tabasco assumed a significant role both in FIDESUR and GERSSE (Andrade Díaz 2005: 236–7). In May 2005, the state of Tabasco represented the states of south-southeast of Mexico in the first Workshop of Competitiveness which led to the foundation of Central American Council of Competitiveness (*Consejo Mezoamerica de Competitividad* – CMC).

To boost the comparative advantage and competitiveness of Tabasco to better integrate the local economy into north and Central American markets, it was necessary to support the local bourgeoisie (Andrade Díaz 2005: 235). 'The Andrade Díaz government played a significant role in coordinating local bourgeoisie to promote the local economy and attract investment to the state' (ibid). The state government developed a Business Competitiveness Program with the participation of eight micro and small businesses. This group diagnosed the deficiencies and needs of local businesses and worked on a strategic plan to help local businesses grow (ibid: 240).The government also directed the articulation of the small and medium sized local enterprises with PEMEX as well as its foreign subcontractors. In March 2005, with the initiation of the state government, PEMEX and local business association agreed on the Development Program of Suppliers and Constructors of PEMEX. With this strategic alliance agreement, PEMEX and its foreign contractors and suppliers began to hire local firms for construction and transportation services (ibid: 271). Five of those small and medium-sized enterprises joined the International Alliance of Supplier Firms to Oil Industry and developed alliances with the US, UK and Venezuelan firms (ibid: 240).

The development projects of the state government also include urban road construction in the agro-industrial regions and the oil and tourism industry areas, and the construction of a new industrial corridor, Canal Victoria, which was launched as a new base for the industrial development in Tabasco (Resumen Ejecutivo 2002: 16).'To take part in the world markets and to avoid being an isolated economy', the development programs in this period attempted 'to transform the agricultural sector from subsistence production towards a business vision' (Resumen Ejecutivo 2002: 23). Local credit mechanisms favored the bigger agricultural bourgeoisie who had already been producing for national and international markets. As a result of these policies, small holders were forced to sell their land and move to the oil-producing cities to work for PEMEX.[28]

---

27 Ibid.
28 Interview with Leyva Leyva.

Mobilization of Peasants, Demobilization Strategies and Party Politics

The previous section showed that decentralization in Tabasco primarily means decentralization of PEMEX activities. Decentralization of development programs shaped the role of the local state as the regulator of the energy-feeder economy for the world market. Meeting the energy demands of the world market became the main concern of the local policy-makers at the cost of demobilizing dominated masses. As neoliberal competition became the only game in town, 'coherent and cohesive bureaucracy' became corrupted into an authoritarian regime with patronage, cronyism and corruption. This corruption was possible only in the absence of strong peasants' and workers' movement.

The lack of peasants' mobilization could be explained by two interrelated factors: first, high expectations of peasants from oil-financed development; second, authoritarian control over peasants by the landed bourgeoisie who actually received the benefits – as compensation – from PEMEX. While local development programs squeezed traditional agriculture, the hope was that PEMEX would bring jobs, schools, food, healthcare and housing. Peasant communities expected that PEMEX would reinvest its profits in the community.[29] These expectations arguably inhibited the development of civil society outside of state control.

By the 1990s, as it became clear that oil-based development had brought Tabasco nothing but ecological destruction and increasing regional inequalities between oil producing municipalities and the rest, peasants discontent started to increase. Increasing environmental awareness and emphasis on sustainable development led local communities in the oil producing areas to demand compensation for disruption. Thousands of fishermen and peasants petitioned PEMEX for damages related to its pollution of the environment. The mobilization of the fishermen and peasants in the oil-polluted areas became one of the most important social upheavals in the region especially in the early 1990s.

Two state commissions were established to contain peasants' discontent and respond to their petitions. In 1984, the state government of Tabasco and federal state agreed on the foundation of the Commission for Development of the Petroleum Zones of the State of Tabasco (*Comisión Para el Desarrollo de las Zonas Petroleras del Estado de Tabasco* – CODEZPET). In 1995, CODEZPET was renamed Inter-institutional Commission for Environment and Social Development (*Comisión Interinstitucional para el Medio Ambiente y el Desarrollo Social* – CIMADES). Both of these commissions had the objective of 'balanced development between the oil industry and the sectors that are not directly dependent on the oil industry'.[30] Despite this purported objective, the commissions worked as a mediator between PEMEX and peasants to resolve the petitions for ecological deterioration.

---

29   Interview with Sanchez López.

30   'Comisión Interinstitucional para el Medio Ambiente y Desarrollo Social' (Interinstitutional Commission for Environment and Social Development), *El Periodico Oficial*, 27 May 1995.

These commissions not only functioned to silence the peasants through limited compensations to reward loyal constituencies, but more importantly channeled the oil revenues towards the agro-industrial bourgeoisie. The second factor that explains the lack of effective peasants' movement in Tabasco is the cooperation of the landed bourgeoisie and PEMEX.[31] The state governments maintained their ties with the big landowners and agricultural producers of the region by directing oil revenue from PEMEX to agriculture sector subsidies.[32] This strategy reconciled the agriculture sector with the oil industry in the state development programs. Therefore, rural power relations were never totally swept from the stage when the oil industry took the lead in development programs. To the contrary, these ties between the agriculture sector and the local state have been reinforced by the growing importance of PEMEX as a state enterprise. Landowning families delivered the political support of the resentful peasants and smallholders in return for support for agro-industry from PEMEX projects.

Increasing resentment among peasant communities towards PEMEX posed deeper political questions about the legitimacy of the local state and strengthened the opposition party, the PRD, in some municipalities. Towards the mid 1980s, the President of the Tabasco chapter of the PRI, Andrés Manuel López Obrador mobilized peasants to negotiate with PEMEX regarding the compensations it should pay for ecological deterioration caused by oil production (Assad 1996: 266, 205). The central PRI organization was uneasy about these mobilization efforts of the PRI leaders in Tabasco.[33] These conflicts eventually led to a breakaway of dissidents from the PRI and formation of an opposition party which then formed the PRD in 1988.[34] From then on, all the protest movements against PEMEX united under the PRD.

Peasant resistance increased in intensity in 1988, 1991 and 1994 following the allegedly fraudulent state elections. The first signs of unrest appeared during the Salvador Neme Castillo government (1989–92). In order to bypass the opposition groups within the PRI in Tabasco, the federal government imposed Neme Castillo as the PRI candidate for the governor's office (Gómez Tagle 1994: 81). López Obrador, who had joined with the other PRI dissidents led by Cuauhtémoc Cárdenas, ran against Neme Castillo for the governorship on the National Democratic Front

---

31　Such arguments were made by various informants in the interviews.

32　Interview with Leyva Leyva.

33　Interview with Camacho Solis.

34　In 1987, Andrés Manuel López Obrador, left the party to organize the opposition movement. The governor, Enrique González Pedrero, chose to stay in the PRI to influence the party's political and economic agenda during the presidential elections. He resigned from the governorship and declared his candidacy for the presidency. Yet the party nominated Carlos Salinas de Gortari for presidency. After the elections, the new president Salinas attempted to weaken the influence of González Pedrero in the party by appointing him to Political, Economic and Social Studies Institute in Mexico City. González Pedrero later joined the PRD in 1990 and became one the closest advisors of Andrés Manuel López Obrador.

(*Frente Democrático Nacional* – FDN) ticket. Arguably owing to the success of the González Pedrero government, Salvador Neme Castillo won the governorship with nearly 80 per cent of the vote. However, shortly after the elections, the Neme government was found to be characterized by nepotism, corruption which created discord within the Tabasco chapter of the PRI as well as between party leaders at the state and national levels (Curzio Gutiérrez 1994b: 65–7). The fact that the state development programs concentrated on the oil industry while abandoning the other sectors gave momentum to the López Obrador-led opposition movement.[35] López Obrador mobilized the resentful local peasant communities against the PRI and PEMEX (Gómez Tagle 1994: 81–2).

The November 1991 municipality elections corresponded to a turning point in local politics (Curzio Gutiérrez 1994a). For the first time in the history of the state, PRI rule was challenged significantly albeit at the municipality level. As a result of loud accusations of fraud by various national and international organizations, President Carlos Salinas de Gortari had to annul the elections. López Obrador organized a 50-day march by 500 peasants from Tabasco to Mexico City, where they joined a demonstration with 20,000 opponents of the PRI. With the pressure of the demonstrations, Neme Castillo came to an agreement with the opposition regarding the disputed three municipalities, and the municipality of Cárdenas was handed over to the PRD after a recount of the votes. Later in January 1992, Neme Castillo stepped down from the governorship and appointed to the General Director of Livestock Policy at the Secretary of Agriculture and Water Resources.

In the 1990s, PEMEX speeded up its drilling operations in order to meet foreign debt payments, an act which amplified the protests of the local communities against the PRI and PEMEX. The increased integration of the energy-feeder local economy into the world market undermined the ability of the local state to prevent the degradation of the environment and the exploitation of natural resources. In 1994 and 1996, demonstrators blocked the oil wells to show their disapproval of the local governments. After the controversial 1994 gubernatorial elections where the PRI candidate Roberto Madrazo, who was well connected with local businessmen by friendship and kinship,[36] won the governorship, the PRD candidate López Obrador once again organized demonstrations protesting the fraudulent elections (Arias Rodríguez and Gusmán 2004).[37] Later, in 1996, thousands of workers, peasants and indigenous people took over 60 installations of PEMEX. The PRD accused the government of Roberto Madrazo Pintado of diverting 30 per cent of the compensation funds that PEMEX had agreed to pay

---

35   Interview with Sanchez López.

36   Madrazo's cousin Carlos Madrazo Cadena was director of the Tabasco chapter of COPARMEX; his other cousin Manuel Felipe Ordóñez Galán was president of the Tabasco Construction Consortium (Eisenstadt 1999: 270–285).

37   The main controversy was around the election campaign budget of the PRI candidate Roberto Madrazo who was accused of having spent 33 times the legal campaign spending limit. Nevertheless, these allegations have not changed the results of the elections.

in order to pave roads in an upscale Villahermosa neighborhood inhabited by the top government and PEMEX bureaucrats (Wheat 1996). The occupiers protested against the PRI–PEMEX alliance that had marginalized dominated masses in favor of foreign oil companies.[38]

However, these protests and resistance were typically met with repression to defend the 'social order' against the dominated masses. The local policy-makers responded to these conflicts by criminalizing the protests and militarizing the state of Tabasco. The army has been called in on several occasions to restore order.

The Federal Electoral Tribunal annulled the October 2000 Tabasco gubernatorial election results, ruling that the elections were fraught with errors and that the PRI illegally used government resources to support its candidate.[39] The second elections were held in August 2001 and the PRI candidate Manuel Andrade Díaz won the election. However, the opposition groups did not accept the official results and claimed that the PRD candidate Cesar Raúl Ojeda Zubieta had actually won. Andrade was succeeded by Andrés Rafael Granier Melo who in 2006 successfully ran for Governor of Tabasco on the PRI ticket.

The structure of the oil industry has allowed PEMEX and local government to buy off the opposition and contain the dissident groups through state employment. A type of labor aristocracy of PEMEX workers has been created with high salaries. The local governments used oil workers to demobilize the dominated classes. The leaders of the STPRM delivered the support of the oil workers to the PRI governments. In the interview with a member of the STPRM, he claimed that 'The Union [STPRM] works like a mafia mollifying the opposition groups that they supposed to mobilize.' An editorial article of a local newspaper makes a similar claim: 'The mafiosi union leaders established their own state within the state', which prevented PEMEX workers from uniting with the PRD-led opposition movement.[40] 'The local PRI organization mobilized a counter resistance protesting against the PRD with the participation of the STPRM leaders, big-land owners, business leaders, ranchers, merchants, and the PRI legislators.'[41]

Although the opposition were not effective in toppling PRI rule in the state, local politics in Tabasco since the late 1980s have undergone a significant transformation. In 1987, an internal conflict within the PRI erupted and intensified the dissident movement. In 1989, this oppositional front became the bastion of the PRD. In the 1990s, the PRD developed into a strong opposition party in Tabasco. As a result of tight PRD–PRI electoral competitions, in 1994, 2000 and 2006 the gubernatorial elections turned out to be very controversial. In the face of widespread protests, the national PRI leaders showed some signs of willingness to negotiate with the PRD leaders. If local development programs continue to abandon large sections of the peasants, smallholders and workers, the opposition movement would be

---

38   Interview with Sanchez López.
39   *La Jornada*, 18 October 2001.
40   *Rumbo Nuevo*, 20 February 1997.
41   Interview with Sanchez López.

able to take over the governor's office and defy national policies, shifting the local regime towards more participatory models with sufficient financial resources and without fear of reprisal. This local resistance was also backed by international environmentalist organizations, which increased its influence on local and national policy-makers. The support of international environmental organizations and civil society associations and media publicity for sustainable development provided local struggles with additional force to empower the dominated masses.[42]

Despite these resistance movements, a large part of PEMEX income is utilized to pay its own debts or the interest on national and foreign debts, or it goes to foreign companies that monopolize the petroleum and petrochemical industries. The economic benefits of decentralization have been enjoyed by these bourgeois classes while an array of burdens – disruption of traditional ways of life, environmental devastation, and so on – were carried by still dominated masses.

Conclusion

This chapter concludes that development programs in Tabasco, which aimed to increase the competitiveness of the local economy, have been crafted by the local policy-makers with very limited participation of social forces. Rich natural resources in Tabasco shaped the local state institutions and conferred capacities to conduct development programs on the local state managers.

If 'historically deep tradition of solid state institutions' is important in producing a local pluralism in the process of decentralization, why is Tabasco so often characterized as authoritarian and so rarely as a participatory democracy? The principal answers to this conundrum lie in the characteristics of the local economy. Decentralization did not improve the policy framework and did not lead to an efficient and egalitarian use of local resources.

Tabasco provides a case which reveals how strong local state institutions evolve in the process of decentralization and whether the local state opens space for local pluralism and participatory democracy. It explains how the local state served as a mediator dealing simultaneously with local, national and foreign bourgeoisie. The decentralization policies did not bring a reallocation of decision-making power in Tabasco. Instead, these new authorities functioned to enlarge the administrative apparatuses of the local state and strengthened state intervention. Furthermore, authoritarian local policy-makers prevailed as a result of decentralization. These policies transferred to local governments the autonomy and responsibility largely to govern the big financial resources of the oil industry. With decentralization, the local policy-makers, particularly the governors, came to be the strongest local agents determining the local development programs. Despite the formal existence of civil society associations, local governments kept them at arms' length and did not open space for the representation of their conflicting interests.

---

42   Interview with González Pedrero.

The case of Tabasco shows that when the local state appears to be the principal agent of development, it is potentially due a development pact among foreign and domestic bourgeoisie mediated through the local policy-makers. The discourse that emphasizes the cross-class alliance behind the local state was largely weakened. The local state assumed the promoter functions of the development and became an intermediary political agency mediating between foreign capital and investors and the domestic bourgeoisie.

The experience of Tabasco provides insight into how corrupt and authoritarian local regimes emerge with decentralization policies. It shows that strong state institutions cannot facilitate the emergence of local pluralism. In these cases, decentralization was not able to curb to abuses of authority by bringing decision-making closer to the citizenry. In fact, strong state institutions provided the means for the local power networks to hold on to their power.

However, authoritarian state-led local development produces its own contradictions. Growing involvement of the local state to stimulate the local economy sharpened the class contradictions and led to a significant loss of legitimacy of the local state in the view of peasants and fishermen. Development based on the expansion of PEMEX activities increased the environmental degradation which had a direct negative impact on the livelihood of fishermen and peasants. To contain politicization of these groups required authoritarian control of the local state over every sphere of socioeconomic life. However, these attempts were not successful in preventing the rise of popular struggles of local groups who felt themselves unfavored by the local state. As the local regime starts to base its power merely on domination, popular struggles may start to organize around political organizations of the opposition. As discussed in the next chapter, it is not strong state institutions but the mobilization of the local dominated classes which is central in attaining more participatory local development models.

Chapter 6

When Business Class Allies with a Strong Indigenous Peasant Movement: Contested Local Development in Guerrero

In Guerrero, the pattern of local development following the implementation of the decentralization policies differed dramatically from the cases of Chihuahua and Tabasco. The local regime of Guerrero can be characterized by continuous contesting among various social classes in the local state apparatuses as well as within the local chapters of the political parties. Although increasing the competitiveness of the local economy to attract more investments to the region became the main objective of the local agents, these motivations did not result in entrepreneurial or authoritarian state-led local development. Unlike Chihuahua and Tabasco, dominated masses in Guerrero have historically been militant and organized which turned local development committees into an arena of struggle expressing different classes, factional interests and alliances. In Guerrero, the decentralization policies led to what I call 'contested local development'.

This chapter is motivated by the idea that Guerrero's experience with decentralization provides us with insights into how decentralization policies could lead to an opening in the local authoritarian regimes by strengthening the local dominated masses despite local tourism bourgeoisie's attempts to take over the local development programs. Recent studies of Guerrero emphasize the increasing importance of local opposition groups in prying open local regimes (Fernández Gómez 2004, Selee 2011, Snyder 2001b). Fernández Gómez (2004) focuses on the role of local dissident groups in fortifying the bases of the PRD and bringing about electoral success. Andrew Selee (2011: 160–201) argues that local politics in Chilpancingo, the capital city of Guerrero, became more pluralistic. Snyder (2001a: 97–134) claims that after the central government 'withdrew' from local political and economic regulation, the opposition parties challenged the local neo-corporatist organizations that emerged to control the local political economy. In sum, the literature on Guerrero singles out the importance of the local opposition groups and the PRD as factors contributing to the evolution of the local regime after the decentralization policies.

This chapter aims to add to this literature by examining the transformation of the local regime with a particular focus on the strategies of the domestic and foreign bourgeoisie. It attempts to show that the main factor that explains the emergence of the contested local development is the strategic alliance of the domestic and foreign bourgeoisie invested in the tourism industry with the strong indigenous peasant movement. When the local economy was poised to integrate into the world market with its tourism industry, foreign tourism bourgeoisie invested heavily in the Acapulco region in partnership with domestic capital groups. Both the local bourgeoisie and their foreign partners joined the already existing peasant movement in order to break apart the local PRI network. Furthermore, the local-global network of the tourism sector needed to ally with the peasant movement to increase the competitiveness of the local economy for investment and tourists. This alliance, which took place under the PRD particularly around the tourism enclaves, weakened the authoritarian PRI networks in the big municipalities, while strengthening the influence of the peasant organizations and enabling the hitherto strong peasants to contest the local development programs. This chapter underlines how decentralization policies may provide an opportunity for previously excluded social classes to organize and form alliances against local authoritarian rules.

This chapter is organized in five sections. The first section traces the formation of local state-society relations shaped by the geographic and demographic characteristics of the state and looks at how local state institutions were formed within these relations. The second section looks at the emerging tourism industry and its demands for decentralization policies in the late 1970s. The third section provides an analysis of how decentralization of the tourism industry changed the direction of the local development programs. It then focuses on the changing balances of social forces as a result of which local development programs have become a matter of struggle among peasant groups and tourism sector bourgeoisie vis-à-vis traditional PRI circles after the decentralization policies. The fourth section discusses the impact of decentralization on party politics and the possible opportunities that decentralization policies can bring both for previously marginalized dominated and bourgeois classes who have a vested interest in local politics. The final section outlines the main findings from the Guerrero case.

Formation of Local Class Relations and Local State Institutions

Examining the geographic and demographic characteristics of the state of Guerrero is an important first step in tracing the formation of local class relations and the local state institutions. Guerrero is located in the south of Mexico. The state is bordered by the states of Michoacán to the west, México, Morelos and Puebla to the north, Oaxaca to the east and the Pacific Ocean to the south. It is divided into seven administrative regions – Costa Chica, Costa Grande, Acapulco, the Central Zone, Chilapa, Tierra Caliente and Mountain. The state capital is the city of Chilpancingo, and other important cities are the three tourist enclaves, Acapulco, Ixtapa and Taxco, which form the 'Triangle of the Sun'. Since the 1940s, the Triangle of the Sun has become one of the significant tourism centers of Mexico.

Guerrero has a significant indigenous peasant population coupled with a valuable tourism sector. There are 7,452 indigenous communities grouped together in 80 municipalities, found principally in the Mountain region (Flores

Félix and Canabál Cristiani 2000: 258). According to the INEGI 2010 data, it has a total population of 3,388,768, of which 15.1 per cent are speaking an indigenous language and 31.4 per cent of indigenous population is monolingual (25.4 per cent men; 37.4 per cent women) (INEGI 2010).

The region is characterized by its militant indigenous and Afro-*mestizo* movement.[1] In the early nineteenth century, the growing number of Afro-*mestizos* infused the Guerrero region with the spirit of independence. They suffered a greater degree of racist degradations than the *mestizo*s and indigenous groups. Indigenous masses joined the Afro-*mestizo* resistance against the colonists. The phrase '*Guerrero bronco*' has long been associated with the resistance movements in the region. The term '*bronco*' refers to the wild and uncontrollable mustang which characterizes the state's volatile history (Bartra 1996).

Vicente Guerrero, a leading general of the wars of independence, who gave his last name to the state, passionately supported the autonomy of village councils, 'declaring that the interests of the people were best served by the closest political body that represented them' (Vincent 2001: 152).[2] The autonomy ideals of the *caudillo*s like Guerrero himself brought about unlimited political power to smallholder *cacique* families. Furthermore, the economic program of the Porfiriato enabled these rancher families to turn into the 'new village elite' (Jacobs 1982). They put aside their differences and aimed to control the political economy of their region jointly (Bartra 1996). Networks of these families and their relations with the Díaz regime shaped the institutions of the local state to a great extent. The close alliance between Díaz and the northern bourgeoisie has gradually generated resentment among these bourgeoning *cacique*s in Guerrero whereby the Revolution was centered on resistance against Díaz's attempts to subordinate the regional powers to national central politics.

The Revolution did not displace the entrenched system of *caciquismo* in Guerrero. Although the belligerent revolutionary forces attempted to destroy the majority of the regional *cacique*s, the established families in Guerrero were 'absorbed' and 'molded into the new political system' (Jacobs 1982: 167). The Figueroa family, for instance, managed to survive and controlled the establishment of the local regime in the aftermath of the revolution, Francisco Figueroa becoming the provisional governor (Valverde 1989: 36).[3]

When the Figueroa family assumed unchallenged power in the region, the social and economic disparities, inequitable land distribution, political manipulation

---

1   Africans were brought to Mexico in the late sixteenth century to recuperate the loss of labor power because of a demographic decline of the Indians. Mixing of the different races created Afro-*mestizo*s among others.

2   When the commander Guerrero became the first black Indian president of Mexico in 1829, he abolished slavery.

3   Bartra identifies the family of Figueroa as one made of small *cacique*s, while Jacobs defines them as rancheros, small property owners, and businessmen (Bartra 1996: 35–51; Jacobs 1982).

and ethnic discrimination started to become significant sources of discontent among school teachers and peasant communities. The Workers' Party of Acapulco (*Partido Obrero de Acapulco* – POA), founded in 1919 with active participation of the teachers' union, received significant electoral support in the 1920s. For the party, the Revolution in Guerrero was a bourgeois revolution, and the 'socialist revolution' was left incomplete.[4] Attempts at a 'socialist revolution' in Guerrero started in the 1920s and teachers' mobilization ushered in militant peasants' movement towards the 1930s. In the early 1930s, many members of the teachers' federation and the peasants' organizations joined PCM, where they constituted an important bloc between 1936 and 1939 (Bartra 1996: 87, Raby 1974: 91–4). The Party supported the formation of the peasant league in Guerrero (Hamilton 1982: 272). Eventually, the Socialist Party of Guerrero (*Partido Socialista de Guerrero* – PSG) embraced the teachers' and peasants' movements and organized another episode of mobilization.

The response of the local policy makers to these local movements was excessively repressive, which in turn marginalized and radicalized the opposition. These radical organizations survived through the centralized corporatist institutions state form. Even after the establishment of the corporatism at the national level, the peasants' and teachers' resistance continued to have a strong presence in Guerrero. Unlike in Tabasco, the hegemony of the local implementation of the corporatist regime in Guerrero was sustained based on coercion. The local regime in Guerrero could be characterized as force-based domination. The central government actively supported, relied on and closely monitored the local policy makers in Guerrero to ensure the suppression of the resistance movements, which would otherwise spread out to the neighboring states. State repression was chosen as the strategy of agro-industry bourgeoisie for countering the opposition.[5] However, repression did not dissolve the resistance. On the contrary, it created stronger resistance challenging the very existence of the state in Guerrero.

While local state power in Tabasco created a centripetal force that prevented dominated masses from establishing their independent organizations, PRI rule in Guerrero created a centrifugal force marginalizing dissidents. Although some opposition leaders continued to struggle within electoral politics outside the PRI, as a result of the persistent forceful actions that the local policy makers undertook, peasants' resistance movements lost confidence in the rules of 'democratic' game. The repeated PRI victories between 1940s and 1990s mean exclusion of the opposition from decision-making and led to an alternative manifestation of discontent: clandestine guerrilla action (Blacker Hanson 2005: ix). The guerrilla

---

4   *Avance/Guerrero*, 'La Revolución no ha Cumplido: FDC', 29 April 1978.

5   Political violence is for which the state is known included extreme cases such as deaths in Chilpancingo during the 1960 movement against the governor, Caballero Aburto; the victims of the military assaults on protesters in Iguala in 1962; the deaths in the central plaza of Atoyac on May; massacre of copper workers in 1967 in Acapulco; and hundreds of the disappeared (Blacker Hanson 2005: xii).

groups founded the Party of the Poor (*Partido de los Pobres* – PDLP) which actively organized the rural and urban communities until 1989.

Despite the existence of strong resistance movements, the reason why the PRI won all the local elections from the 1940s until the 1990s was the extensive two-way control networks. Top-down control is the central government's control over governor's and the governors' control over mayors. The local policy makers maintained close relations with the central state to sustain their local power. Many of the governors had to end their governance before their tenure ended because they were replaced by the center. With the legitimacy they received from the federal level, as Selee argues (2011: 173–74), the state government and key political leaders maintained tight control over municipal elections; governors frequently removed mayors either by decree or due to unofficial pressure.

Bottom-up control of *caciquismo* has been a well-established structure which shaped social relations in Guerrero until the 1980s. The biggest *cacique* family ruled Guerrero for over 40 years. In the 1970s, the name Figueroa is intimately linked with the state of Guerrero as well as with the authoritarianism, backwardness and violence that rule the state. The *cacique* families took direct control of leading political positions. To nominate the candidates for mayors and city council members in most of the municipalities required a negotiation among these families, mediated by local policy makers (Estrada Castañón 1994: 58, Selee 2011: 173). Their political power enabled these families to further their capital accumulation. They used several strategies to control the local producers: they were the informal agricultural bankers;[6] they – especially the Figueroa family – had the monopoly over the fertilizer market, essential for agricultural production;[7] and they provided the only access to the markets for producers.[8] Through these strategies smallholder *cacique* families of the 1920s became the 'agro-industry bourgeoisie' of Guerrero in the 1940s. These families also attempted to weaken the cohesion of traditional collectives through extra-economic strategies. All the big *cacique* families trained and armed their own private police, called white guards (*guardia blanca*) which posed a latent threat of violence towards peasants and the guerrilla movement sympathizers.[9]

How have other local economic agents complied with these power networks? The answer lies in the nature of the local economy. Even if a certain level of

---

6   In the 1940s, the Agricultural Credit Bank failed to meet the demands of many small peasants in Guerrero. For money-lending, these peasants and *ejiditarios* became dependent on the local *caciques*, who charged high interest rates in order to create a mechanism of control (cf. Hamilton 1982: 193).

7   Interviews with Ríos Piter and Ortega.

8   In coffee and cocoa production, the big producers, known as *acaparadores*, purchase the products from producers and transport them to national and global markets (Bartra 1996: 160, 165; Snyder 2001a). This power has been extensive because until the 1990s, and small producers lacked any other options to sell their products.

9   Interview with Ojela Rivera.

discontent among certain factions of bourgeoisie had existed, there was not a single faction that could lead local development and organize a coalition of the bourgeois classes. As Estrada Castañón notes, bourgeoisie in Guerrero has been 'parochial' and 'local' in their businesses and 'weak' and 'fragmented' in organization which had curtailed their capacity within corporatist associations to lead a bourgeois coalition in the state (Estrada Castañón 1994: 87–8). Similarly, Fernández mentions since 'economic sectors such as commerce, service and industry were disarticulated agro-industry bourgeoisie led the coalition of the dominant classes.[10]

The local state institutions of Guerrero were formed as a result of the condensation of these power relations. Local state's organizational capacity was weak due to its impact on capital accumulation and social structure. The local state apparatuses were overwhelmingly involved in the power networks of the agro-industry bourgeoisie. Decisions were generally in the hands of powerful *caciques* who were accountable only to the central government. Political relations were based on personal contacts and clientelist relations between policy makers and the agro-industry bourgeoisie. While smallholder-turned-agro-industry-*caciques* realized their objective interests through the state apparatus, they failed to maintain the conditions required for capital accumulation in commerce or industry. Their discretionary control led the state security forces to become notoriously corrupt and repressive. Local state institutions in Guerrero served to reinforce inequalities and political exclusion (cf. Estrada Castañón 1994: 56–7, Rendón Alarcón, 2003: 111–17).

Growing Tourism Industry, Local Problems and Challenges

The Mexican state 'pushed' tourism through central planning in the 1940s (Bennett and Sharpe 1982). As the Secretary of Internal Affairs between 1940 and 1946, Miguel Aleman started a dramatic change in Mexico's tourism policies, switching from historical cultural heritage to nature tourism. The first investments in the port of Acapulco were made during Aleman's presidency (1946–52). Later in the 1960s, parallel to the rise in worldwide tourist flows as product of developments in air transportation, the Mexican state invested heavily in tourism development in Acapulco. The state also offered incentives for developers to build hotels and resorts. In 1969, the national development agency, the Tourism Infrastructure Trust (*Fondo de Promoción de Infrastructura Turística* – INFRATUR) was formed to carry out the planning. In 1974, the Ministry of Tourism (*Secretaría de Turismo* – SECTUR) was founded together with the National Tourism Fund (*Fondo de Nacional Turística* – FONATUR), an agency stemming from the INFRATUR and the Tourism Guarantee and Promotion Fund (*Fondo de Garantía y Fomento del Turismo* – FOGATUR).

Since the 1970s, tourism and related sectors have become major components of the economy of Guerrero. Tourism has become the fastest growing economic

---

10   Interview with Fernández.

activity and Mexico has gradually become one of the most popular destinations in the world (Clancy 2001: 130). Foreign investors in the tourism sector started to create strong local allies. Hotel chains such as Holiday Inn, Hilton International, Inter-Continental, Hyatt International and Marriott invested in the region not through direct ownership and management, but by allying with domestic investors who sign some combination of management contracts or leasing, franchise or technical service agreement. The Monterrey Group has powerful enterprises outside the area of Monterrey. The group participated in a joint venture with Hyatt International and took over management of the Continental Hotel in Acapulco. In addition to these two hotel chains, large sums of capital were invested in Acapulco by the Monterrey Group in 1980.[11] Furthermore, these hotel chains provide other services, such as banking, car rental, tour operation, catering and so on. As a result of the growth of tourism, other sectors such as banking, commerce, restaurants, transportation, and local arts and crafts in Acapulco also flourished. Therefore, the tourism industry in Acapulco has generated benefits for established local bourgeoisie and new capital groups as well as for professionals, middle strata and some enterprising poor people.

Tourism sector bourgeoisie were uninterested in local politics until the late 1970s and did not cultivated close relations with the local PRI elites, because the development decisions and investments in the tourism sector were handled by the central state. Yet, in the second half of the 1970s, tourism sector bourgeoisie faced two local problems that would threaten the competitiveness of the region for both foreign investments and tourists: insecurity and infrastructure problems.

In the 1960s and 1970s, the representation crisis manifested itself most radically in Guerrero through the growing militant student and indigenous movements. In October 1960, the students of the Autonomous University of Guerrero (*Universidad Autónoma de Guerrero* – UAG) in collaboration with teachers and peasants launched a fight against the repressive rule of the governor Caballero Aburto (1957–61). Several municipalities supported this struggle to protest the governor and the mayors that the governor had appointed without the consent of the local communities. 'These movements turned into a rebellion of the municipalities against the state and central governments'.[12] Following the students, the guerrilla organizations, in the 1970s, focused their demands on democratization and participation. The national army launched an extensive attack against the guerrilla leaders, an act known as the Dirty War (*Guerra Sucia*) because of the tactics that the army generals and paramilitary groups used against the local communities (Bartra 1996: 163; Castro Hipolito 1982: 68–74). Especially in this period, the most visible image of the local and central state in Guerrero came to be the army. The authoritarian rule of the Rubén Figueroa Figueroa government (1975–81), and harsh military force exercised over the opposition threatened the growing tourism sector. The 'Acapulco Document', which was produced at

---

11   *Acapulco News*, 'Hotels Attract Big Investors', 2 February 1980.
12   Interview with Ortega.

the World Tourism Meeting in Acapulco in 1982, underlined that the 'growing number of armed conflicts ... constitutes obstacles to the development of tourism' (Acapulco Document 1982).

Underdevelopment of infrastructure in Acapulco came to be another important concern of the tourism bourgeoisie. Thousands of poor Mexicans flooded into Acapulco in the 1960s and 1970s in search of work.[13] Nevertheless, infrastructure construction did not keep pace with growth. The city was not capable of handling such large numbers of newcomers. The central development agencies were not able to regulate growth in Acapulco. The result was a flurry of construction of elaborate, exclusive hotels which led to over-building, environmental degradation and marginalization of native Acapulquenos (Hundt 1996: 108). The city of Acapulco and its adjacent towns had very poor public services such as health, sewers, potable water, electricity, schools or recreation facilities (ibid). These infrastructure problems were considered a handicap for Acapulco in attracting tourists as new investments in tourism promoted other regions like Yucatan Peninsula providing modern amenities for tourists.

With the conviction that 'these local problems required local solution',[14] as bourgeoisie investing the tourism industry strived to gain control over local politics, they faced two challenges: authoritarian power networks of the PRI and lack of resources at the disposal of the local governments. The local capital groups seconded the criticisms coming from dissident organizations regarding the impact of *caciquismo* and corruption in constraining local development. In the late 1970s, agro-industry families and private initiatives in tourism had uneasy relationships which hindered the search for solutions to the development problems concerning the tourism sector.[15] The Rubén Figueroa Figueroa government generated discontent among the capital groups in Acapulco (Bartra 1996: 164). In 1977, these groups complained that the autonomy of the municipality of Acapulco was not respected by the governor.[16] In 1978, the president of the local chapter of CANACO, Vicente Rueda Saucedo, claimed that 'the CANACO is a body of consultation; not of antagonism. Thus, the governor should consult us about the revenues and spending of the municipality of Acapulco'.[17] In a conference, 'the Municipality and the Trust' (*el Municipio y el Fideicomiso*), organized by Acapulco capital groups, one of the participants, Miguel Garcia Maldonado, summarized the demands of these capital groups succinctly. He noted that the state of Guerrero did not recognize the autonomy of the municipality of Acapulco.

---

13 According to *Avance/Guerrero* (1 September 1979), more than 20,000 immigrants came to Acapulco in 1979.

14 This argument was made by a leading businessman in Acapulco.

15 Ibid.

16 *Revolución-Diario de Guerrero* 'No se respeta la autonomía del municipio: CANACO', 3 December 1977.

17 *Avance/Guerrero* 'Reanudan relaciones Canaco y gobierno; transformar Guerrero, tarea de varios sexenios: Rubén Figueroa', 23 March 1978.

The intervention of the state in the matters of the municipality was harmful for the development of Acapulco. He suggested that 'there should be a reorganization and revision of the laws regulating the economic-administrative relations among the state, federation and the municipality for a better redistribution of resources of the country'.[18] Participants in the meeting agreed that the local power relations of the PRI in Guerrero should be dissolved in order to achieve socioeconomic development. The meeting called for the decentralization of financial resources and tourism regulations to solve local infrastructural problems.[19]

As the tourism sector has become one of the key activities in the integration of Mexico into the world economy, these criticisms became more important for the PRI leaders who were already suffering from a loss of national support. President López Portillo (1977–82) established closer relations with the tourism sector bourgeoisie of Acapulco. He visited Acapulco in 1978 (16 October) and 1979 (2 September) to meet with the sector representatives. It seems that such meetings served their purpose and that the tourism industrialists were successful in convincing the President of the local problems and constraints they were facing. In 1982, in his opening addresses of the World Tourism Organization meeting held in Acapulco, Portillo acknowledged that the growing tourism industry generates multiplier effects which could make it a centerpiece of an integral development process in the region and the fight against *caciquismo* and said that decentralized financial resources and development plans are important ways to achieve better social and economic development (Acapulco Document 1982).

Local Development Programs

At the *Consulta Popular* meeting held in Guerrero on 15 December 1981, presidential candidate Miguel de la Madrid addressed social development issues in Guerrero, comparing the social development indicators at the national level with those of Guerrero (de la Madrid 1983: 5–11). The presidential candidate noted that 'the level of marginalization in Guerrero did not decrease with the Mexican Revolution'. He placed special emphasis on *caciquismo* as a 'constraint against development'. *Caciquismo*, he claimed, refers to 'underdevelopment of politics'. Then, he turned to the rich natural resources and potential development strategies of the state, which had not been used efficiently. He referred to tourism as 'the new direction for local development'. He pointed out that investment in tourism would 'bring about better social development in communication and transportation'. Finally, he noted that decentralization reforms in Guerrero could not 'lead to a healthy local development without an improvement of the local state institutions'.

---

18   *Avance/Acapulco* 'El Fideicomiso es dañino a la autoridad municipal', 14 September 1981.

19   *El Sol de Acapulco*, 'Piden Descentralizar la Ley Federal de Turismo', 29 August 1983.

He underlined that 'democratic governance and the participation of various local groups' were key elements to improve local state institutions. In his speech de la Madrid diagnosed the main problems and prospects of Guerrero in the process of decentralization rather accurately.

This section shows that, initially the decentralization policies presented both challenges and opportunities for the authoritarian PRI enclaves in small municipalities. Towards the end of the 1980s, however, local dissident groups organized local indigenous peasants especially around the two largest cities, Acapulco and Chilpancingo to participate in politics, which brought electoral success to the PRD in various municipalities in the region. As a parallel story the decentralization policies increased the strategic importance of local politics for the tourism sector. Eventually, tourism industrialists, who had been in the periphery of the power networks of the PRI, became involved in the PRD and started to play a central role in local politics. As a result of the strategies and alliances of the local and global tourism industrialists and indigenous peasant groups, this section shows that the local regime evolved towards contestation among inherently conflicting social interests.

Plan Guerrero: Challenges to Caciquismo and Corporatism

In the early 1980s, the level of marginalization and potential for disruption in the context of a harsh economic crisis constrained the government to respond to some of the demands of local indigenous peasant groups. In line with President de la Madrid, Governor Cervantes Delgado (1981–87) presented the decentralization policies as a way to stimulate local participation and democratization.[20] In an attempt to provide them with alternative channels of representation, Cervantes incorporated certain opposition groups as his advisors. Many of his top advisors had leftist backgrounds; some had played prominent roles in the national student movement of 1968, while others had been militant in opposition parties (Calderón Mólgara 1994: 77). Following the decentralization policies, the local congress redesigned the Law of Citizen Participation and the internal regulations of the Development Planning Committee of Guerrero (Comité de Planeación para el Desarrollo del Estado de Guerrero – COPLADEG) by reforming 50 articles of the Constitution of Guerrero (SPP 1988: 155).[21]

The Cervantes Delgado government formulated the Socioeconomic Plan of the State of Guerrero (*Plan de Desarrollo Socioeconómico del Estado Guerrero* or better known as *Plan Guerrero*) which would be effective between 1984 and 1987. Its objectives were identified as improving public health and education services, increasing infrastructure construction and supporting industrial development

---

20 *Novedades Acapulco*, 'Desconcentración de Administración Pública Municipal é les Próximo', 21 December 1984.

21 Ibid., 'Reforma casi total de la Constitución', 31 January 1984.

(SPP 1988: 155–58).[22] This first decentralized development program had serious implications for the power relations in Guerrero with regard to control of local *caciques*.

Within the Plan, a development program called Municipal Strengthening (*Fortalecimiento Municipal*) was launched to curb the authoritarian power of the *cacique* families by increasing the capacity of municipal public administration. Municipal Strengthening aimed to enable the municipalities to manage their own income resources and local communities to solve their own problems.[23] To achieve this, the Plan instituted development accords whereby each municipality would negotiate their development projects with the state government.[24]

In the interviews, various local actors mentioned that the new financial resources of the municipalities were at the discretionary disposal of corrupt local authorities and *cacique* families in municipalities (cf. Rodríguez Wallenius 2005: 159–60).[25] There were two measures that were installed to counteract to this tendency. First, in order to prevent corruption and fraud in municipalities, the Cervantes government established an audit mechanism for the municipalities.[26] Since then, every November, the month of the audits, the first pages of the local newspapers are filled with news of irregularities revealed by the auditors in the municipalities. Although the auditing mechanism did not resolve the problem, it surely made these problems more visible to the public and provided legitimate causes for demonstrations against the corrupt local authorities. The second measure challenged the extra-economic control mechanisms of the local *cacique* families. With a new law of public security, private armed guards (*guardia blanca*) were forced to disarm.[27] This regulation while improving the capacities of the municipalities weakened the discretionary repressive control of the *cacique* families. However, fear factors in the municipalities did not completely fade away since the local *caciques* were still powerful enough to control the security forces of the municipalities.

The state government of Guerrero allied with the Union of *Ejidos* to strengthen them vis-à-vis the *cacique* families. The Union was founded in 1979 in the Costa Grande region and expanded to the Mountain region with the support of the Cervantes government (Bartra 1996: 165, Snyder 2001b: 104). By the mid 1980s, the Union represented 90 per cent of Guerrero's coffee producing families (Cono and Paz Paredes 1991: 55). As noted above, local *caciques* had been controlling the peasants by providing them with credit and links to world markets. The Plan

---

22   Ibid., '$50 mil millones para Guerrero en 84 Anuncio ante MMH en Chilpancingo', 14 January 1984.

23   *El Sol de Acapulco*, 'Invierten $350 Millones en Municipios', 6 July 1983.

24   *Novedades Acapulco*, 'El Congreso Local reformó las leyes de Hacienda del Estado y Municipal', 22 December 1984.

25   Interviews with Fernández and Gusman Visairo.

26   *El Sol de Acapulco*, 'Auditarías a los 75 municipios', 28 July 1983.

27   Interview with Ojela Rivera.

Guerrero aimed to improve credit mechanisms. The development program of Credit on Your Word (*Credito a la Palabra*) assisted small producers in obtaining cheap credit from the Union of *Ejidos*. Producers started to organize the credits collectively within the Union (Snyder 2001b). At the same time, the Union provided a network for small producers to transport their products to the market for better prices (Bartra 1996: 167). The *caciques* thus ceased to be the only bankers or link to the market for small producers. As the Union of *Ejidos* became a strong power against the local branch of the CNC, the CNC leaders were forced to make manifest declarations against the control of the *caciques* in order to co-opt the autonomous peasants' organizations.[28]

The Governor of Tabasco, Enrique González Pedrero (1982–87) and Governor Cervantes Delgado shared a similar vision in communicating with the local communities. Like González Pedrero, Cervantes Delgado traveled to small villages to meet with the peasantry and listen to their problems (cf. Snyder 2001b: 101). They both involved the local communities into local decisions. Despite these similarities, Enrique González Pedrero rendered dominated classes dependent to the local state, while the latter strengthened social organizations outside the state institutions. This difference does not simply stem from each governor's personal conviction. What explains this difference is that the indigenous peasants in Guerrero have gained a privileged position through previous mobilization by progressive grassroots organizations. As discussed below, with the decentralization of the tourism sector, this characteristic of Guerrero was to become more significant in shaping the path of local development.

Decentralization of the Tourism Sector: Restructuring of the Local Economy

The decentralization policies increased the importance of local politics for the tourism sector. In 1983, the tourism industrialists demanded a separate municipality for the tourism areas of Acapulco to be able to allocate more financial resources to their sector. The mayor of Acapulco delivered this demand to the State Congress, with a proposal to divide Acapulco into two different municipalities for the 'better treatment of the tourism sector as well as for the improvement of rural and agricultural development'.[29] When this proposal was not accepted by the State Congress, the tourism industrialists raised their voice. The President of the Association of Hotel Sales Executives (*Asociación of Ejecutivos de Ventas de Hoteles*) boldly declared that 'the next mayor of Acapulco should be a businessman from the tourism sector, because the infrastructure problems affecting the tourism sector can only be taken into account by someone who is familiar with the sector'. At the same time, he refrained from upsetting the local PRI elite, noting that 'the

---

28   In 1983, the candidate for the leader of the local chapter of CNC, Mario Hernández Posada, promised to fight against *caciquismo*. *El Sol de Acapulco*, 'Guerra al Caciquismo, Promote el Candidato de la CNC', 19 July 1983.

29   *El Sol de Acapulco*, 'Propone dividir en 2 a Acapulco', 2 August 1983.

businessmen of Guerrero do not have political ambitions and the majority of them are without political party affiliation'.[30] Since the PRI was still strong in local politics, the capital groups did not dare to support an opposition party, but instead chose to pressure the PRI from within.[31]

What motivated further the tourism industrialists to become involved in local politics was the decentralization of the institutions of tourism development with the launching of a coordination office of The Secretary of Tourism (*Secretaria de Turismo* – SECTUR) in Acapulco. To minimize possible coordination problems between the federal and local governments in shaping the development programs for the tourism sector, SECTUR was decentralized in 1985. A coordination office of the SECTUR in Acapulco was opened to coordinate the offices of Guerrero, Oaxaca and Chiapas and mediate among them.[32]

After the decentralization of SECTUR,[33] there was a significant shift in the development projects away from agriculture and towards the tourism sector. The shift became visible in the development programs of the José Francisco Ruíz Massieu government (1987–93).[34] The first two years of the Ruíz Massieu government can be characterized by measures to increase the competitiveness of the local economy. While subsidies for agriculture were eliminated, public resources were allocated largely for urban development programs, such as mega-projects intended to attract foreign capital to the tourism sector. The biggest such investments were a shopping complex, in Acapulco, Ixtapa Marína and the Cuernavaca–Acapulco superhighway (*Autopista del Sol*).

Integration of the local economy into the world market via the tourism industry unleashed certain local and global agents which would gradually weaken *cacique* families both politically and economically. The owners and managers of the international hotel chains such as Holiday Inn, Hilton International, Inter-Continental, Hyatt International and Marriott became influential agents in local politics. As a parallel process, the rule of the *cacique* families in rural areas around tourism centers was seriously undermined. The generally agreed view was that unconstrained power of the local *caciques* was damaging the image of the region for foreign investors. The government attempted to strengthen the private sector vis-à-vis the *cacique* families by decreasing the size of the public sector: 17 of the 36 state economic enterprises were privatized between 1987 and 1989 (Estrada

---

30   Ibid., 'El Próximo Alcalde Debe ser Empresario: Propone la Asociación de Hoteles', 21 August 1983.

31   Interview with a leading business investing in the tourism sector.

32   *Novedades Acapulco*, 'Descentralización en la SECTUR', 16 December 1984.

33   Interview with Garcia Maldonado and Gusman Visairo.

34   As in Tabasco, Carlos Salinas de Gortari (1988–94) carefully handpicked the gubernatorial candidate for Guerrero, José Francisco Ruíz Massieu (1987–93), in order to prevent possible pressures from the agro-business class who had had tight networks with the local chapter of the PRI. Ruíz Massieu was a close colleague and the brother-in-law of Carlos Salinas de Gortari.

Castañón 1994: 142–43). The economic power of the Figueroa family was largely curtailed by the privatization of the Fertilizers of Guerrero.[35] These policies tilted the balance of power towards the private sector and tourism industrialists. The close relations between the state government and the peasants that characterized the Cervantes government were replaced by joint ventures between the Ruíz Massieu government and large foreign firms and their local partners investing in the tourism sector.

In 1993, the SECTUR undertook further efforts to decentralize a number of its functions to state governments. Tourism activities were to be regulated by the state governments with the municipality and state development programs. State Consultative Tourism Boards (in short, Tourism Boards) were established to promote participation of local and global tourism sector representatives in local development programs more effectively. Through these public–private consultative boards, local tourism industrialists and representatives of international hotel chains started to provide consultation, advisory and technical-support services to state tourism agencies. The SECTUR organized annual meetings with major tourism-oriented municipalities in order to define new development programs for each region.

The Tourism Board of Acapulco organized tourism promotion activities, including annual fairs in Acapulco that were previously in the hands of the Secretary (OECD 2001). In the 1995 Tourism Board meeting, the federal, state and municipality of Acapulco authorities and tourism sector representatives agreed that local and regional socio-economic development plans were essential in attracting more foreign direct investment and tourists to the region. The meetings also underlined the need to emphasize the cultural richness of the region in the development of tourism.[36] In 1998 the mayor called for the participation of the tourism sector in this committee to tailor the development programs of the municipality of Acapulco. For that purpose, the mayor of Acapulco created a development agency to support the tourism sector.[37]

Indigenous Peasants' Mobilization

The new direction of the development programs generated new dynamics of popular resistance. The development programs increased the socio-economic polarization in the region by channeling local resources to the tourism industry. The marginalization of indigenous peasant communities in many mountain region municipalities increased (Camposortega and Jiménez 1998). Polarization and marginalization created strong discontent among these communities. At the same time, the weakened control of the *caciques* lifted the previously existing constraints on mobilization among the indigenous peasant groups. With the privatization of the state initiatives, the local

---

35   Interview with Ríos Piter.

36   The reports on these meetings are available at www.cddhcu.gob.mx/camdip/comdip/comtur1.

37   *Novedades Acapulco*, 'Acapulco es un gran destino turístico', 28 November 1998.

state has lost most of its previous modes of regulation to arbitrate the discontent (Estrada Castañón 1994: 153). Under these conditions, indigenous peasants and the local political parties that have had organic ties with the guerrilla movement in the region organized around the PRD and radicalized their demands.

At the end of the 1980s, Cuauhtémoc Cárdenas initiated a strong dynamism among the local leftist political parties and militant indigenous organizations. In the 1988 presidential elections, Cuauhtémoc Cárdenas won 36 per cent of the votes in Guerrero (Bartra 1996: 141). During the election period, the PRD became established in the state through 10 district assemblies in areas where the organized opposition existed. Previously existing socialist parties like the PCM and its heirs PSUM and the Mexican Socialist Party (*Partido Mexicano Socialista* – PMS), disbanded themselves to integrate into the PRD.

The PRD played a vanguard role in organizing local communities' protests against the local regime. The party expanded its power by mobilizing the other southern states of Mexico, particularly Oaxaca and Chiapas, and combining the forces of the resistance movements in these states. In the 1990s, with the effect of the PRD, the indigenous movement in Guerrero organized collectively to define the terms of the local development. The PRD strengthened the power of the indigenous peasants by helping to formation of new organizations. The most prominent organizations were the Council of Nahua Peoples in Alto Balsas (*Consejo de Pueblos de Nahua en Alto Balsas* – CPNAB), the Guerrero Council of 500 Years of Indigenous Resistance (*Consejo Guerrerense 500 Años de Resistencia Indígena* – CG500ARI) and the Tlachinollan Human Rights Center of the Mountains (*Tlachinollan Centro de Derechos Humanos de la Montaña*). These organizations became active in defending the rights of the rural activists who were often threatened, jailed, killed or disappeared (Selee 2011: 177). The directors of these organizations acted as liaisons between state development agencies and community members. They functioned to channel government funds to community projects like road repair, piped water systems, latrines, electrification, wood stoves and cultural maintenance (Overmeyer-Velazquez 2003: 5). To protest against the San Juan Tetelcingo hydro-electric dam project, on 2–12 October, 1992 they organized a 'March for the Dignity and Resistance of Indigenous Peoples' from Chilpancingo to Mexico City showing the strength of the indigenous movement in Guerrero.[38] The next day, the hydro-electric project was officially suspended.

The political representation of the indigenous groups through the PRD in the local congress enabled them to intervene in politics more effectively. Various indigenous communities in the Mountain region had already been demanding territorial autonomy. As the decentralization policies increased the importance of the autonomy, these demands steadily increased. In 1993, the PRD deputies in the State Congress submitted a proposal for the creation of the municipality of Acatepec in the Mountain Region, which was approved by the Congress.

---

38 For a concise analysis on indigenous mobilization in Guerrero against the Tetelcingo Dam, see Hindley 1999.

Following Acatepec, with the support of the PRD, the indigenous habitants of *Rancho Nuevo de Democracia* and Mixtecapa localities in the Mountain region formed their own de facto municipalities with their traditional leaders (Flores Félix and Canabál Cristiani 2000: 257).

The Zapatista movement provided an additional push to the indigenous mobilization in Guerrero. In early 1994, with the impetus that the Zapatista Army of National Liberation (*Ejército Zapatista de Liberación Nacional* – EZLN) rebellion added to the indigenous movement in the region, peasant organizations in Guerrero expanded their demands for territorial self-determination, autonomy and direct participation. In 1995, the Popular Revolutionary Army (*Ejército Popular Revolucionario* – EPR) was formed to defend the rights of the indigenous peoples in Guerrero. The EPR demanded that the *caciquismo* in Guerrero should end and that the sovereignty and rights of indigenous communities should be guaranteed by the state institutions.[39]

When the state government chose to repress these mobilizations with brutal force, indigenous peasants chose to play a proactive role instead of going underground. The state government replaced the principal military commands in Guerrero with the generals who had been involved in the Dirty War of the 1970s. Once again the army became the only visible face of the state of Guerrero for the indigenous people.[40] However, this time round, indigenous movement leaders did not choose to launch a guerrilla movement. In response to increasing violence and corruption, in October 1995 indigenous groups formed the Community Police in 52 communities in the Mountain region to ensure the safety of the people. Coffee and corn producers' organizations joined the effort, along with the CG500ARI. The local communities created their own police, exercising their right to self-governance, as recognized by the *International Labor Organization* (ILO) in Convention 169. Under constant social pressure, the governor Rubén Figueroa Alcocer resigned in March 1996, and Angel Aguirre Rivero (1996–99) substituted him as interim governor of Guerrero.[41]

---

39   *Novedades Acapulco*, 'Que termine el cacicazgo o habrá un asalto final, advierte el EPR', 26 November 1998.

40   On 28 June 1995, the Massacre of Aguas Blancas took place in Costa Grande. According to the National Commission on Human Rights (*Comisión Nacional de los Derechos Humanos* – CNDH) report, while a group of farmers associated with the *Farmers Organization of the Southern Sierra (Organización de Campesinos en Sierra Sureño OCSS)* were traveling to Atoyac for a demonstration, they were attacked at the check point by police, and 17 farmers died and 21 were seriously injured. As a result of the investigation, some 20 state government officials were found responsible for the massacre and guilty of obscuring evidence in the investigation. The responsible officials included Guerrero's Secretary of State, and State Attorney General. For the annual report of the commission, see Comisión Nacional de Derechos Humanos, Informe Anual 1995. [Online]. Available at: www.cndh.org.mx.

41   Despite this change in the governors' office, the repression on peasants has continued during the Aguirre Rivero government. See Schatz (2011: 213–214).

In the midst of this turmoil, the PRD functioned as a channel for the dissident groups to influence local politics. In 1997 and 1998, various militant groups entered the PRD. The Party organized marches for peace, justice and better public services for the marginalized municipalities.[42] In a December 1997 demonstration organized by the PRD, several demonstrators took over the municipality of Atoyac for a short period and declared that if the mayors and the governor did not respond to their demand for transparency and justice, they would take over other municipalities. The state government negotiated with the demonstrators and agreed to launch an investigation into their allegations.[43] In 1999, the CG500ARI and the PRD leader Félix Salgado declared an alliance in order to promote the direct representation of the indigenous groups in Guerrero (Díaz de Jesús 2000: 173).

Tourism Industrialists Encroaching on the PRD

In the 1990s, tourism industrialists repeatedly raised concerns that so long as social unrest and political instability continued, the tourism sector could not flourish in Guerrero. The tourism sector of Acapulco chose to organize politically to break apart the PRI network, because they considered that the security problems were closely related to the PRI dominance in the region. As the interviews with various agents indicate, the tourism sector bourgeoisie had supported the PRI until a viable alternative emerged. When the PRD started receiving increasing support from dominated masses in the rural areas, the tourism industrialists began to organize within the PRD.[44]

Yet the capital groups refrained from linking with the PRD through their representative associations, arguably to prevent possible resistance from the social base of the party. Instead, they established a civil society association in 1992, the Civic Front of Acapulco (*Frente Cívico de Acapulco*). Its founder was Zeferino Torreblanca Galindo, who had worked in the rank-and-file of the CONCANACO and COPARMEX of Guerrero. The Civil Front of Acapulco built a network of sympathizers with the PRD in Acapulco that worked parallel to and complementary with the PRD organization (Fernández 2004).

Since the mid 1990s, tourism industrialists have become important agents within the PRD. The Civic Front of Acapulco allied with the indigenous organizations to determine the strategies and candidates of the Party in the local elections. In the 1993 elections, while Félix Salgado, the leader of the PRD in Guerrero, nominated as the candidate for governor supported by the radical left parties and indigenous organizations, the founder of the Civil Front, Torreblanca Galindo

---

42   *Novedades Acapulco*, 'Otra marcha en la capital: indígenas piden servicios público', 12 November 1997.

43   *Novedades Acapulco*, 'Encierren Perredistas al Alcalde de Atoyac', 20 November 1997; 'Amenazan Perredistas con tomar el palacio municipal de Chilapa', 8 December 1997; 'Protesta contra el alcalde de Tlalchapa', 9 December 1997.

44   Interview with Gusman Visairo.

ran for the mayor of Acapulco on the PRD ticket. The Civic Front supported the candidacy of Salgado for governor's office and in turn, the militant bases of the PRD supported Torreblanca Galindo.[45] Although both candidates were defeated by the PRI, Torreblanca Galindo secured a seat in the Chamber of Deputies of Mexico via proportional representation in 1994. In this period, he was distinguished for his participation in the issues related to commerce and tourism as well as efforts against corruption and irregularities in the state government and the municipality of Acapulco.[46]

The beginning of the 2000s witnessed an important transformation in the local political regime of Guerrero. As a result of the alliance between the peasants and tourism sector bourgeoisie, Zeferino Torreblanca Galindo assumed the presidency of the municipality of Acapulco on the PRD ticket in 1999.[47] Through the PRD, the indigenous movement representatives and the tourism industrialists became involved in determining the development priorities of Guerrero. On the other hand, the local *cacique* families controlling the agro-industry sector of the local economy tried to regain their political and economic power.

The state development plan of René Juárez Cisneros government (1999–2005) was shaped in a major battle among key local agents and their representative organizations. As in Chihuahua, the state development programs stressed the importance of business initiatives in development. The stated goals of the state development program of 1999–2005 were 'to strengthen the competitiveness and sustainability of tourism services in order to create jobs, attract foreign exchange, and promote regional development'(Juárez Cisneros 2001: 17). For these purposes, private and the public sectors started to work together to define the development programs.

However, unlike in Chihuahua, local capital groups' active involvement in local politics did not quieten the dominated classes, particularly indigenous peasants. The disparity between increasing demands for participation and the lack of participatory channels carried the risk of leading to local anarchy. Faced with strong demands for participation and mobilization coming from the indigenous communities, in February 2000, the government enacted an Internal Regulation of the Citizen Council for the Public Works Vigilance and the Acquisitions of the State of Guerrero (*Reglamento Interior del Consejo Ciudadano de Vigilancia de la Obra Pública y las Adquisiciones del Estado de Guerrero*). According to this regulation, the State and Municipality Councils of Citizen Participation and Consultation included various groups in the local decision-making processes. The Citizen Councils were first established in Chilpancingo and Acapulco and later installed in all seven regions of the state.

---

45   Interview with César Aguirre.

46   See the story of his political career at the official website of the government of the State of Guerrero. [Online]. Available at: www.guerrero.gob.mx/?P=titulardetalle&key=20 [Accessed: 22 January 2007].

47   The PRD has won the municipal elections in Acapulco since then.

Furthermore, indigenous communities gained other participation channels. The government created the Secretary of Indigenous Matters as an organ charged with acting to defend and preserve the rights and culture of the indigenous communities as well as promoting integral development in rural areas (Carreño Rangel 2001: 119). The indigenous communities were included in the development programs through the Community Development Committees (Juárez Cisneros 2001: 17). Furthermore, the State Council of Indigenous Communities was formed in order to build a bridge between the indigenous communities and the state of Guerrero (Carreño Rangel 2001: 119). Due to vibrant local organizations and local identities, by 2003, some 28,000 Community Development Committees were formed in Guerrero (Juárez Cisneros 2003: 29). The Council of Indigenous Communities included 82 producer organizations, 122 social agencies and 25 other organizations that had the common objective of improving the living conditions of indigenous communities.[48]

In 2005, the PRD won the governorship putting an end to PRI rule. Zeferino Torreblanca became the first non-PRI governor of Guerrero. The interviews with key agents within the PRD reveal that although the indigenous peasants' organizations were not content with the political agenda of the PRD candidate, they supported him since his governorship would give them a channel to influence the decisions through the internal mechanisms of the PRD.[49] 'After all, the PRD was not the PAN and business people would not dominate the indigenous communities in the party organization.'[50] The PRD received strong support in the 2002 local state legislative and mayoral elections. The ability of the PRD to overcome potentially fatal internal disputes regarding the governor's candidacy brought the party an electoral victory in the 2005 gubernatorial elections.

The main motivation of the Torreblanca government was to improve procedures in order to revise the image of Guerrero in the eyes of the foreign investors. The government aimed 'to introduce a new approach to addressing political, social and economic issues in Guerrero'. In this 'new approach', Torreblanca placed significant emphasis on the efficiency of decision-making procedures (Torreblanca 2006a). For that purpose, he emphasized that Guerrero needed a 'different political class' that is 'not only concerned with the elections but concerned with delivering the best service possible' (Torreblanca 2006b: 2). In 2006, the institutional structure of the COPLADEG was reorganized to bring about 'efficient outcomes'. In this process, professional members and business associations came to be the major

---

48   Some of the organizations in the State Indigenous Council are the Regional Council of the Mountain (*Consejo Regional de la Montaña*), the Organization ZANSEKAN TINEMI, the CG500ARI, the Light Organization of the Mountain (*la Organización Luz de la Montaña*), the Union of Ejidos and Communities of the Costa Chica (*la Unión de Ejidos y Comunidades de la Costa Chica*), and the Regional Council of the Nahuas Peoples of the Alto Bases, among others.

49   Interview with César Aguirre.

50   Ibid.

participants of the COPLADEG meetings. The organizations that would represent the peasants and indigenous communities were handpicked in order to reduce the number of organizations and create more 'efficient deliberation'.[51]

The agenda of the PRD governor has caused serious discontent among the indigenous peasant base of the PRD. Empowered indigenous communities continue to contest the local capital groups within the PRD structure. In November 2006, 140 representatives of 34 indigenous, peasant, environmentalist and human rights organizations gathered in Chilpancingo in a statewide forum called 'Towards a Democratic and Transparent Guerrero' and raised their demands for more democratic participation and transparency.

Nevertheless, peasants' discontent within the PRD did not lead to a favorable outcome for the 2011 elections. The PRD was able to keep the governors' office in the elections. Yet, the newly elected governor of PRD, Angel Aguirre Rivero, is familiar with governor's office of Guerrero; he served as the interim governor between 1996 and 1999, then on the PRI ticket. The problem was not the past political party affiliation of Aguirre Rivero. But his interim government had notoriously exerted political pressure on the dissident peasants while giving tourism industrialists an upper hand in local politics.

The Aguirre Rivero government (2011–2017) has started with grave human rights violations and criminalization of social protest. On 12 December 2011, when the students of the Rural Teacher Training School (*Normales*) at Ayotzinapa, Guerrero blocked the Cuernavaca–Acapulco superhighway demanding job guarantee for the graduates of these schools and more funds to improve their infrastructural conditions and education quality, the governor ordered the Director of the State Police to clean up the highway.[52] Upon this order, the local police opened fire on the students which killed two protesters and wounded four. 24 students were beaten and arrested.[53] The CNDH report documents the rights violations and claims that this incident reveals the intentions of criminalization of social protest in the State of Guerrero (CNDH 2012).

The Aguirre Rivero government pledged 'to reestablish Acapulco to its former prominence'. Since he assumed the office in April 2011, Aguirre Rivero has been endeavoring to attract capital to 'change the face of Acapulco'. In line with this purpose, the Consulting Board for the Restoration of Traditional Acapulco was established in February 2012. The Board, composing of the representatives of the government of Guerrero, municipality of Acapulco, as well as the representatives of civil society, is chaired by Carlos Slim to whom Governor Aguirre thanked for 'his efforts in support of Guerrero's social programs for the neediest'.[54] The

---

51   Interview with Quevedo Mena.

52   *El Sur*, 'El Gobierno me pidió limpiar y la carretera está limpia'. 13 December 2011.

53   *La Jornada*, 'Guerrero: Matan a 2 alumnos normalistás en acción represiva', 13 December 2011.

54   Carlos Slim is a Mexican businessman who is ranked by *Forbes* as the richest person in the world since 2010. see also http://www.carlosslim.com/preg_resp_vueltamexico_

concern about the conditions of the neediest seems to contradict with human rights violations and criminalization of social protest.

Party Politics

It must be noted that, unlike in Tabasco and Chihuahua, increasing involvement of bourgeoisie of the sunrise sector, tourism has also enabled local dominated classes in the touristic regions to participate in local development. The tourism industrialists allied with the strong indigenous movement so they could stop the local conflicts, which threatened the tourism industry. The development projects had to preserve the environment, to help develop the potentials of the indigenous communities and to provide an enabling environment for the promotion of local entrepreneurship. Such development policies called for greater involvement by the local authorities. The tourism sector bourgeoisie were historically distinct from the traditional PRI networks, and their party preference shifted towards the PRD which had already been receiving support from the dominated classes. Tourism industrialists and other local capital groups intervened in local politics by supporting the PRD against the PRI.

The tourism bourgeoisie's involvement in local politics loosened the grip of traditional PRI networks which further unleashed the power of the indigenous groups. Tourism industrialists pushed local governments towards adopting policies and regulations which would allow the tourism sector to operate effectively. For this purpose, they called for a publicly accountable, bottom up, deliberative system to replace the patronage, clientelism and corruption that had systematically curbed the development potentials of the region compared to other states of the country.[55] As an indigenous movement leader from Guerrero said, 'the methods and mechanisms that existed until now has blocked us. They did not let us have our direct representatives. Since the local elections have become important, we started to have more indigenous people reaching the political power' (Díaz de Jesús 2000: 174). The PRD supported the formation of indigenous peasants' organizations through which marginalized

---

telmex_ing.html [Accessed: 4 June 2012].

55   To strengthen the bureaucratic administration of the state of Guerrero, Governor Ruíz Massieu (1987–93) brought a group of technocrats from Mexico City who had received their education in North American universities. His technocrats attempted to construct the institutional structure of the local state by providing clear task definitions for each department and committees of the state. The government enacted 'a law that establishes the bases of the Support for the Community Participation' on 13 May 1987 (Julián Bernal 2001: 61). In March 1991, the Planning Law was amended with detailed explanations of responsibilities and functions of the COPLADEG. The structure of the democratic planning was clarified with a detailed organizational structure which was also sent to the municipality governments.

groups and communities could be incorporated into the development programs. In brief, the PRD provided indigenous peasants with a way to reach to political power.

There is a serious challenge to the social empowerment of the local indigenous groups through the PRD. The contestation about local development is not solely between the PRI and PRD. Similar to party politics, politics within parties is not immune to struggle of antagonistic interests. The support of the tourism industrialists for the PRD was conditional on the candidates. They claimed that their main concern was not the party ideology itself but the political and economic agenda of the candidates.[56] In the interviews, several local agents mentioned that Zeferino Torreblanca is closer to the PAN than PRD in terms of his ideological inclinations. Nevertheless, since the PAN does not have a base of support in Guerrero, the tourism industrialists support the PRD rather than the PAN, since the former has more potential to challenge the PRI. Therefore, the decentralization process in Guerrero revealed the tendency of the process to bring about a *stickiness of the party preference* in local politics. Local capital groups may bypass internal party structure to press their interests within the PRD. Indeed, in 2011 local elections, the PAN candidate for governor dropped his bid endorsing the winning PRD candidate Aguirre Rivero. The involvement of tourism industrialists in politics and their strategic alliance with indigenous peasants may eventually marginalize the participation of the dominated classes as in Tabasco and Chihuahua. Tourism industrialists may take over the PRD and pit it against the PRI, which would lead to a similar situation the one in Chihuahua.

However, strong local communities and organizations in Guerrero can still counteract to the tendency to create of public–private partnerships and entrepreneurial local development seen in Chihuahua. The indigenous organizations, local leftist parties and the PRD itself have constructed the spaces for class struggle.

Conclusion

The path of local development in Guerrero is shaped by the alliances and conflicts between tourism sector bourgeoisie and indigenous' peasants within the PRD structure as opposed to the traditional PRI elite. Although Guerrero occupied an important place in the history of Mexican politics due to the local indigenous peasants' mobilization, it is one of the states where the local political regime has controlled by the PRI until the late 1980s. The indigenous peasants' movements and various local agents such as teachers and students in Guerrero have historically been very strong and well-organized. Nevertheless, before the introduction of decentralization policies, their potential had been restrained by repressive state and agro-industry bourgeoisie. The first effect of decentralization policies was to weaken the economic power of the agro-industry bourgeoisie and their extra-economic domination strategies. In the late 1980s, as the pressure on the power

---

56   Interview with Gusman Visairo.

of the dominated classes was partially lifted, these local organizations gained strength and gathered under the umbrella of the PRD.

This chapter aimed at revealing another aspect that was at work in shaping the pattern of decentralization in Guerrero: the involvement of local and foreign tourism sector bourgeoisie in local politics and their strategic alliance with peasants under the PRD. Decentralization in Guerrero also meant the decentralization of The SECTUR which increased the strategic importance of the local development programs for the tourism sector. Yet the tourism industrialists were not influential within the local chapter of the PRI. In other words, they lacked channels to intervene in local politics. When the PRD started to become a viable alternative to the PRI, the tourism sector bourgeoisie and their representative associations gave their support to it in order to challenge PRI rule. Their support for the PRD enabled the party to topple the PRI at the state government level. Nevertheless, it should be underlined that the agro-industry bourgeoisie and the PRI elite have not lost their power completely in various municipalities that are distant to the touristic enclaves. As the indigenous peasant communities and local and foreign tourism bourgeoisie have gained increasing access to local policy making and have exercised their capacity by making collective interventions in politics, decentralization has evolved towards a contested local development.

The degree of pluralism in Guerrero has become remarkable. The process of decentralization has unleashed the capacities of already existing yet locally marginalized agents such as tourism bourgeoisie and indigenous peasants. These policies brought about a contest between these newly unleashed social forces and previous networks and then a struggle among the former contesting to determine the development priorities of the region according to their inherently antagonistic interests.

The increased pluralism in local politics has not automatically lead to an increase in the efficiency of the policy outcomes. The major problems of local politics are unsolved. The state's reputation for corruption, political violence and drug trafficking seems to be still strong. The increase in financial resources available for the state government has not translated into a significant increase in the level of social development of the municipalities.

The conclusion we can derive from the case of Guerrero is that in the process of decentralization, strong local authoritarianism can slowly be challenged by the inclusion of previously excluded social forces. The determining conditions that brought about this pattern are the rich repertoire of local resistance, an absence of hegemonic bourgeois faction that could take over the development programs, a lack of organizational capacity in the state institutions orchestrating development and a strategic alliance between local capital groups and dominated classes. Under these conditions, dominated classes can exercise their capacity for proactive action by making effective individual and collective interventions. We should note that decentralization is an unfinished evolutionary development. The local development model in Guerrero should be seen as a transitional form in the evolution of an open-ended system. The strategic alliances of tourism industrialists with indigenous peasants may bring about struggles that could continuously transform local power relations, which would have strong implications for the national and global political economy. Thus, contested development in the process of decentralization may evolve towards an alternative form of development that is socially empowering and transformative of the broader institutional structure of the state.

Chapter 7
Conclusion

The central concerns of this book have been twofold: to examine the relationship between evolving international economic system and decentralization processes for understanding policy change towards decentralization, and to explain the impact of decentralization policies on local, national and global political economic relations and on social regulation. The main finding regarding the first concern is that neoliberal transition carries a strong tendency towards decentralization policies. These policies appeared to be viable policy options for policy-makers to perpetuate their political power while rearranging both state intervention into the market economy and interest representation in response to the crisis of the late 1970s. Regarding the second concern, this book makes the case that the outcome of decentralization policies was to draw the local level directly into global capitalism, mediated by the local state. These policies redefined the role of the local state in relation to development which became dependent on the economic competitiveness of the region. Decentralization diffused the 'politics of global competitiveness' into localities by forcing local agents to abide by the rules of neoliberal competition to bring about local development. Attracting capital investment became the main motivation behind the actions of local agents. These constraints prevented localities from pursuing policies that were not in accordance with market relations. This process led to different local development patterns which varied according to the nature of the local economy and the social composition of the locality. The way each local economy is integrated into the world market, the strategies and alliances of agents in this integration process became determining factors of the outcome.

This book has aimed to go beyond most recent works on decentralization. Previous analyses converge on the idea that decentralization is a political process that leads to democratization at the local level either directly or through strong state institutions. These analyses have predominantly focused on how politicians and institutions shape the outcomes of decentralization. Therefore, such studies do not provide a satisfactory framework for addressing the questions of why decentralization policies were implemented in various countries parallel to the transition to neoliberalism and how local class relations have evolved and what kind of local development patterns have come about in the process of decentralization. This book has attempted to contribute to the literature by filling this gap providing conceptual and analytic tools derived from of the case studies illustrated.

This book has employed a realist political economy approach that is suggested as an alternative to the liberal-individualist and statist approaches to decentralization. The relational ontology of social reality in realist methodology strengthened the explanatory leverage of the analyses on the observed differences and similarities of the patterns of local development in three states of Mexico. This comparative analysis has aimed to reveal both universalizing and *sui generis* characteristics of the cases. These observed characteristics are explained by underlying universalizing mechanisms – that is the integration of the local economy into the world economy – and forces – that is class strategies and alliances shaped by the expectations of the agents from this integration process. These mechanisms and forces carry potentials that constrained but did not determine a particular outcome in local regimes. In fact as it has been shown in the case study chapters, decentralization policies led to various local development patterns with contrasting consequences for dominant and dominated social classes. The evidence analyzed in this book shows that the way in which the local economy is integrated into the world economy affects the character of local democracy and potential for democratization.

In this chapter, broader implications of these patterns for understanding integration of the developing countries into the world market will be explored. To do this aim, a cross-case perspective, highlighting the key factors that account for the contrasting effects of decentralization and underscoring a certain underlying uniformity across different cases will be laid out. The remainder of this chapter is organized as follows. In the first section draws attention both to the convergences and divergences across cases by focusing on changing modes of interest representation and state intervention. The second section revisits the distinct patterns of local development. The third section briefly discusses further research questions that are brought to the fore by the findings and analyses of this book.

Changing Forms of State Intervention and Interest Representation

This book underlines that the world economy is a totality of local economies. 'Global' agents of the world economy reside and produce in localities. With decentralization policies global dynamics are increasingly driven by forces within, and relations among, local economies. The case study chapters have examined the ways 'politics of global competitiveness' manifest themselves in specific local forms. This reveals that national and global politics do not float above local politics but are continuously shaped and reshaped within local politics. The changes at the local level are part and parcel of the transformations in national and global level politics.

Different local development patterns shaped in the decentralization process help us to define the dynamics of the neoliberal era. In the case of Chihuahua, the cross-border cooperation among non-governmental organization as well as between municipalities in shaping local development programs recalls the arguments regarding blurring national borders and 'hollowing out' of nation states in the era of neoliberal globalization. Cross-border collaboration among regional, urban or local spaces shows the 'post-national' character of economic and social policy-making. As the interface of the public and private sector has been restructured, the significance of 'non-state mechanisms in compensating for market failures' increased (Jessop 2002: 254). Yet paradoxically, controlling these cross-border collaboration and non-state mechanisms can lead to enhanced role for nation states. As, the case of Tabasco shows, local governments have become important agents in designing the local development plans to aid the local bourgeoisie and maintain the cohesion of the social system. The boundaries of the state have not simply been rolled back. Instead, the regulation mechanisms of the state have been redefined in different scales. The central state becomes the primus inter pares in the intergovernmental relations (ibid. 253). Finally, the experience of Guerrero suggests that decentralization brings its own contradictions mediated in and through various forms of political organization and mobilization. While the contested local development pattern in Guerrero carries the risk of obscuring class relations, it could also cause a significant transformation in the local regime as the indigenous peasant movement acquires the potential to link its struggle with global anti-capitalist movements. Therefore, in the course of neoliberalization by decentralization, a diverse array of localized struggles in different contexts could be embraced and connected in a bigger concern that would uncover the class content of these struggles. Therefore, significant policy change can also come about through the action of local governments responding to the pressures of the local dominated classes.

Boosting competitiveness through decentralization is mediated by the local states in differing forms. With the inclusion of local, regional and global agents in decision-making at the local level, states have rescaled themselves, changing forms of intervention strategies. It should be noted that state intervention does not mean translations of the economic interests of dominant classes into political processes. There is always contention and conflict between opposing forces, and negotiation and compromise, in ways which are specific to the history of particular regions. Local state interventions aim at boosting legitimacy and obscuring the class role of the state as well as facilitating capital accumulation.

Decentralization policies were considered a way to release the pressure of local demands. Faced with the demands for better housing, health and education, expenditures of local authorities would be expanded. However, as the Decentralization and Subnational Thematic Group of World Bank (Rodden, Eskeland and Litvack 2003) suggests, local authorities are also expected to maintain a 'fiscal discipline' and 'hard budget constraints' through increasing reliable and effective 'revenue raising capacity'. To accomplish this aim, local governments started to build up their own development strategies with the inclusion of local, regional and national agents. Advisory committees, including business, labor and peasant organizations, other civil society associations, and local policy-makers along with academic members, were established to work with local offices of national governments in devising and implementing local development programs (cf. Keating 1997: 22).

'Social reproduction' policies of states have been transferred to subnational level state authorities. Poverty reduction programs are becoming increasingly important to the World Bank's policy dialogue and lending operations in its client countries. The stated objectives of 'these programs are to overcome economic and social disparities across regions, and among urban and rural areas'. Nevertheless, as this book underlines, decentralization policies created inequalities across regions and within localities. Furthermore, the cases of Chihuahua and Guerrero also revealed that in strategic regions, social policies can play a significant role in improving the image of the locality. This book aims to raise the possibility that the allocation of the poverty reduction programs would also be directed by the dictates of neoliberal competition.

This book reveals that the articulation of the local with the world economy for dynamic competitive advantages reflects a subtle but profound change in the orientation of the state policies towards creating local differences to capture flows and embed mobile capital. The case studies show that the emphasis on promoting a locality in order to attract private investment is likely to increase territorial inequalities. In all three cases examined here, decentralized development programs concerned particularly the municipalities that carry potential to boost the competitiveness of the locality which would have direct impact on the equality of service quality and development level within the state. This local discretion over development programs helped areas with dynamic markets to increase their competitiveness. In Chihuahua, the local development programs favored the *maquiladora* areas in Ciudad Juárez and Chihuahua City; in Tabasco the local development programs favored the oil-producing municipalities; and in Guerrero the touristy municipalities, principally Acapulco and Textla, were the main recipients of the development programs.

As the local economy turned into the main focus of development, localities have become the base from which agents can exercise their capacity by making effective individual and collective interventions within and beyond that base (Cooke 1989: 12). Thus, with decentralization, it would not be surprising to observe changes in the balance of social forces in local politics that would affect the forms of interest representation.

Case studies examined in this book reveal the significance of alliance networks of dominated as well as bourgeois classes along the local-global axis. Decentralization policies could favor market-oriented agents that had had limited power in local politics before these policies were put into effect. On the other hand, previously marginalized dominated classes who are able to connect their local struggles to bigger concerns of new global social movements such as human rights, anti-militarism and environmentalism could retain the capacity to transform their narrow interest to collective will formation so as to pave the ground for the formation of a counter-hegemonic strategy of development in local politics.

In addition to local and regional agents, decentralization policies opened space for various 'global' agents in local politics. The local development committees started to include significant 'global' agents. These agents could have a democratizing as well as an anti-democratizing impact on local politics. While involvement of the globally organized environmental and human rights organizations can strengthen dominated classes by linking their struggle to global issues, multinational corporates' involvement in local politics can have the effect of tilting the balance of local struggle towards local bourgeoisie.

The cases provide different examples of market-oriented agents being favored in local politics. In the case of Chihuahua, foreign capital groups got involved in local politics. Big corporations investing in the *maquiladora* industry and multinational marketing companies have been the market oriented agents that were helped in local politics. The case of Tabasco shows that international oil companies have gained a privileged position in the decision-making processes of the oil producing local economy. In Tabasco, foreign oil corporations play an indirect role in determining the local development of an oil-dependent economy. These global agents did not have a direct presence in local politics as in Chihuahua. Nevertheless, they affected local policy-making through constraining the strategic selectivity of the local state. In Guerrero, international tourism bourgeoisie came to be the agents that decentralization policies helped. Hotel chains such as Holiday Inn, Hilton International, Inter-Continental, Hyatt International and Marriott created strong local allies with management contracts, leasing, franchise and technical service agreements. These alliances of market-oriented agents along the local-global axis shaped the policy shifts in local policies.

The local-global alliance networks of previously marginalized dominated classes have become significant in democratizing local politics in differing ways. Each pattern of local development carries a different potential for democratization. Chihuahua presents the least favorable case in terms of its democratization potential. Since the decentralization process has been dominated by local and foreign capital groups seeking to reinforce entrepreneurial local development, democratization was confined within the sphere of electoral politics. On the other hand, human rights organizations in Guerrero and environmentalist organizations in Tabasco strengthened the local struggle of the dominated classes. The international human right organizations and the environmentalist groups strengthened local struggles by connecting them to bigger global concerns of human rights, anti-militarism and environmental degradation.

Previous research maintains that the strength of the corporatist relations shows variations across different regions of Mexico. Cornelius (1999: 4), for example, suggests that the Mexican state displays a 'Swiss-cheese' type of local control, 'effective in some regions but ineffective in others'. It is generally acknowledged that despite the regional variations, the overall impact of the decentralization policies has been to weaken previous corporatist relations in Mexico. The findings of this book show that neoliberalization by decentralization has a varying impact on the corporatist control mechanisms of the PRI elites and *cacique* families depending on the nature of the local economy. It is true that decentralization of the development programs gave more power to local organizations which could weaken the centralist corporatist networks based on top-down control. Nevertheless, bottom-up neocorporatism that connects localities around the premises of competitiveness could potentially emerge (Jessop 2003: 261).

Each case study chapter reveals important features of the transformation of the corporatist structure at the local level. The cases of Chihuahua and Guerrero show that top-down corporatist relations were weakened by a shift in the direction of the development programs. The local capital groups in Chihuahua and coalition of tourism industrialist and indigenous peasants in Guerrero pursued their own agendas challenging the previous control mechanisms. In interviews with various local actors in Guerrero and Chihuahua, it was mentioned that the local *caciques* have not lost control completely of their municipalities, yet their influence in shaping local level politics has been curtailed because of the general shift in the local development pattern.

Although corporatism had been relatively weaker in Chihuahua than many other states, particularly in Guerrero, the public investments in the agriculture and animal husbandry sectors were the means of keeping corporatist relations intact in the region. In the process of decentralization, local bourgeois classes saw the linkages between their own private economic interests and establishment of the public–private partnership that would shift the orientation of local development policies towards the border economy. This collective agreement extends beyond business associations and trade unions which curtailed the control mechanisms of the PRI even in non-*maquiladora* economy municipalities. A similar process has been experienced in Guerrero, as public investment has diverted from agriculture to integrate the sunrise sector of tourism. In Guerrero, the corporatist organizations had been the central control mechanisms of the PRI. When the decentralization policies increased the role of the local state in development, the tourism sector was accepted as the motor of development which led to a sharp decrease in public investment in the agricultural sector. Both in Chihuahua and Guerrero self-reflexive understanding of the local communities to collaborate to boost the competitiveness of their local economy required less direct state involvement. States resources and actions are used to back or support the decisions reached though corporatist negotiation (cf. ibid).

Tabasco differs from the other two cases in terms of the reorganization of corporatist relations at the local level. Corporatist relations have been stronger in Tabasco than most other states due to state ownership of oil resources. The decentralization policies transferred more authority to local policy makers to regulate the increased local income received from oil production. This financial autonomy turned out to be the trigger for local capital groups to organize around the local state which provided the local state with more power to re-regulate local development. In this process, corporatist control mechanisms have not weakened significantly. Furthermore, the tacit coalition, established between the oil industry and the big landed bourgeoisie in order to be able to pacify the peasants in the region, established new local control mechanisms.

The literature on decentralization stresses that local political organizations are an effective means of representing collective interest of the dominated classes (Chávez 2004, Fung and Wright 2003). The case studies show that political parties could play a central role in local politics and have profound effects on the way local decisions are made. They generate a very particular type of political dynamics at the local level according to the balance of social forces. The experiences of Guerrero and Tabasco confirm the emphasis in the literature in that the PRD has assumed the role of the vanguard of the masses. The PRD was able to gather the disintegrated local dissident groups and mobilize them around a common program.

However, studies of the relations between bourgeois classes and the political parties at the local level are rare. The case study chapters provide some insights about the changing relations between the political parties and local bourgeoisie. The case of Chihuahua shows that the local bourgeoisie could use opposition political parties as a vehicle to challenge the previously established coalitions and to destroy top-down corporatist relations in local politics. The case of Chihuahua also reveals that public–private partnerships retain a non-partisan character. The fact that tight networks of local capital groups with foreign bourgeoisie could facilitate the integration of the local economy into the world market, strengthen the structural affinity between the political interest of the policy makers and the economic interest of local bourgeoisie. In Chihuahua, when the PAN lost its base of public support and the PRI regained the governorship, the relationship between the local government and the capital groups has not changed essentially. The entrepreneurial character of the local development pattern remained intact. Similarly, the case of Guerrero reveals that local capital groups' encroachment in local politics is non-partisan. In Guerrero, as the PRD came to be a viable alternative to the PRI, local bourgeois classes supported the PRD to challenge the PRI elite. With the effect of these newcomers to the party, the policy agenda and political ideology of the local chapter of the PRD has significantly diverged from its national organization.

In the process of decentralization, the conventional view of party politics as essentially taking place at the national level, between national parties, over national issues, appears increasingly inadequate. Political parties serve to represent sets of politically defined social interests, but how can these national parties deal with often conflicting regional and local interests? The answer to this question lies in four trends launched by the decentralization process. First, as decentralization policies diffuse neoliberal competition rules to the local economy, the policy priorities of political parties at the local level have converged to a large extent. The main concern of local governments and policy makers has become to attract investment to their region for development. The transfer of economic development issues to local governments leads to the convergence in strategic selectivity between different local governments regardless of the party controlling them. Therefore, neoliberalization by decentralization limits the room for political maneuver of local policy makers by making local development dependent on competitiveness. Second, nationally organized parties have started to display substantial variations across different regions within a country which are weakening the internal consistency of party politics. Third, the decentralization process renders political parties central for local dominated classes for mobilization and involvement in local politics. Local and regional parties can gain control of local governments dispelling nationally organized political parties from local politics. Therefore, emergence of subnational political parties could pose challenges to existing party politics. Fourth, as decentralization puts an emphasis on local participation not necessarily through political parties, the latter are no longer the only political body that mobilizes social groups. Local social organizations can grow and replace the functions of the nationally organized political parties. These trends launched with decentralization appear to challenge the political party system.

Three Patterns of Local Development

The comparative analysis of the three Mexican states confirmed the value of the framework built in Chapters 1 and 2 by showing how the alternative theoretical approach helps explain why decentralization led to entrepreneurial, authoritarian state-led and contested local development in different states of Mexico. The emphasis on promoting a locality in order to attract private capital tends to facilitate the spread of market principles of the type associated with the neoliberalization. The lessons from the study of the three local development patterns offered intriguing insights about how boosting competitiveness through decentralization manifests itself in a wide range of outcomes.

In this section, three patterns of neoliberal local development that result from decentralization policies are identified and examined. In the first pattern, 'entrepreneurial local development', local capital groups take over the state institutions and marginalize other social classes from political decisions through a 'public–private partnership'. The second pattern of decentralization where local policy makers make the political decisions on behalf of dominant factions of bourgeoisie can be called 'authoritarian state-led local development'. The third pattern of decentralization policies, 'contested local development', carries the tendency to open up new spaces for transformative social struggle. This pattern indicates that decentralization policies can unleash social agents and new struggles at the local level and can lead to the transformation of the main elements of the local regime. The evidence from Mexico suggests that countries that implement decentralization policies might give rise to multiple local development pathways which in turn create distinct opportunities for the social classes in different localities.

Pattern 1: Entrepreneurial Local Development

The decentralization process has a tendency to evolve towards weakening of the local state structure and turn the local state into a network of local capital groups and their foreign allies. Decentralization in some regions can decrease the level of government initiatives and bring market-oriented groups closer to political decisions. The close alliances between globally mobile capital and local capitalists form the central dynamic that brings about the entrepreneurial local state. The networks which link factions of capital dependent on local markets with foreign mobile capital create new forms of integration of some localities into the world economy. Border zones have such a tendency to develop alliances between bourgeois classes on both sides of the border to increase the competitiveness of their zone.

This form of local politics is characterized by the concept of 'public–private partnership'. In this partnership, the local state is transformed into a 'strategic enabler' (Cochrane 1993). Local governments encourage private investment in infrastructure. Local policy makers become one of many agents, but not necessarily the most dominant. The 'private-public partnership' and other 'self organizing governance mechanisms' can emerge along with new development institutions as a way to meet local needs (Jessop 2002: 248). This restructuring process results in entrepreneurial local development pattern.

The entrepreneurial local development pattern does not suggest that the local states simply become instruments of capital. Instead, due to the increasing structural power of the local bourgeoisie, the political interests of local policy-makers and the economic interests of local capitalists converge. Eventually, stronger coordination among local firms and foreign capital replace local state institutions and marginalize interests of the dominated masses.

Pattern 2: Authoritarian State-Led Local Development[1]

Where foreign oligarchs[2] have a vested interest in the local economy and local bourgeoisie is entirely dependent on foreign capital, local state institutions remain well-developed and policy makers are able to retain control over local development. Under these conditions, decentralization tends to bring about *authoritarian state-led local development*.

Neoliberal decentralization policies do not necessarily lead to decrease in state regulations or to transfer of power to social agents. Although decentralization seems to make it harder to impose state authority, paradoxically, under certain circumstances, they can ascribe more powers to local policy makers to re-regulate the local development (Harvey 1985: 259).

Where foreign oligarchs have a vested interest in local economy and local capital groups are entirely dependent upon foreign capital, these conditions necessitate growing involvement on the part of the local state. When this class coalition necessitates growing involvement of the local governments, the local state institutions acquire the capacity to implement their agenda. Under these conditions, the task of creating a business-friendly local regime may require the local state to intervene actively to restructure the local economy which leads to authoritarian state-led local development. Therefore decentralization can bolster greater control of local states over every sphere of socioeconomic life combined

---

1 This pattern of local development draws from Poulantzas' elaborations on Authoritarian Statism. See Poulantzas (1978: 203–16).

2 I use the term oligarchy to describe the few and large multinational corporations which dominate a given sector.

with radical decline of the institutions of political democracy. In this pattern of development, the authoritarian local state becomes an agent if not an appendage of foreign interest serving to prevent a possible rise in class struggles.

The local state assumes an increased role in restructuring the industry in order to increase relative surplus-value, furthering capital accumulation. The local state acts as a stimulator of the local economy. It takes measures such as offering cheap credits for investment in the region, subsidies and tax-cuts for the local exporters to encourage businesses already in the region to stay and to attract new firms. With these measures the local state takes on a decisive weight in internationalization of the local bourgeoisie.

In most cases, neoliberal decentralization policies are not effective in providing local governments with sufficient resources of their own. In order to be capable of handling the local development programs, local policy makers would have to generate local income. However, if the local government has important revenues, that would increase the capacity of its institutions to craft the local development programs. This pattern of local development can be observed if the local economy is dependent on a sector which the state manages. Since the state commands vital resources and is strongly organized, the local capital groups tend to be junior partners of local development. The state-run energy sector in collaboration with foreign oligarchs is a classic example of this sort of activity.

Involvement of the state in local development may sharpen the intra- and inter-class contradictions. States' role in favor of foreign bourgeoisie may heighten the uneven development within the locality where foreign bourgeoisie is reproduced. Designation of particular regions as 'development areas' to the detriment of others may awaken popular movements and lead to politicization of dominated masses in the marginalized regions. Selective aids to individual businessman, policies to favor certain factions, may induce an intra-class conflict within the domestic bourgeoisie. Since the development programs are crafted by the state, unfavored groups confront the local state directly which could eventually result in sizeable representation crisis for different sections of the society.

Pattern 3: Contested Local Development

According to Fung and Wright (2003), decentralization policies may deepen the ways in which 'ordinary people' can effectively participate in and influence policies which directly affect their lives. These processes empower 'disadvantaged groups' and encourage more political participation because they rely upon the commitment and capacities of ordinary people to make sensible decisions through reasoned deliberation (ibid: 5).

This pattern is made possible by strong class struggle which pushes the bourgeois class to strategically ally with the dominated classes in local politics. Competition and a business-friendly environment also require cross-class cooperation of political, economic and social agents devoted to development in a specific location. The local bourgeoisie may cooperate with the other social classes to promote the region. This cooperation may include locally based, non-local bourgeois interests, trade unions, local and national politicians, as well as local peasants and indigenous movements. The liberal 'local community' notion stems from these alliances of various social classes, which seek to increase the competitiveness of the local economy. Dominant masses also gather round a 'common interest' and define their locality in terms of the politics of global competitiveness.

The agents that engage in local politics are not concerned solely with economic development. The strategic alliances among various social agents can function to improve the quality of labor and the environment in the region, which are important factors in businesses' decisions to invest. For some sectors, these two areas interact since the ability to attract the required types of highly skilled engineers and technologies depends in a good part on a locality's housing, schools and level of amenities (Teitz 1987: 13). In the tourism sector, for instance, traditional culture may similarly be a source of economic success, giving a region a specific niche in the international market. Moreover, middle-class tourists are interested in arms-length representation, aestheticized poverty and contrived authenticity that filter out the real world of human rights violations, violent inequalities, deeply rooted racism and intense class and political conflicts. (Robinson 2003: 203). 'Like other investors, they, [tourists], avoid regions that contain the poorest of the poor' (Harrison 1994: 239). In these cases, if development projects fail to reconcile the needs of the dominated classes, it may risk fragmenting cooperation and damaging the competitiveness of the region in terms of investments.

In the localities where dominated classes managed to gain a privileged position through struggle or historical accident, decentralization may open space for these social agents and struggles. Under these conditions, local dominated masses can exert pressure on the local state and use it to oppose the state from within; they can act in a collective organized way to represent their interests. Where workers and peasants are strong enough to become the prime movers in the local coalition, development policies would give more favor to the needs of these classes than simply capital attraction. Depending on the relative weight of these non-capitalist interests, the contested local development pattern may be realized as an unintended consequence of these strategic alliances.

Political organizations are one of the most effective means of representing the collective interests of non-capitalist interests. Decentralization reforms reinvigorated electoral politics and enabled the leftist parties to compete. Observing the opportunity for transformation, parties of the social democratic left have moved away from centralization to support decentralization and regionalism (Chávez 2004, Keating 2001). Since the early 1980s, local politics have become for the left a privileged space in which to experiment with social reforms and learn how to govern (Chávez 2004). The political parties that have closer connections with local grassroots movements have assumed the 'role of vanguard of the masses' (ibid).

Organized under regionally effective political parties, relatively poorer regions are enabled to use their political weight to compensate for their economic weaknesses. This tendency is dependent on the importance of regions to the national governing coalition, their marginality and their potential for disruption or separatism (Keating 1997: 19). Therefore, through decentralization policies, poor regions can gain investment, jobs and improved living standards. Furthermore, due to the strong effect of the peasants' movements allied with urban trade unions, 'alternatives to neoliberal capitalist democracy will likely emerge from the countryside' (Goldfrank 2004: 194). These rural-based movements can neutralize the power imbalances of capitalism (O'Malley 2001: 218).

Decentralization therefore is a process evolving through contradictions and struggles of opposites. The first two patterns of decentralization suggest that 'the spatial organization is not neutral with respect to different classes' (Harvey 2000: 36). The decentralization process can break up workers' nationally organized trade unions and peasants' groups by inducing mutual competition through numerous local struggles (ibid: 37). Decentralized development programs can thus lead to the marginalization of various social groups. In the absence of a significant challenge from the dominated classes, local and foreign bourgeoisie could capture a central role in crafting the local development programs and create socially disintegrated local politics. Yet, incorporation of local agents into decisions is a 'double-edged sword', albeit the one edge of this sword is still sharper. The closer the dominated classes come to inclusion within the state system, the better they could organize to counteract the structural constraints.

Suggestions for Future Research Agenda

This book began with the observation that decentralization policies have been implemented in various countries with important implications on development. It then showed how existing studies leave us without a framework for understanding both the policy change towards decentralization parallel to the transition to neoliberalism and the new local development patterns that emerge after decentralization. The rest of the analysis sought to fill this gap by developing an alternative theoretical approach to decentralization using the case of Mexico and a subnational comparison of three states of Mexico.

An important agenda for future research is the impact of decentralization policies on uneven development. The subnational comparison of local development in Mexico shows that fostering competition between localities is likely to exacerbate the uneven development between richer and poorer regions. Mexico started to have highly competitive economies in some regions while other regions were largely marginalized. With neoliberalization through decentralization, it is more probable to find a developed region, alongside an exploited undeveloped region within the same national borders. The integration of local economies into the world economy qualifies the division of labor among regions in the world economy bringing various patterns of local development of different regions within a single country.

Identifying three different local development patterns in one country provides a strong basis for expecting that different decentralization policies brought about a rich variety of local development patterns in other countries. Although these three patterns cannot exhaust the full range of local development patterns, they provide a wide range of possibilities to which decentralization tends to lead. An intriguing area for future research would be to conduct further case and comparative studies in order to test the general validity of the proposed relations in this book. Does decentralization in other countries result in local development patterns similar to those identified in this book? In cases of more 'extensive' decentralization policies, where local governments have greater independence from the center in terms of financial resources and development decisions, would decentralization bring different dynamics, and other patterns of local development than those examined and theorized in this book?

Appendix

Author's Interviews

Abardía Hernandez, Emiliano. Director of Programming, Municipality of Paraiso. Interview date: 4 March 2006. Paraiso, Tabasco.

Aguirre, Julio César. Former PRD City Council Member of the Municipality of Chilpancingo. Interview date: 22 June 2006. Chilpancingo, Guerrero.

Alarcon Pastor, Jaime. General Director of Sectoral and Institutional Operation of the COPLADEG. Interview date: 21 June 2006. Chilpancingo, Guerrero.

Álvarez Alejandro. Professor, Department of Economics, UNAM. Interview date: 18 January 2006. Mexico City.

Álvarez Monje, Fernando. President, Chihuahua Executive Committee of the PAN. Interview date: 17 February 2006. Chihuahua City.

Angel Maldivía de Dios, Miguel. PRI Deputy, State Congress of Tabasco, former president of Tabasco chapter of CANACINTRA. Interview date: 8 March 2006. Villahermosa, Tabasco.

Anonymous Interviewee. A leading tourism businessmen in Acapulco, Interview date: 15 June 2006. Acapulco, Guerrero.

Anonymous Interviewee. A member of the Oil Workers' Union. Interview date: 3 March 2006. Villahermosa, Tabasco.

Anonymous Interviewee. CEO of a company investing in the *maquiladora* sector in Chihuahua. 19 February 2006. Chihuahua City.

Anonymous Interviewee. Local businessman from Chihuahua. Interview date: 10 February 2006. Chihuahua City.

Arellano Barnola, Luis Arturo. Regular Trustee, Ciudad Juárez chapter of CANACO. Interview date: 22 February 2006. Ciudad Juárez.

Atilano, Letisia. Director, Regional Museum of Guerrero, former member of Subcommittee of Culture of the State of Tabasco (1986–92). Interview date: 23 June 2006. Chilpancingo, Guerrero.

Aziz Nassif, Alberto. Professor, Center for Research and Advanced Studies in Social Antropology (CIESAS). Interview date: 28 June 2005. Mexico City.

Balcázar Antonio, Elías. Professor, Juárez Autonomous University of Tabasco. Interview date: 11 March 2011. Villahermosa, Tabasco.

Cabrero Morín, Ricardo. Undersecretary of Revenues of the State of Guerrero. Interview date: 22 June 2006. Chilpancingo, Guerrero.

Cabrero, Enrique. Director, Center for Research and Teaching in Economics. Interview date: 16 June 2005. Mexico City.

Camacho Solis, Manuel. PRD Deputy, National Congress of Mexico, former Undersecretary of Regional Development (1984–88). Interview date: 18 July 2005. Mexico City.

Carbajal, Jesús León. Former Mayor, Municipality of Quecgultenango (1999–2002). Interview date: 21 June 2006. Chilpancingo, Guerrero.

Cázares Quintana, Roberto. President, El Barzon; PRD Deputy, State Congress of Chihuahua. Interview date: 21 February 2006. Chihuahua City.

Chablé, José. Advisor, the Coordinator of the COPLADE of Tabasco. Interview date: 2 March 2006. Villahermosa, Tabasco.

Comaduran Amaya, José Antonio. PRI Deputy, State Congress of Chihuahua. Interview date: 21 February 2006. Chihuahua City.

de la Madrid, Miguel. Former President of Mexico (1982–88). Interview date: 30 June 2005. Mexico City.

de la Rocha Montiel, Alejandro. General Director, Chihuahua chapter of COPARMEX. Interview date: 16 February 2006. Chihuahua City.

Donrentea Velez, Efrain. PRI City Council Member of the Municipality of Acapulco, president CNC of Acapulco (2004–2007). Interview date: 16 June 2006. Acapulco, Guerrero.

Fernández, Raúl. Chairperson, Advanced Political Studies Institute, University of Guerrero. Interview date: 12 June 2006. Acapulco, Guerrero.

Galicia, Ignacio. Former advisor, FDC of Chihuahua (1992–2001). Interview date: 16 February 2006. Chihuahua City.

Gallegas Garcia, Carlos. Deputy candidate from the PAN for State Senate from District No: 8. Interview date: 17 June 2006. Acapulco, Guerrero.

Garcia Maldonado, Miguel. Public Notary No 10, former General Secretary, Municipality of Acapulco (1977), former president, State Council of Elections (1996–99), former president, PROTUR. Interview date: 15 June 2006. Acapulco, Guerrero.

Godoy Zeferino, Ulises. Director of Planning and Programing. Interview date: 14 June 2006. Acapulco, Guerrero.

Gómez, Alma. Former PRD Deputy, State Congress of Chihuahua (1998–2001). Interview date: 16 February 2006. Chihuahua City.

Gómez, Gabino. Director, El Barzon. Interview date: 14 February 2006. Chihuahua City.

González Avelar, Miguel. Former leader of the Senate (1982–88), former Secretary of Education (1984–88). Interview dates: 30 June 2005; 8 July 2005. Mexico City.

González Ballina, Darvin. Former Mayor of Balancan, Tabasco (1986–87). Interview date: 8 July 2006. Mexico City.

González Compeán, Miguel. Chief of the Director for the Coordination of Regional Delegations, former Secretary of Treasury and Public Credit. Interview date: 24 June 2005. Mexico City.

González Pedrero, Enrique. Former Governor of Tabasco (1983–87). Interview date: 27 July 2005. Mexico City.

Granadas Pineda, Sergio. President of the Chihuahua Executive Committee of the the PRI. Interview date: 17 February 2006. Chihuahua City.

Gusman Visairo, Maria Antonieta. Council member of Civic Front. Interview date: 16 June 2006. Acapulco, Guerrero.

Hernandez Hernandez, Ulises. President, CCE of Tabasco. Interview date: 9 March 2006. Villahermosa, Tabasco.

Hernandez Ortega, Delfino. PRD City Council member of Municipality of Acapulco. Interview date: 15 June 2006. Acapulco, Guerrero.

Hernandez Salgado, Oscar. PRI City Council member of Municipality of Acapulco, former president of the Acapulco chapter of the PRI (2004–2006). Interview date: 15 June 2006. Acapulco, Guerrero.

Ignacio Marvan. Professor, Center for Research and Teaching in Economics, former Secretary of the Commission of Social Well-being, for the elaboration of the Government Plan (1988–94). Interview date: 4 July 2005. Mexico City.

Jacobo Zaidenweber. Former president, CONCAMIN (1983–88). Interview date: 13 August 2005. Mexico City.

Kalisch Valdez, Samuel G. Former president, Camara de Comercial, (1974), former president, CODECH (1992), former president FECHAC (1990–2002). Interview date: 11 February 2006. Chihuahua City.

Lara Armendrais, Luis. President, CODECH, Chairman of the Board and CEO, American Industries. Interview date: 21 February 2006. Chihuahua City.

Leyva Leyva, Marco Antonio. PRI Deputy, State Congress of Tabasco. Interview date: 2 March 2006. Villahermosa, Tabasco.

Llergo Latournerie, Mario. Sub-Coordinator, General Coordination of the COPLADET. Interview date: 3 March 2006. Villehermosa, Tabasco.

López Baez, Antonio. PAN Deputy, State Congress of Tabasco. Interview dates: 7 March 2006. 15 March 2011. Villahermosa, Tabasco.

López, José Antonio. Coordinator of Rural Development of Chihuahua. Interview date: 14 February 2006. Chihuahua City.

Madero Muñoz, Gustavo. PAN Deputy, National Congress of Mexico. Interview date: 13 February 2006. Chihuahua City.

Manzanedo Figueroa, Luis. Coordinator of Planning, Budget and System Control. Interview date: 14 June 2006. Acapulco, Guerrero.

Mazur Rivera, Miguel Salim. PRD Deputy, State Congress of Tabasco. 8 March 2006. Villahermosa, Tabasco.

Mendez Lopez, Lazaro. PRD Deputy, State Congress of Tabasco. Interview date: 7 March 2006. Villahermosa, Tabasco.

Merino, Maurico. The Coordinator of the COPLADET. Interview date: 14 June 2005. Mexico City.

Moguel Perez, Patricio. Mayor of Municipality of Balancan. Interview date: 10 March 2006. Villahermosa, Tabasco.

Murgia, Carlos. Former President, Ciudad Juárez chapter of the CANACINTRA (1994–96), president, DECJ. Interview date: 22 February 2006. Ciudad Juárez.

Muriguial, Daniel. Businessman. Interview date: 22 February 2006. Ciudad Juárez.

Narváez Cruz, Manuel. Director of Programming and Treasury of the Municipality of Jalapa. Interview date: 10 March 2006. Jalapa, Tabasco.

Núñez Baca, Beatriz del Carmen. Chief of Regional Links and Social Organization of Chihuahua. Interview date: 17 February 2006. Chihuahua City

Ojeda Rivera, Rosa Icela. Director, Advanced Political Studies Institute, University of Guerrero; advisor, State Commission of Human Rights; General Secretary, Communist Party of Mexico. Interview date: 13 June 2006. Acapulco, Guerrero.

Oka Urioste, Eki. Sub-Coordinator of Advisors, Municipality of Acapulco. Interview date: 15 June 2006. Acapulco, Guerrero.

Oliver Arellano, Enrique. Advisor to the Mayor of Balancan. Interview date: 11 March 2006. Balancan, Tabasco.

Ortega, Rojelio. Director, Advanced Political Studies Institute, University of Guerrero. Interview date: 13 June 2006. Acapulco, Guerrero.

Ortuño, Teresa. Former PAN Federal Deputy, National Congress of Mexico (1982–85; 1988–91). Interview date: 13 February 2006 Chihuahua City.

Osbaldo, Oscar. General Director, Ciudad Juárez chapter of CANACO. Interview date: 22 February 2006. Ciudad Juárez.

Pastor López, Luz Maria. PRD City Council member of the Municipality of Chilpancingo (2001–2003). Interview date: 23 June 2006. Chilpancingo, Guerrero.

Pedro Ignacio Quesada. Mayor, Municipality of Maguarichi. Interview date: 21 February 2006. Chihuahua City.

Perez Bocanegra, Hector. President, Association Animal Husbandry, Jalapa. Interview date: 10 March 2006. Jalapa, Tabasco.

Priego, Oscar. Director, Academic Division of Economics and Administrative Sciences. Interview dates: 28 February 2006. March, 30, 2011. Villahermosa, Tabasco.

Puga, Christina. Professor, Department of Economics, UNAM. Interview date: 28 June 2005. Mexico City.

Quevedo Mena, Luis Angel. Operative Coordinator of the COPLADEG. Interview date: 21 June 2006. Chilpancingo, Guerrero.

Quintana, Victor. President of PDF of Chihuahua. Interview date: 16 February 2006. Chihuahua City.

Ramos Vaca, Alonso. Former President, CODECH. Interview date: 18 February 2006. Chihuahua City.

Rascón, Marco. Former PRD Deputy, National Congress of Mexico, Mexico City. Interview date: 24 January 2006. Mexico City.

Reyes López, Carlos. Director, Plastics Industry of Chihuahua; former president, Chihuahua chapter of COPARMEX (2004–2005). Interview date: 16 February 2006. Chihuahua City.

Ríos Piter, Armando. The Secretary of Rural Development of the State of Guerrero. Interview date: 22 June 2006. Chilpancingo, Guerrero.

Riquelme, Carlos. President, Ciudad Juarez chapter of CODECH. Interview date: 22 February 2006. Ciudad Juárez.

Rodas Ornales, Rodolfo. Advisor to the Mayor of the Municipality of Chihuahua City. Interview date: 14 February 2006. Chihuahua City.

Rodríguez Zentalla, Ramón. General Coordinator, Secretary of Economic Development and Tourism. Interview date: 8 March 2006. Villahermosa, Tabasco.

Rojas, Carlos. Financial Coordinator for PAN's election office. Interview date: 4 September 2005. Mexico City.

Romero, Alejandro. Sub-Director of Planning, Municipality of Villahermosa. Interview date: 3 March 2007. Villahermosa, Tabasco.

Ruíz Mendez, Antonio. General Coordinator of the COPLADEG. Interview date: 21 June 2006. Chilpancingo, Guerrero.

Ruíz Valencia, Mario. PRD City Council member of the Municipality of Chilpancingo. Interview date: 23 June 2006. Chilpancingo, Guerrero.

Sanchez López, José Luis. PRD Deputy, State Congress of Tabasco. Interview date: 3 March 2006. Villahermosa, Tabasco.

Scherrer, Dora M. PAN Deputy, State Congress of Tabasco. Interview date: 2 March 2006. Villahermosa,Tabasco.

Serna Maganda, Frank. Chief of Budget Control Department of the State of Guerrero. Interview date: Interview date: 14 June 2006. Acapulco, Guerrero.

Sevilla Carillo, Jorge. Director General, Construction and Real Estate Sevilla Sociados S.A de C.V. Interview date: 4 March 2006. Paraiso, Tabasco.

Torpey Andrede, José. Former Mayor of Jalapa (1993–94). Interview date: 7 March 2006. Villahermosa, Tabasco.

Torres Armendariz, Clara. National Secretary of Political Promotion of Women, PAN. Interview date: 22 February 2006. Ciudad Juárez.

Trevizo Gutiérrez, Jesús. Advisor, State Executive Committee of PAN. Interview date: 13 February 2006. Chihuahua City.

Valdés Ugalde, Francisco. Professor, Institute for Social Research, UNAM, Mexico   City. Interview date: 20 June 2005. Mexico City.

Valenzuela, Luis Raúl. President, Municipal Committee of Chihuahua City of PAN. Interview date: 13 February 2006. Chihuahua City.

Valero, Ricardo. Former Undersecretary of Foreign Affairs (1983–88). Interview date: 12 July 2005. Mexico City.

Vidal Serrat. Coordinator of Advisors, UAG. Interview date: 16 June 2006. Acapulco, Guerrero.

Villalobos Madero, Guillermo. Former Director, Business Center of Chihuahua City (1979–95); former PAN Deputy, State Congress of Chihuahua (1995–98). Interview date: 14 February 2006. Chihuahua City.

Villanueva Manjarrez, Carlos. Director of Planning of the State of Chihuahua. Interview date: 24 February 2006. Chihuahua City.

Villegas Montes, Luis. Secretary of Electoral Action of the Chihuahua Executive Committee of the PAN. Interview date: 14 February 2006. Chihuahua City.

Bibliography

'Acapulco Document'. 1982. Adopted at the World Tourism Meeting, Acapulco, August 21–7.

Adib, M. et al. (eds). 2008. *Decentralization and Local Democracy in the World*. Barcelona: World Bank and United Cities and Local Governments.

Aguirre, Adrián. 2006. Fundación del Empresariado Chihuahuense: From Welfare to Well-being. *Alliance*, 11(1). [Online]. Available at: www.alliancemagazine. org/node/990 [Accessed: 11 November 2011].

Alanís Enciso, F.S. 1999. *El Primer Programa Bracero y el Gobierno de México, 1917–1918*. San Luis Potosí: Colegio de San Luis.

Alba Vega, C. and A. Aziz Nassif. 2000. Cultura Política: Una Mirada a los Empresarios, in *Desarrollo y Política en la Frontera Norte*, ed. C. Alba-Vega and A. Aziz-Nassif. Mexico City: Ciesas IRD-UACH.

Alfie, C.M. 1996. Desarrollo y Medio Ambiente: Ciudad Juárez-El Pase ¿Cooperación o Conflicto?, in *Desarrollo Fronterizo y Globalización*, ed. A. Mungaray and G. García de León. Mexico City: ANUIES.

Álvarez, A. 1987. *La Crisis Global del Capitalismo en México: 1968/1985*. Mexico City: Ediciones Era.

Andrade Diaz, M. 2005. Logros en el Desarrollo Armónico y Equilibrado, 4to. Informe de Gobierno. [Online]. Available at: http://saf.tabasco.gob. mx/saf per cent20pdfs/004rendicion_cuentas/ informes per cent20de per cent20gobierno/2005/2-Introduccion.pdf [Accessed: 11 November 2011].

Appendini, A.K. et al. 1972. Desarrollo Desigual in México. *Demografía y Economía* 6 (1): 1–39.

Arias Gómez, M.E. et al. 1987. *Tabasco: Una Historia Compartida*. Villahermosa: Gobierno del Estado de Tabasco.

Arias Rodríguez, J.M. and I. Gusmán Hugo. 2004. *Los Donativos y Donaciones de PEMEX en Tabasco*. Villahermosa: Asociación Ecológica Santo Tomás A.C.

Assad, M. 1996. *Breve Historia de Tabasco*. Mexico City: El Colegio de México.

Baerresen, V.D. 1971. *The Border Industrialization Program of Mexico*. Lexington, Massachusetts: Lexington Books, D.C. Health and Company.

Baeza Terrazas, José Reyes. 2005a. *Plan Estatal de Desarrollo 2004–2010*. Chihuahua: Gobierno del Estado de Chihuahua.

Baeza Terrazas, José Reyes. 2005b. *Tercer Informe Político*. Chihuahua: Gobierno del Estado de Chihuahua.

Balcázar Antonio, E. 2003. *Tabasco en Sepia: Economía y Sociedad (1880–1940)*. Villahermosa: UJA.

Bardhan, P. and D. Mookherjee (eds). 2006. *Decentralization and Local Governance in Developing Countries: A Comparative Perspective.* Boston: MIT Press.

Barkin, D. 1986. Mexico's Albatros: The U.S. Economy, in *Modern Mexico: State, Economy, and Social Conflict,* ed. N. Hamilton and T.F. Harding. Newbury Park, London, New Delhi: Sage.

Barry, N. 1988. *The Invisible Hand in Economics and Politics, Hobart Paper, No. 111.* London: The Institute of Economic Affairs.

Bartra, A. 1996. *Guerrero Bronco: Campesinos, Ciudadanos, y Guerrilleros en la Costa Grande.* Mexico City: Ediciones Era S.A. De C.V.

Bennett, D. and K. Sharpe. 1985. *Transnational Corporations versus the State: The Political Economy of the Mexican Auto Industry.* Princeton, NJ: Princeton University Press.

Bertran, U. and S. Portilla. 1986. El Proyecto de Descentralización del Gobierno Mexicano (1983–1984), in *Descentralización y Democratización en México,* ed. B. Torres. Mexico City: El Colegio de México.

Blacker Hanson, O. 2005. La Lucha Sigue! (The Struggle Continues!): Teacher Activism in Guerrero and the Continuum of Democratic Struggle in Mexico. Unpublished PhD thesis, University of Washington.

Blair, H. 2000. Participation and Accountability at the Periphery: Democratic and Local Governance in Six Countries. *World Development* 28(1): 21–39.

Boone, C. 2003. Decentralization as a Political Strategy in West Africa. *Comparative Political Studies* 36(4): 355–80.

Bosch, N. and J.M. Duran (eds). 2008. *Fiscal Federalism and Political Decentralization: Lessons from Spain, Germany and Canada.* Cheltenham, UK and Northhampton, MA: Edward Elgar.

Brenner, N. 2000. Building 'Euro-Regions': Locational Politics and the Political Geography of Neoliberalism in Post-Unification Germany. *European Urban and Regional Studies* 7(4): 319–45.

Brenner, N. 2004. *New State Spaces: Urban Governance and the Rescaling of Statehood.* Oxford: Oxford University Press.

Buchanan, J. 1991. *Constitutional Economics.* London: Blackwell.

Bulki, S., G. Perry and W. Dillenger. 1999. *Beyond the Center Decentralizing the State.* Washington, DC: World Bank.

Cabrero, E. 2000. Los Dilemmas de la Descentralización en México. *Revista O&S* 7(19): 123–141.

Calderón Mólgara, M.A. 1994. *Violencia Política y Elecciones Municipales.* Zamora. Michoacán: El Colegio de Michoacán.

Callaghy, M.T. 1989. Toward State Capability and Embedded Liberalism in the Third World: Lessons for Adjustment, in *Fragile Coalitions: The Politics of Economic Adjustment,* ed. J.M. Nelson et al. Washington, DC: Overseas Development Council.

Cammack, P. 2006. The Politics of Global Competitiveness. *Papers in the Politics of Global Competitiveness 1.* [Online] Available at: http://e-space.mmu.

ac.uk/e-space/bitstream/2173/6190/3/The%20Politics%20of%20Global%20
Competitiveness.pdf [Accessed: 11 November 2011].

Cammack, P. 2010. The Shape of Capitalism to Come. *Antipode* 41 (S1): 262–80.

Camp, R. 2005. Enhorabuena Juárez. [Online]. Available at: www.planjuarez.org/
ver_nota.ssp?id=116 [Accessed: 25 June 2006].

Camp, R.A. 2003. *Politics in Mexico: The Democratic Transformation*. 4th edn.
Oxford: Oxford University Press.

Campbell, T. 1997. Innovations and Risk Taking: The Engine of Reforms in Local
Government in Latin America and the Caribbean. *The World Bank Discussion
Paper* No: 357. Washington, DC: World Bank.

Campbell, T. 2003. *The Quite Revolution: Decentralization and the Rise of
Political Participation in Latin American Cities*. Pittsburgh: University of
Pittsburgh Press.

Campbell, T. 2008. Conclusion, in *Decentralization and Local Democracy in the
World*. Barcelona: World Bank and United Cities and Local Governments.

Camposortega, S. and R. Jiménez. 1998. *Combate a la Pobreza y al Rezago Social
en el Estado de Guerrero*. Mexico City: UNAM, UAA.

Canel, E. 2010. *Barrio Democracy in Latin America: Participatory
Decentralization and Community Activism in Montevideo*. University Park,
PA: Penn State University Press.

Canudas Sandoval E. 1989. *Trópico Rojo: Historia Política y Social de Tabasco*.
Villahermosa: Gobierno del Estado de Tabasco.

Carr, B. 1986. The Mexican Economic Debacle and the Labor Movement: A New
Era or More of the Same?, in *Modern Mexico: State, Economy, and Social
Conflict*, ed. N. Hamilton and T.F. Harding. Newbury Park, London, New
Delhi: Sage.

Carreño Rangel, T. 2001. La Participación Social Indígena, in *Foro Nacional de
Participación Social Cuarto Foro Regional*. Mexico City: CEDEMUN.

Castells, M. 1977. *The Urban Question: A Marxist Approach*. Cambridge, MA:
MIT Press.

Castro Hipolito, S. 1982. *Guerrero, Amnistia y Repression*. Mexico City,
Barcelona, Buenas Aires: Editorial Grijalbo, S.A.

Celis Salgado, L. 1988. *La Industria Petrolera en Mexico: una Crónica Volume 1*.
Mexico City: CONACULTA.

CEPAC, 2005. Resultados de la 4a Evaluación al Municipio de Chihuahua en Materia
de Transparencia, 6 October 2005. [Online]. Available at: http://cimtramx.tripod.
com/ sitebuildercontent/sitebuilderfiles/boletincimtrachihuahua4avuelta.pdf).
[Accessed: 11 November 2011].

Chand, V.K. 2001. *Mexico's Political Awakening*. Notre Dame, IN: University of
Notre Dame Press.

Chaparro, E. 1997. Chihuahua Ejemplo Mundial de Desarrollo Económico. *El
Diario de Chihuahua*, 19 November 1997: 4.

Chávez, D. 2004. Introduction: Local Left Politics in a Democratising Region, in *The Left in the City: Participatory Local Government in Latin America*, ed. D. Chávez and B. Goldfrank. London: Latin American Bureau.

Chávez, D. and B. Goldfrank (eds). 2004. *The Left in the City: Participatory Local Governments in Latin America*. London: Latin America Bureau.

Cheema, S.G. and D.A. Rondinelli (eds). 1983. *Decentralization and Development: Policy Implementation in Developing Countries*. Beverly Hills, London, New Delhi: Sage.

Cheema, S.G. and D.A. Rondinelli. 1997. From Government Decentralization to Decentralized Governance, in *Decentralizing Governance: Emerging Concepts and Practices*, ed. S.G. Cheema and D.A. Rondinelli. Washington, DC: Brookings Institution.

Clancy, M. 2001. Mexican Tourism: Export Growth and Structural Change since 1970, *Latin American Research Review* 36 (1): 128–50.

CNDH, Recomendación No.1 VG/2012, 27 March 2012. [Online].Available at: http://www.cndh.org.mx/node/694.[Accessed: 6 June 2012].

Cockburn, C. 1977. *The Local State: Management of Cities and People*. London: Pluto.

Cochrane, A. 1993. *Whatever Happened to Local Government*. Buckingham, Philadelphia: Open University Press.

Cockroft, J.D. 1983. *Mexico, Class Formation, Capital Accumulation and the State*. New York: Monthly Review.

CODEZPET. 1985. *Diagnostica Sobre la Influencia de la Actividad Petrolera en el Desarrollo de Tabasco*. Villahermosa: Subcomités de Políticas de Desarrollo.

Connerly, E., K. Eaton and P. Smoke (eds). 2010. *Making Decentralization Work: Democracy, Development and Security*. Boulder, CO: Lynne Rienner.

Cono, R. and L. Paz Paredes, 1991. El Curso de la Organización Cafetalera en la Costa Grande de Guerrero, *Cuardernos Agrarios* 3: 51–70.

Consulta Popular. 1982. Mexico City: PRI.

Cooke, P. 1989. Localities. London: Unwin Hyman.

Cordero, S.H., R. Santin and R. Tirado. 1983. *El Poder Empresarial en México*. Mexico City: Terra Nova.

Cornelius, A.W. 1999. Subnational Politics and Democratization: Tensions between Center and Periphery in the Mexican Political System, in *Subnational Politics and Democratization in Mexico*, ed. W.A. Cornelius, T.A. Eisenstadt and J. Hindley. San Diego: University of California Press.

Cornelius, W.A, A.L. Craig and J. Fox (eds). 1994. *Transforming State-Society Relations in Mexico: The National Solidarity Strategy*. San Diego, CA: Center for US–Mexican Studies.

Craig, R.B. 1971. *The Bracero Program: Interest Groups and Foreign Policy*. Austin, TX: University of Texas Press.

Crook, R.C. and J. Manor. 1998. *Democracy and Decentralisation in South Asia and West Africa: Participation, Accountability, and Performance*. Cambridge, UK: Cambridge University Press.

Curzio Gutiérrez, L. 1994a. Las elecciones locales de 1991 en Tabasco, in *Elecciones con Alternativas: Algunas Experiencias en la República Mexicana*, ed. J. Alonso and J. Tamayo. Mexico City: La Jornada Ediciones.

Curzio Gutiérrez, L. 1994b. Tabasco, in *La república mexicana: modernización y democracia de Aguascalientes a Zacatecas*, ed. P. González Casanova and J. Cadena Roa. Mexico City: Centro de Investigaciones Interdisciplinarias en Humanidades, UNAM.

Cypher, J.M. 1990. *State and Capital in Mexico: Development Policy since 1940*. Boulder, San Francisco and Oxford: Westview.

Danson, W.M. 1998. Debates and Review, *Regional Studies* 32(8): 759–68.

de la Madrid, M. 1982. *Pensamiento Político*, Mexico City: Coordinación General de Documentación y Análisis.

de la Madrid, M. 1983. *Manual Síntesis de Pensamiento Político*, Mexico City: PRI, Coordinación General de Documentación y Análisis.

Delarbe, R.T. 1986. The Mexican Labour Movement, in *Modern Mexico: State, Economy, and Social Conflict*, ed. N. Hamilton and T.F. Harding. Newbury Park, London, New Delhi: Sage.

Díaz de Jesús, M. 2000. Como Nosotros, Indígenas, Nos Fuimos Abriendo Espacio Político en Guerrero, in *Dilemas de la Democracia en México: Los Actores ante la Representación Política*, ed. A. Hémond and D. Recondo. Mexico City: IFE.

Díaz Serrano, J. 1992. *La Privatización del Petróleo Mexicano*. Mexico City: Editorial Planeta.

Dickovick, J.T. 2007. Municipalization as Central Government Strategy: Central-Regional-Local Politics in Peru, Brazil and South Africa, *Journal of Federalism* 37(1): 1–25.

Dowd, D. 2004. *Capitalism and its Economic: A Critical History*. London Ann Harbor, MI: Pluto.

Dresser, D. 1994a. Embellishment, Empowerment, or Euthanasia of the PRI? Neoliberalism and Party Reform in Mexico, in *The Politics of Economic Restructuring in Mexico*, ed. K. Middlebrook, J. Molinar and M. Cook. La Jolla: University of California San Diego, Center for US–Mexican Studies.

Duncan, S. and M. Goodwin. 1988. *The Local State and Uneven Development: Behind the Local Government Crisis*. Cambridge: Polity.

Eaton, K. 2003. Designing Subnational Institutions: Regional and Municipal Reforms on Postauthoritarian Chile, *Comparative Political Studies* 34(2): 218–44.

Eaton, K. 2004. The Link between Political and Fiscal Decentralization in South America, in *Decentralization and Democracy in Latin America*, ed. A.P. Montero and J.D. Samuels. Notre Dame, IN: University of Notre Dame Press.

Edmonds-Poli, E. 2006. Decentralization under the Fox Administration. Progress or Stagnation, *Mexican Studies / Estudios Mexicanos* 22(2): 387–416.

Eisenstadt, T.A. 1999. Electoral Federalism or Abdication of Presidential Authority? Gubernatorial Elections in Tabasco, in *Subnational Politics and Democratication in Mexico*, ed. W.A. Cornelius, E.A. Todd and H. Janu. La Jolla: University of California San Diego, Center for US–Mexican Studies.

Estrada Castañón, A.T. 1994. *Guerrero: Sociedad, Economía, Política, Cultura.* Mexico City: Centro de Investigaciones Interdisciplinarias en Humanidades, UNAM.

Evans, P.B., D. Rueschemeyer and T. Skocpol (eds). 1985. *Bringing the State Back in.* Cambridge: Cambridge University Press.

Falletti,T.G. 2004. Federalism and Decentralization in Argentina: Historical Background and New Intergovernmental Relations, in *Decentralization and Democratic Governance in Latin America* ed. J.S. Tulchin and A. Selee. Washington, DC: Woodrow Wilson.

Falletti, T.G. 2010. *Decentralization and Subnational Politics in Latin America.* Cambridge: Cambridge University Press.

Fernández Gómez, R. 2004. *Elecciones y Alternancia Guerrero.* Mexico City: Nuevo Horizonte.

Fine, B. 1999. The Developmental State is Dead: Long Live Social Capital? *Development and Change* 30: 1–19.

Flores Félix, J.J. and B. Canabál Cristiani. 2000. Organizaciones Indígenas en la Montaña de Guerrero, in *Dilemas de la Democracia en México: Los Actores ante la representación política*, ed. A. Hémond and D. Recondo. Mexico City: IFE.

Fox, J. 1997. The World Bank and Social Capital: Contesting the Concept in Practice, *Journal of International Development* 9(7): 963 71.

Fox, J. and J. Aranda. 1996. *Decentralization and Rural Development in Mexico: Community Participation in Oaxaca's Municipal Funds Program.* San Diego: University of California Press.

Fox, V. 2003. *Segundo Informe de Gobierno.* Mexico City: Presidencia de la Republica.

Fung, A. and E.O. Wright (eds). 2003. *Deepening Democracy: Institutional Innovations in Empowered Participatory Governance.* London, New York: Verso.

Gamas-Torruco, J. 1975. *El Federalismo Mexicano.* Mexico City: Secretaría de Educación.

Garza, G. 2003. The Dialectics of Urban and Regional Disparities in Mexico, in *Confronting Development: Assessing Mexico's Economic and Social Policy Challenges*, ed. K.J. Middlebrook and E. Zepeda. Stanford, CA: Stanford University Press.

Gaspar, G. and L. Valdés. 1987. 'Las Venturas Recientes del Bloque en el Poder', *Estudios Sociológicos* 5 (15): 499–524.

Gereffi, G. 1996. Mexico's 'Old' and 'New' Maquiladora Industries: Contrasting Approaches to North American Integration, in *Neo-Liberalism Revisited: Economic Restructuring and Mexico's Political Future*, ed. G. Otero. Oxford: Westview.

Gereffi, G. 2003. Mexico's Industrial Development: Climbing Ahead of Falling Behind in the World Economy?, in *Confronting Development: Assessing Mexico's Economic and Social Policy Challenges*, ed. K.J. Middlebrook and E. Zapata. Stanford, CA: Stanford University Press.

Giddens, A. 1984. *Central Problems in Social Theory: Action, Structure, and Contradiction in Social Analysis*. Basingstoke: Macmillan.

Goldfrank, B. 2004. Conclusion, in *The Left in the City: Participatory Local Government in Latin America*, ed. D. Chavez and B. Goldfrank. London: Latin American Bureau.

Goldfrank, B. 2011. *Deepening Local Democracy in Latin America: Participation, Decentralization and the Left*. University Park, PA: Penn State University Press.

Gómez Tagle, S.T. 1994. *De la Alquimia al Fraude en las Elecciones Mexicanas*. Mexico City: G.V. Editores.

González Calzada, M. 1940. *Tomás Garrido: Al Derecho y al Revés*. Mexico City: Publicaciones and Ediciones Especiales.

González Casanova, P. 1970. *Democracy in Mexico*. New York: Oxford University Press.

González Pedrero, E. 1987a. *Discursos Por Tabasco 1983/1987 Volumen 1*. Villahermosa: Gobierno del Estado de Tabasco.

González Pedrero, E. 1987b. *Discursos Por Tabasco 1983/1987 Volumen 2*. Villahermosa: Gobierno del Estado de Tabasco.

Gottdiner, M. 1986. *Cities in Stress: A New Look at the Urban Crisis*. Beverly Hills, CA: Sage.

Gramsci, A. 1971. *Further Selections from the Prison Notebook*. New York: International Publisher.

Gray, J. 1995. *Liberalism*. 2nd edn. Buckingham: Open University Press.

Grindle, M.S. 2009. *Going Local: Decentralization, Democratization and the Promise of Good Governance*. Princeton and Oxford: Princeton University Press.

Griswold, D.T. 2002. NAFTA at 10: An Economic and Foreign Policy Success. *CATO Institute Free Trade Bulletin* 1. [Online]. Available at: www.cato.org/pub_display.php? pub_id=10687 [Accessed: 10 November 2011].

Guigale, M. and S. Webb. 2000. *Achievements and Challenges of Fiscal Decentralization in Mexico*. Washington, DC: World Bank.

Guillén, T. and A. Ziccardi. 2004. Introducción Parámetros de la Reforma Municipal en México, in *Innovación y Continuidad del Municipio Mexicano: Análisis de la Reforma Municipal de 13 Estados de la República*, ed. T. Guillén and A. Ziccardi. Mexico City: M.A. Porrua-IIS.UNAM.

Haggard, S. and S. Webb (eds). 1994. *Voting for Reform: Democracy, Political Liberalization, and Economic Adjustment, A World Bank Book*. New York: Oxford University Press.

Hamilton, N. 1982. *The Limits of State Autonomy: Post-Revolutionary Mexico*. Princeton, NJ: Princeton University Press.

Hamilton, N. 1986a. The Limits of State Autonomy, in *Modern Mexico: State, Economy, and Social Conflict*, ed. N. Hamilton and T.F. Harding. Newbury Park, London, New Delhi: Sage.

Hancock, R.H. 1959. *The Role of the Bracero and Cultural Dynamics of Mexico: A Case Study of Chihuahua*. Stanford, CA: Hispanic American Society.

Harding, A. 1996. Is There a 'New Community Power' and Why Should We Need One? *International Journal of Urban and Regional Studies* 20: 637–55.

Harrison, D. 1994. Tourism, Capitalism and Development, in *Capitalism and Development*,ed. L. Sklair. New York: Routledge.

Harvey, D. 1985. *The Urbanization of Capital*. Baltimore: Johns Hopkins University Press.

Harvey, D. 1999. *Limits to Capital*. London, New York: Verso.

Harvey, D. 2000. *Spaces of Hope*. Berkeley, CA: University of California Press.

Hernández Trillo F., A. Diaz Cayeros and R. Gamboa González. 2002. Determinants and Consequences of Bailing out States in Mexico, *Eastern Economic Journal* 28 (3): 365–8.

Herod, A. and M.W. Wright. 2002. Placing Scale: An Introduction, in *Geographies of Power: Placing Scale*, ed. A. Herod and M.W. Wright. Oxford: Blackwell Publishing.

Hindley, J. 1999. Indigenous Mobilization, Development and Democratization in Guerrero: The Nahua Peasants vs. the Tetelcingo Dam, in *Subnational Politics and Democratization in Mexico*, ed. W. Cornelius, T.A. Eisenstadt and J. Hindley. La Jolla: Center for US–Mexican Studies University of California, San Diego.

Hundt, A. 1996. Impact of Tourism Development on the Economy and Health of Third World Nations, *Journal of Travel Medicine* 3(2): 107–12.

INEGI. 2010. *Censo de Población y Vivienda*. Mexico City: INEG.

Interamerican Development Bank. 1994. Fiscal Decentralization: The Search for Equity and Efficiency, in *Economic and Social Progress in Latin America: 1994 Report*. Washington, DC: Interamerican Development Bank.

Jacobs, I. 1982. *Ranchero Revolt: The Mexican Revolution in Guerrero*. Austin, TX: University of Texas.

Jessop, B. 1990. *State Theory: Putting the Capitalist State in its Place*. Cambridge: Polity

Jessop, B. 1999. Narrating the Future of the National Economy and the National State: Remarks on Remapping Regulation and Reinventing Governance, in *State/Culture: State Formation after the Cultural Turn*, ed. G. Steinmetz. Ithaca, NY: Cornell University Press.

Jessop, B. 2002. *The Future of the Capitalist State*. Cambridge: Polity.

Jessop, B. and Ngai-Ling Sum. 2000. An Entrepreneurial City in Action: Hong Kong's Emerging Strategies in and for (Inter) Urban Competition, *Urban Studies* 37 (12): 2287–2313.

Juárez Cisneros, R. 2001. *Tercer Informe de Gobierno*. Chilpancingo: Estado de Guerrero.

Juárez Cisneros, R. 2003. *Informe de Gobierno de Estado de Guerrero*. Chilpancingo: Estado de Guerrero.

Julián Bernal, C. 2001. La Sociedad Civil Organizada, su Participación y Relación con el Estado caso de Guerrero. *Foro Nacional de Participación Social Cuarto Foro Regional*. Mexico City: CEDEMUN.

Kähkönen, S. and A. Lanyi. 2001. Decentralization and Governance: Does Decentralization Improve Public Service Delivery? Premnotes Public Sector World Bank 55.

Katz, F. 1981. *The Secret War in Mexico: Europe, the United States, and the Mexican Revolution*. Chicago, London: University of Chicago Press.

Kaufman, R.R. and G. Trejo. 1997. Regionalism, Regime Transformation and PRONASOL: The Politics of National Solidarity Programme in Four Mexican States, *Journal of Latin American Studies* 29: 717–45.

Keating, M. 2001. *Beyond Sovereignty: Plurinational Democracy in Post-Sovereign World*. Montréal: McGill University Press.

Keating, M. 1997. The Political Economy of Regionalism, in *The Political Economy of Regionalism*, ed. M. Keating and J. Loughlin. London: Frank Cass.

Koonings, K. and D. Kruijt. 2006. Introduction: The duality of Latin American city scapes, in *Fractured Cities: Social Exclusion, Urban Violence and Contested Spaces in Latin America*, ed. K. Koonings and D. Kruijt. New York: Zed Books.

Leal, J.F. 1986. The Mexican State, 1915–1973: A Historical Interpretation, in *Modern Mexico: State, Economy, and Social Conflict*, ed. N. Hamilton and T.F. Harding. Newbury Park, London, New Delhi: Sage Publications.

Lindblom, C.E. 1977. *Politics and Markets: The World's Political-Economic System*. New York: Basic.

Logan, J. and H. Molotch. 1987. *Urban Fortunes*. Berkeley: University of California Press.

López Ochoa, M.A. 1987. Palabras de despedida, in *Encuentro de Presidente Municipales: Los Municipios de la Frontera Norte III*. Nogales, Sonora: Municipio de Nogales, Sonora.

Loughlin, J. and P.G. Peters. 1997. State Traditions, Administrative Reforms and Regionalization, in *The Political Economy of Regionalism*, ed. M. Keating and J. Loughlin. London: Frank Cass.

Loveman, B. 1993. *The Constitution of Tyranny, Regimes of Exception in Spanish America*. Pittsburgh: University of Pittsburgh Press.

Luna, M. 2004. Business and Politics in Mexico, in *Dilemmas of Political Change in Mexico*, ed. K. Middlebrook. London: Institute of Latin American Studies University of London, Center for US–Mexican Studies University of California.

Madrazo Pintado, R. 2000a. *6 Anos de Trabajo 6 Anos de Gobierno*. Villahermosa: Gobierno de Estado de Tabasco.

Madrazo Pintado, R. 2000b. *Sexto Año de Gobierno*. Villahermosa: Gobierno de Estado de Tabasco.

Magid, H. 1987. John Stuard Mill, in *History of Political Philosophy*, ed. L. Strauss and J. Cropsey. Chicago and London: University of Chicago Press.

Mann, M. 1985. The Autonomous Power of the State: Its Origins, Mechanisms and Results. *European Journal of Sociology* 25: 185–213.

Manor, J. 1999. *The Political Economy of Democratic Decentralization.* Washington, DC: The World Bank.

Martínez Laguna, N. 2004. Oil Policies and Privatization Strategies in Mexico: Implications for the Petrochemical Sector and its Production Spaces. *Energy Policy* 32(18): 2035–2047.

Martínez, O.J. 1982. *Ciudad Juárez: El auge de una ciudad fronteriza a partir de 1848.* Mexico City: Fondo de Cultura Económica.

McNulty, S.L. 2011. *Decentralization and Participation in Post-Fujimori Peru: Voice and Vote.* Stanford, CA: Stanford University Press.

Middlebrook, K.J. 1995. *The Paradox of Revolution: Labor, the State and Authoritarianism in Mexico.* Baltimore, London: Johns Hopkins University Press.

Mill, J.S. 1991. *Considerations on Representative Government,* vol. 19. Toronto: University of Toronto Press.

Mizrahi, Y. 1992. The Strengths and Weaknesses of the PAN in Chihuahua. *Documento de Trabajo Estudio Políticos* 1: CIDE.

Mizrahi, Y. 1996. ¿Administrar o Gobernar? El Reto del Gobierno Panista en Chihuahua. *Documento de Trabajo Estudio Políticos* 42: CIDE.

Montero, A.P. 2001. After Decentralization: Patterns of Intergovernmental Conflict in Arjantina, Spain, Brazil and Mexico. *Journal of Federalism* 31(4): 43–64.

Montero, A.P. and D.J. Samuels (eds). 2004a. *Decentralization and Democracy in Latin America.* Notre Dame, IN: University of Notre Dame Press.

Montero, A.P. and D.J. Samuels 2004b. The Politics of Decentralization in Latin America, in *Decentralization and Democracy in Latin America,* ed. A.P. Montero and D. J. Samuels. Notre Dame, IN: University of Notre Dame Press.

Mullen, R.D. 2011. *Decentralization, Local Governance, and Social Wellbeing in India: Do Local Governments Matter?* London: Routledge.

Neal, F.W. 1958. *Titoism in Action: The Reforms in Yugoslavia after 1948.* Berkeley: University of California Press.

O'Malley, A. 2001. Prospects for Community-Based Development, in *Transcending Neoliberalism: Community-Based Development in Latin America,* ed. H. Veltmeyer and A. O'Malley. Bloomfield, CT: Kumarian.

O'Neill, K. 2003. Decentralization as an Electoral Strategy. *Comparative Political Studies* 36(9): 68–109.

O'Neill, K. 2004. Decentralization in Bolivia, in *Decentralization and Democracy in Latin America,* ed. A.P. Montero and D.J. Samuels. Notre Dame, IN: University of Notre Dame Press.

O'Neill, K. 2005. *Decentralizing the State: Elections, Parties and the Local Power in the Andes.* New York: Cornell University Press.

Oates, W.E. 1972. *Fiscal Federalism.* New York: Harcourt Brace Jovanovich.

Ollman, B. 2003. *Dance of Dialectics: Steps in Marx's Method.* Urbana, IL: University of Illinois Press.

Otero, G. 1996. Neoliberal Reform and Politics in Mexico, in *Neoliberalism Revisited: Economic Restructuring and Mexico's Political Future,* ed. G. Otero. Oxford: Westview.

Overmeyer-Velazquez, R.L. 2003. Indian, Nation and State in Guerrero, Mexico. Unpublished PhD thesis, University of California, Santa Barbara.

Oxhorn, P., J.S. Tulchin and A.D. Selee (eds). 2004. *Decentralization and Democratic Governance, and Civil Society in Comparative Perspective: Africa, Asia and Latin America.* Washington, DC: Woodrow Wilson Center.

Parker, A. and R. Serrano. 2000. *Promoting Good Local Governance through Social Funds and Decentralization.* Washington DC: World Bank.

Pazos, L. 1983. *Respuestas a Los Planes de MMH: Critica y Soluciones para. Salir de la Crisis.* Mexico City: Editorial Diana.

Peck, J. 1995. Moving and Shaking: Business Elites, State Localism and Urban Privatism. *Progress in Human Geography* 19 (1): 16–46.

Peck, J. 2001. Neoliberalizing States: Thin Policies / Hard Outcomes. *Progress in Human Geography* 25 (3): 445–55.

Peck, J. 2004. Geography and Public Policy: Constructions of Neoliberalism. *Progress in Human Geography* 28 (3): 392–405.

Peck, J. and A. Tickell. 1992. Local Modes of Social Regulation? Regulation Theory, Thatcherism and Uneven Development. *Geoforum* 23: 347–64.

Peck, J. and A. Tickell. 2002. Neoliberalizing Space: the Free Economy and the Penal State. *Antipode* 34(3): 380–404.

Peterson, G.E. 1997. *Decentralization in Latin America: Learning through Experience.* Washington, DC: World Bank.

Pickvance, C. 1995. Marxist Theories of Urban Politics, in Theories of Urban Politics, ed. J. David. London: Sage.

Pickvance, C. 2001. Four Varieties of Comparative Analysis. *Journal of Housing and the Built Environment* 16: 7–28.

Pickvance, C. and E. Preteceille (eds). 1991. *State Restructuring and Local Power.* London, New York: Pinter.

Poder Ejecutivo Federal. 1989. *Plan Nacional de Desarrollo, 1989–1994.* Mexico City: Secretaría de Programación Presupuesto.

Poder Ejecutivo Federal, 2000. Plan Nacional de Desarrollo, 1995–2000. Mexico City: Secretaría de Programación Presupuesto

Poulantzas, N. 1978. *State, Power, Socialism.* London: Verso.

Prescott, H.W. 2001. *History of the Conquest of Mexico.* New York: Modern Library.

Prud'homme R. 1996. The Economics of Decentralization in Very Low Income Countries. *Revue Région and Dévelopment* 3:155–60.

Raby, D.L. 1974. *Educación y Revolución Social en México: 1921–1940.* Mexico: Sep Setentas.

Ramos Vaca, A.R. 2006 Dialogue, Partnership and the Evolution of Clustering Efforts in Chihuahua, International Workshop on Public–Private Dialogue, Paris, February 1–2, 2006. [Online]. Available at: www.publicprivatedialogue.org/case_ studies/Working per cent20Group per cent2007 per cent20Case per cent20Study per cent20- per cent20Chihuahua.pdf [Accessed: 10 November 2011].

Rendón Alarcón, J. 2003. *Sociedad y Conflicto en el Estado de Guerrero, 1911–1995: Poder Político y Estructura Social de la Entidad*. Mexico City: Plaza y Valdés.

Ribot, J.C. 2004. *Waiting for Democracy: The Politics of Choice in Natural Resource Decentralization*. Washington, DC: World Resources Institute.

Rico Medina, S. 1993. *La Revolución Mexicana en Tabasco: Un Estudio sobre las élites políticas Regionales 1884–1921*. Mexico City: Instituto de Investigaciones José María Luis Mora.

Robinson, I.W. 2003. *Transnational Conflicts: Central America, Social Change and Globalization*. London, New York: Verso.

Rodden, J.A., G.S. Eskeland and J. Litvack (eds). 2003. *Fiscal Decentralization and the Challenge of Hard Budget Constraints*. Cambridge, MA: MIT Press.

Rodríguez Wallenius, C.A. 2005. *La Disputa por el Desarrollo Regional: Movimiento Sociales y Constitución de Poderes Locales en el Oriente de la Costa Chica de Guerrero*. Mexico City, Barcelona: CESEM and PYV.

Rodríguez, E.V. 1997. *Decentralization in Mexico: From Reforma Municipal to Solidaridad to Nuevo Federalismo*. Oxford: Westview.

Rodríguez, E.V. and M.P. Ward. 1995. Introduction: Governments of the Opposition in Mexico, in *Opposition Government in Mexico*, ed. V.E. Rodríguez and P.M. Ward. Albuquerque: University of New Mexico Press.

Ronquillo, V. 1999. *Las Muertas De Juárez: Crónica De Una Larga Pesadilla*. Mexico City: Planeta Mexicana.

Ruíz Durán, C. (2000) *El Paradigma de Desarrollo Regional Basado en la Cooperación Público-Privada: El Caso de Chihuahua, México*. Santiago: United Nations Comisión Económica para. América Latina y el Caribe.

Ruíz, C. and A. Fabregas. 2009. *Historia Política Contemporánea de Tabasco*, Volume 2. Villahermosa: Gobierno Del Estado de Tabasco.

Ruz, M.H. 1989. *Un Rostro Encubierto: Los Indios del Tabasco Colonial*. Mexico City: CIESAS.

Sassen, S. 2006. *Cities in World Economy*. London, New Delhi: Pine Forge.

Sayer, A. 1984. *Method in Social Science: A Realist Approach*. London: Routledge.

Sayer, A. 2000. *Realism and Social Science*. London: Sage.

Sayer, D. 1987. *The Violence of Abstraction: The Analytical Foundation of Historical Materialism*. London: Basil Blackwell.

Schatz, S. 2011. *Murder and Politics in Mexico: Political Killings in the Partido de la Revolución Democrática and its Consequences*. New York, London: Springer.

Scherr, S.J. 1985. *The Oil Syndrome and Agricultural Development: Lessons from Tabasco, Mexico*. New York: Praeger.

Schmidt, S. 2000. *In Search of Decision: The Maquiladora Industry in Mexico*. Ciudad Juárez, Chihuahua: Universidad Autónoma de Ciudad Juárez.

Schmitter, P.C. 1974. Still the Century of Corporatism? *Review of Politics* 36 (1): 85–131.

Selee, A. 2011. *Decentralization, Democratization and Informal Power in Mexico.* University Park, PA: Penn State University Press.

Sellers, M.J. 2002. *Governing from Below: Urban Regions and the Global Economy.* Cambridge: Cambridge University Press.

Shadlen, K.C. 2000. Neoliberalism, Corporatism, and Small Business Activism in Contemporary Mexico. *Latin American Research Review* 35(2): 73–106.

Shotton, R. and A. Rogers. 2007. *Delivering the Goods: Building Local Government Capacity to Achieve the Millenium Development Goals.* New York: UNCD.

Sklair, L. 1989. *Assembling for Development: The Maquiladora Industry in Mexico and the United States.* Massachusetts: Unwin Hyman Inc. Winchester.

Skocpol, T. 1979. *States and Social Revolutions.* Cambridge: Cambridge University Press.

Skocpol, T. 1984. Emerging Agendas and Recurrent Strategies in Historical Sociology, in Vision and Method in Historical Sociology, ed. T. Skocpol. Cambridge: Cambridge University Press.

Skocpol, T. 1985. Bringing the State Back In: Strategies of Analysis in Current Research, in *Bringing the State Back in*, ed. P.B. Evans, D. Rueschemeyer and T. Skocpol. Cambridge: Cambridge University Press.

Smith, N. 1984. *Uneven Development: Nature, Capital and the Production of Space.* Oxford: Blackwell.

Smith, N. 1993. Homeless/Global: Scaling Places, in *Mapping the Future: Local Cultures, Global Changes*, ed. J. Bird et al. London: Routledge, 87–121.

Snyder, R. 2001a. Scaling Down the Subnational Comparative Method. *Studies in Comparative International Development* 36 (1): 93–110.

Snyder, R. 2001b. *Politics after Neoliberalism: Reregulating in Mexico.* Cambridge: Cambridge University Press.

SOCINTEC. 2003. *¿Quién es Juárez? Elementos de reflexión.* Ciudad Juárez: Plan Estratégico de Juáre.

Soederberg, S. 2001. State, Crisis and Capital Accumulation in Mexico. *Historical Materialism* 9: 61–84.

South, R. 1990. Transnational 'Maquiladora' Location. *Annals of American Geographers* 80 (4): 549–70.

SPP. 1983. *Fortalecimiento y Desarrollo Municipal.* Mexico City: Secretaría de Programación Presupuesto.

SPP. 1988. *Mexico: Desarrollo Regional y Descentralización de la Vida Nacional Experiencias de Cambia Estructural 1983–1988.* Mexico City: SPP.

Stohr, W. et al. (eds). 2001. *New Regional Development Paradigms: Decentralization, Governance and the New Planning for Local Level Development.* Westport, CT: Greenwood.

Swyngedouw, E. 1997. Neither Global nor Local: 'Glocalization' and the Politics of Scale, in *Spaces of Globalization*, ed. K.R. Cox. New York: Guilford.

Székely, G. 1985. Recent Finding and Research Suggestions on Oil and Mexico's Economic Development. *Latin American Research Review* 20(3): 235–46.

Taylor, P. 1996. Embedded Statism and Social Sciences: Opening up to New Spaces. *Environment and Planning* 28: 1917–1928.

Teitz, B.M. 1987. The Role of Small Business. *Town Planning Review* 58(1): 5–18.

Tirado, R. 1987. Los Empresarios y La Política Partidaria. *Estudios Sociológicos* 5 (15): 477–97.

Tocqueville, A. 1969. *Democracy in America*, ed. P.J. Mayer. Garden City, NY: Doubleday.

Torreblanca Galindo, Z. 2006a, Reafirma Zeferino Torreblanca compromiso para. impulsar y avanzar en el desarrollo integral del estado, Dirección General de Comunicación Social. *Boletín de Prensa* No. 135–206.

Torreblanca Galindo, Z. 2006b. Zeferino Torreblanca Se Reunió con Integrantes del Frente Cívico, Dirección General de Comunicación Social. *Boletín de Prensa* No. 995–1000.

Treisman, D. 2007. *The Architecture of Government: Rethinking Political Decentralization*. Cambridge: Cambridge University Press.

Tulchin, J.S. and A.D. Selee (eds). 2004. *Decentralization and Democratic Governance on Latin America*. Washington, DC: Woodrow Wilson Center.

Tuleda, F. 1989. *La Modernización Forzada del Trópico el Caso de Tabasco: Proyecto Integrado del Golfo*. Mexico City: Centro de Estudios Demográfico y de Desarrollo Urbano.

UN-Habitat. 2007. Resolution 23/3: *Guidelines on Decentralization and Strengthening of Local Authorities*.[Online]. Available at: www.unhabitat.org/downloads/*docs/5181_19348_Resolution per cent2021–3.pdf*. [Accessed: 8 November 2011].

Valdés Ugalde, F. 1996. The Private Sector and Political Regime Change in Mexico, in *Neoliberalism Revisited: Economic Restructuring and Mexico's Political Future*, ed. G. Otero. Oxford: Westview.

Valdés Ugalde, F. 1997. *Autonomía e Legitimidad: Los Empresarios, La Política y El Estado en México*. Mexico City: Siglo Veintiuno.

Valverde, C.1989. *Juilán Blanco y Revolución en el Estado de Guerrero*. Chilpancingo, Guerrero: H. Ayuntamiento de Chilpancingo.

Véliz, C. 1980. *Centralization in Latin America*. Princeton, NJ: Princeton University Press.

Veltmeyer, H. 2000. The Dynamics of Social Change and Mexico's EZLN. *Latin American Perspectives* 27 (5): 88–110.

Veltmeyer, H. 2001. The Quest for Another Development, in *Transcending Neoliberalism: Community-Based Development in Latin America*, ed. H. Veltmeyer and A. O'Malley. Bloomfield, CT: Kumarian Press.

Vincent T.G. 2001. The Contributions of Mexico's First Black Indian President, Vicente Guerrero. *Journal of Negro History* 86 (2): 148–59.

Ward, P.M. 1990. *Mexico City: The Production and Reproduction of an Urban Environment*. Boston: G.K. Hall & Co.

Warner, M. and J. Gerbasi. 2004. Rescaling and Reforming the State under NAFTA: Implications for Subnational Authority. *International Journal of Urban and Regional Research* 28(4): 853–73.

Wasserman, M. 1984. *Capitalists, Caciques and Revolution: The Native Elite and Foreign Enterprise in Chihuahua, Mexico, 1854–1911.* Chapel Hill and London: University of North Carolina Press.

Webster, N. 1992. Panchayati Raj in West Bengal: Popular Participation for the People and the Party? *Development and Change* 23(4): 129–63.

West, R.C., N.P. Psuty and B.G. Thom. 1976. *Las Tierras Bajas de Tabasco en el Sureste de México.* Villahermosa: Gobierno de Estado de Tabasco.

Wheat, A. 1996. Mexico's Privatization Piñada. *Multinational Monitor* 17 (10): 9–15.

Williams, E.J. 1990. The Resurgent North and Contemporary Mexican Regionalism. *Mexican Studies / Estudios Mexicanos* 6(2): 299–323.

Willis, E., C. Garman and S. Haggard. 1999. The Politics of Decentralization in Latin America. *Latin American Research Review* 34 (1): 7–56.

Wilson Salinas, Patricia. 1983. El Auge Petróleo y la Planeación Regional en México. *Revista Interamerican de Planificación* 17(66): 149–63.

Wilson, R.R. et al. 2008. *Decentralization, Democracy, and Sunational Government in Brazil, Mexico and the USA.* Notre Dame, IN: Notre Dame University Press.

Wood E.M. 2002. Global Capital, National States, in *Historical Materialism and Globalization*, ed. M. Rupert and H. Smith. London and New York: Routledge.

World Bank. 1994a. *Making Development Sustainable: The World Bank Group and the Environment, Fiscal 1994.* Washington, DC: World Bank.

World Bank. 1994b. *Governance: The World Bank's Experience.* Washington, DC: World Bank.

World Bank. 1997. *World Development Report 1997: The State in a Changing World.* Washington, DC: World Bank.

World Bank. 2000. *Reforming Public Institutions and Strengthening Governance: A World Bank Strategy.* Washington, DC: World Bank.

World Bank. 2004. *Measuring Fiscal Decentralization.* Washington, DC: World Bank.

World Bank. 2008. *Decentralization in Client Countries: An Evaluation of World Bank Support 1990–2007.* Washington DC: World Bank.

Wynia, G.W. 1990. *The Politics of Latin American Development.* Cambridge: Cambridge University Press.

Yalman, L.G. 2009. Transition to Neoliberalism: The Case of Turkey in the 1980s. İstanbul: Bilgi University Press.

Zolberg, R.A. 2006. *A Nation by Design: Immigration Policy in the Fashioning of America.* New York, Cambridge and London: Russell Sage Foundation-Harvard University Press.

Index